The Ultimate

HARLEY-DAVIDSON

The Ultimate
HARLEY-DAVIDSON

An encyclopedia of the definitive motorbike from classic to custom – exploring the legend of an American dream

MAC McDIARMID

METRO BOOKS
NEW YORK

ACKNOWLEDGEMENTS

This 2007 edition published by Metro Books, by arrangement with Anness Publishing Ltd

Metro Books
122 Fifth Avenue
New York, NY 10011

ISBN: 978-0-7607-9203-2

Publisher Joanna Lorenz
Project Editors Zoe Antoniou and Polly Willis
Designer Michael Morey

Printed and bound in Singapore

3 5 7 9 10 8 6 4

Publisher's note

In recognition of the uniquely American pedigree of the motorcycles featured on the following pages, engine capacity is generally expressed in imperial units (cubic inches) with the metric equivalent (cc) in brackets. However, even Harley-Davidson employ units somewhat arbitrarily, favouring cu in for heavyweight twins, but ccs for Sportster models, a practice we have also adopted.

The capacity of Harley engines should also be treated with some care. Even from the early days, the inch sizes quoted and used by Harley fans were a sort of numeric shorthand, relating only approximately to measured reality. More recently, even the "80-inch" Evo engine actually measured 81.8cu in – a difference of no less than 29cc. In general, where an engine is referred to as something-inch, this refers to popular usage. Dimensions expressed in cu in and/or cc are as accurate as records permit.

We trust that this historical ambiguity will not reduce the reader's enjoyment.

Although the advice and information in this book are believed to be accurate and true at the time of going to press, neither the authors nor the publisher can accept any legal responsibility or liability for any errors or omissions that may be made.

The Publishers would like to thank the following for their kind permission to reproduce their photographs:

John Bolt
44tr, 45tr, 49b, 59br, 77b, 84bl, 100 (all), 101tl/tr/br, 110-1, 112 (all), 113 (all), 114 (all), 115 (tr/b), 150-1, 153tl, 166t, 168b, 182t.

John Caroll
93b, 102t, 160br, 164t/mr/b, 165bl.

Alan Cathcart
128tl, 250, 251t.

Bob Clarke
30m, 34t, 41tl, 43t, 64t, 84tr/br, 85bl, 89m/b, 96bl, 102bl/br, 103 (all), 105t, 123b, 125bl, 126ml, 140 (all), 163tr, 165m, 168t, 169b, 181b, 188-9, 209m, 231 (all), 234-5, 240t, 241t/b, 243t/m, 245t, 246bl, 248b, 253 (all).

Classic Bike
148b, 184b, 202b, 203t,

Neil Dalleywater
43br, 74br, 160bl, 192t, 233t.

Kobal
96t/m, 97tr, 127t, 127br.

Mac McDiarmid
1c, 8-9, 28t/b, 33, 35b, 41tr, 45b, 47tl/b, 49t, 60t/m/br, 61tr, 62 (all), 63tl/b, 64b, 65 (all), 66 (all), 67 (all), 71 (all), 72t, 73br, 74t/bl, 76t, 78t, 82 (all), 83 (all), 84tl, 86-7, 94-5, 97tl/bl/br, 101bl, 105b, 106 (all), 107 (all), 108tr/b, 109 (all), 115tl, 120b, 122t, 123tl, 124 (all), 125m/br, 128b, 135tr, 138t, 146b, 147tr, 152t, 153tr/b, 157t, 170-1, 172 (all), 174t, 175tl, 177t, 178m, 179t, 182m/b, 193t, 194t, 195tl, 196bl/br, 197tr, 206 (all), 207t/m, 210-1, 212m/b, 213m, 214t/m, 215t/m, 218-219, 220t, 221t, 228-9, 244 (all), 245m/b, 247m, 249tl/m, 251bl/br.

Don Morley
2, 13br, 21b, 35t, 42b, 59tl, 128tr, 132-3, 141, 155, 183, 246t/br, 247b, 248t, 249tr.

B. R. Nicholls
121t, 126b.

Quadrant
6, 130, 180t, 227.

Tony Stone
50-51, 159.

Garry Stuart
3b, 5b, 11t/ml, 12tl/tr, 13bl, 14bl/br, 15t, 16t/bl, 18b, 19 (all), 20 (all), 21t, 22t/b, 23t, 24 (all), 25 (all), 26 (all), 27 (all), 29 (all), 30t/b, 31 (all), 32 (all), 34b, 36 (all), 37 (all), 38 (all), 39 (all), 40 (all), 41b, 42t, 43bl, 44tl/b, 45tl, 46 (all), 47tr, 48 (all), 50tl/b, 58b, 60bl, 61tl/b, 68-9, 70 (all), 72b, 73t/bl, 75 (all), 76b, 77t, 78b, 85tl/tr/br, 88br, 90 (all), 91tl/m, 92t/b, 93t, 98 (all), 99 (all), 104b, 108tl, 116-7, 119t/b, 121b, 122b, 123tr, 125t, 126t/mr, 129tr/b, 134 (all), 135tl/b, 136 (all), 137 (all), 138b, 139 (all), 142-3, 144 (all), 145 (all), 146t/m, 147tl/b, 148t, 149 (all), 152m/b, 153m, 154 (all), 156t/b, 157m/bl/br, 158t/b, 160t, 161 (all), 162 (all), 163tl, 163m/b, 164ml, 165bl, 166m/b, 167t/b, 168m, 169t, 173t/b, 174b, 175tr/b, 176 (all), 177b, 178t, 180b, 181tl/tr, 186 (all), 187 (all), 190 (all), 191 (all), 192b, 193b, 194b, 195tr/b, 196t, 197tl/b, 198t, 199ml, 200-1, 203b, 204 (all), 205 (all), 207b, 208m/b, 209t, 213b, 214b, 222 (all), 223 (all), 224b, 236 (all), 237 (all), 238 (all), 239 (all), 240bl, 241m, 242m/b, 243b, 247t, 249, 252.

All other photographs courtesy of Harley-Davidson, Inc.

t=top b=bottom l=left r=right m=middle tr= top right tl=top left ml=middle left mr=middle right bl=bottom left br=bottom right lm=left middle tmr=top middle right tml=top middle left

Thanks also to Keith Ryan (editor), Shaun Barrington (editorial consultant), Richard McGinlay (reader) and Geoffrey Meadon (indexer).

Contents

The World of Harley-Davidson

The Models

American
Classics
SCHOTT
USA
HARLEY-DAVIDSON

THE WORLD OF HARLEY-DAVIDSON

"If you have to ask..." said the Harley-Davidson slogan, "...you wouldn't understand." Just what is it that makes Harley-Davidson so special? The company makes motorcycles, true, but it is much more than a mere motorcycle manufacturer – Milwaukee makes legends. The company that has become an American icon crafts heavy metal into love affairs, forges lifestyles and fulfils dreams. As much myth as motorcycle – often imitated, never copied – there is simply nothing quite like a Harley-Davidson.

Today, Harleys are as recognizable around the world as the Stars and Stripes, as ubiquitous as McDonald's and as prized for their rugged honesty as Zippo lighters and Levi's. They appear in movies and advertising; they're the wheels of choice for celebrities and stars. Elvis owned one and, according to the T-shirt at least, God rides one too. Men have raced them almost as soon as the first one came out of the shop. They have been a unique facet of American life through two world wars and a crippling Depression.

Harley-Davidson's is the longest history in motorcycling, almost the story of motorcycling itself, and *The World of Harley-Davidson* is the epic tale of the making of an American legend.

The Evolution of Harley-Davidson

From uncertain beginnings in a Milwaukee basement in 1903, Harley-Davidson has witnessed and withstood everything a turbulent century could throw at it. Once the world's largest producer of motorcycles, Harley's sales shrank to a mere 10,000 per year during the 1950s. Increasing competition – first from Europe, then from Japan – brought the once-proud giant to the brink of ruin. By the 1970s, changes of ownership, confusion about its markets and a moribund model range made Harley-Davidson almost a joke to all but its most devoted fans. As recently as the mid-1980s this vibrant dream factory was effectively broke.

Today, the company is booming. Inspired styling and brilliant marketing, combined with modern manufacturing techniques, see Milwaukee's finest thundering confidently into the future.

EARLY YEARS

In the early days of the 20th century, young men in dingy workshops across the industrialized world tinkered with an endless array of new-fangled mechanical contraptions. There may have been hundreds of such enthusiastic amateurs in Wisconsin alone, but it was the relatively untutored tinkering of two young Milwaukee men in particular that would give rise to an American legend.

The story begins in 1900 – 15 years after Gottlieb Daimler created the world's first powered two-wheeler and only six years after the first production machine – when William Sylvester Harley and Arthur Davidson got together in a Milwaukee basement with motorcycling in mind.

Information from these early years is sketchy, so the inspiration for their enthusiasm is unclear. A primitive motorcycle was demonstrated by its creator, Edward Joel Pennington, on nearby Wisconsin Avenue as early as 1895, though it's not clear whether the duo actually witnessed the event. They are known to have been impressed by a variety act five years later, however, in which comedienne Anna Held rode a French-built motorcycle across the stage of Milwaukee's Bijou theatre.

Harley was just 20 at the time, Davidson a year younger. The pair had been friends since their school days and, by accident or fate, had already accumulated some of the skills their

■ ABOVE *The founders, from left: Arthur Davidson, Walter Davidson, William Harley and William Davidson.*

■ BELOW *What is believed to be the very first production Harley-Davidson, now fully restored, enjoys pride of place in the Juneau Avenue lobby.*

■ RIGHT AND BELOW *The Model 5D twin from 1909 was essentially two singles on a common crankcase. Valve gear problems meant that only 27 were built. Production of an improved version began for 1911 with the Model 7D.*

■ RIGHT *America's early road network was primitive, but motorcycles proved easier to manhandle than cars.*

dreams required by the time they began working together in that Milwaukee basement. Harley worked as a draughtsman and had six years of experience in bicycle manufacturing; Davidson was a pattern maker with the same company as Harley, working on small petrol (gas) engines. They were also fortunate enough to have working alongside them a German colleague familiar with pioneering European motorcycles. Work on the first Harley-Davidson engine began in 1900 or 1901 and was probably based on one of the do-it-yourself kits then available, itself roughly based on the French De Dion-Bouton design. A drawing dated 20 July 1901 shows a 7.07cu in (115.8cc) engine with a bore and stroke of 2 x 2.25in (50 x 55mm). When installed in a bicycle, power proved deeply disappointing.

At least one more prototype followed, including a machine capable of "thrilling speeds up to 25mph" and measuring 10.2cu in (167cc). It soon became clear that their venture required more expertise if it was ever going to get up to speed – beginning with the need for a skilled mechanic. Fortunately, Arthur's brother, Walter Davidson, was just such a man.

Walter was working as a railroad machinist in Parsons, Kansas, at the time, but was due in Milwaukee for the wedding of a third Davidson

■ ABOVE *By 1913 all Harley twins enjoyed all-chain drive, although the basic Model 9A single (right) continued with leather belt drive.*

brother, William A. (Bill). Arthur wrote to Walter, offering him a ride on their new motorcycle. It was only later that he discovered ("imagine my chagrin") that he would have to help build it first. He must have liked the idea though –, enough to find work in Milwaukee and join the team. The founders became four when William, the eldest Davidson brother and a foreman railway toolmaker, jumped on board – and the four began the ride of their lives.

The machine recognized as the first true Harley-Davidson engine was built during 1902-3, by which time locally built Merkel and Mitchell motorcycles were already a familiar feature of Milwaukee life. Bore and stroke were 3 x 3.5in (76.2 x 88.9mm) for a displacement of 24.74cu in (405cc) but the Harley-Davidson engine incorporated many technical refinements. The new engine was of F-head layout, with much larger cooling fins than before, as well as much larger flywheels – almost 10in (250mm) across. Some of the machining was done on a lathe belonging to a friend, Henry Melk, while other parts were crafted illicitly as parts for foreign sales in the toolrooms of William A. Davidson's employers, the Chicago, Milwaukee and St Paul Railroad. Legend has it that the first carburettor was made from a discarded tomato can (although this could as easily refer to the 1901 engine), and Bill Harley later described its spark plug, which had cost the princely sum of $3.00, as being "as big as a doorknob".

Assistance with the design came from Arthur's childhood friend, Ole Evinrude, who was already making liquid-cooled engines of his own and would later find fame with his outboard motors. Evinrude is credited with setting up the carburettor, but other components – notably the roller tappets still used on Harleys today – may have been his idea as well. Scaling 49lbs (22kg), this engine was installed in a loop frame similar to the existing Merkel design, in the Davidson family's back yard at 315 37th Street. The site, known as 38th Street today, is now owned by the giant Miller Brewery and is little more than a stone's throw from Juneau Avenue.

■ BELOW *A well-to-do couple with a Model 9A, pictured in 1913.*

■ LEFT *Team Harley in 1915, from left: Otto Walker, Harry Crandall, Joe Walter, Red Parkhurst, Alva Stratton and Ralph Cooper.*

■ **THE HARLEY-DAVIDSON MOTOR CO.**

So it was that in 1903 – the same year the Wright brothers took to the air – the Harley-Davidson team created its first motorcycle and readied itself to produce similar machines for public consumption. This handsome machine was gloss black with gold pinstriping, a single-loop tubular steel frame, unsprung forks and leather belt final drive directly from the crankshaft. Additional power was offered by pedals, which also provided the only braking force. It is unclear how many machines were built during 1904 – sources suggest figures anywhere from one to eight, although anything over three seems unlikely. However many there were, each was assembled in a 15 x 10ft shed erected in the Davidson back yard by the boys' father, a cabinet-maker. Modest though it was, the shed bore the legend "Harley-Davidson Motor Co." on its front (and only) door with typical understated pride.

The first production Harley has a tale to tell all its own. It carried its first owner, a Mr Mayer, for almost 6,000 miles before passing to George Lyon, who covered another 15,000 miles. It was sold in turn to a Dr Webster, followed by Louis Fluke and Stephen Sparrow, who between them clocked up almost another 62,000 relatively untroubled miles (a total of 134,000 km). By 1913, the company decided to advertise the bike's exploits, promoting an image of dependable travel:

■ BELOW *This celebratory restoration of a 1913 single shows an image of the first factory (which was located on Juneau Avenue, Milwaukee) on the tank.*

■ ABOVE *The inlet-over-exhaust valve layout is clearly seen on this early "Renault Gray" single.*

■ LEFT *William S. Harley on the left and Walter Davidson on the right getting a motorcycle over the rocks of a creek, 1912.*

"100,000 miles on its original bearings and no major components replaced". Harley-Davidson engines were also produced for use in "buckboards" (four-wheel wagons) and the company's earliest advertisements also proposed their use in boats.

Motorcycle production soared to seven in 1905 as the company took on its first outside employee and attracted its first dealer, C.H. Lang of Chicago, who would become the largest motorcycle dealer in the country within a dozen years. A year later, in 1906, "Renault gray with red pinstriping" joined black as a colour option, and the model became known as "the Silent Gray Fellow", a name that reflected its quietness and dependability.

Engine capacity had by now increased to 26.84cu in (440cc) and the list price for the latest models was $200.

Production had soared to 50 units by 1906, prompting a move from the company's original hut on 37th Street and Highway Boulevard into its first proper building on the present Juneau Avenue site. The new factory turned out to be sitting partially on land belonging to the railroad. Fortunately, the "factory" was a wooden structure, and at 28 x 80ft (9 x 25 metres) eight or ten people were able to carry it the few feet to its proper location.

Finance for expansion came from a relative, James McLay, known as "the honey uncle" due to his generosity and hobby of beekeeping. This affectionate tribute was more appropriate than anyone could imagine, for Juneau Avenue was to become a veritable hive of activity, seven days a week, 365 days a year.

■ BELOW RIGHT AND LEFT *An unrestored and original 1915 61-inch F-head twin. Note that pedal assistance is still retained.*

■ FORGING AHEAD

By 1907, the company was getting serious: it became Harley-Davidson Inc. Walter was the largest stockholder, followed by Arthur, with the two Williams a joint third. A Davidson sister, Elizabeth, also had the good sense to buy Harley-Davidson shares early in the firm's

■ ABOVE *A rare 1914 Model 10C single with hugely complex two-speed rear hub.*

■ BELOW *Harley-Davidson motorcycles and sidecars were used by the rural postal service.*

life. (By 1916, Davidson family stockholders would outnumber Harleys seventeen to three.) It was a heady time. The company had already taken on extra staff; William Harley had begun an engineering degree at the University of Wisconsin in Madison; Walter was exploring the mysteries of heat treatment on metals; and the enterprise, and Arthur, as company secretary and sales manager, was taking a more

professional approach to production and training. The company may have begun as four young men with more enthusiasm than talent, but they had ambitions for the company they had created. That year, they produced no fewer than 150 machines and within 12 months had sold the first of many thousands for police duty.

Even so, it was clear that further progress demanded a more ambitious new motorcycle than the existing single, which in 1909 expanded to 30.17cu in (495cc). By 1908, William Harley had graduated and continued work on a more potent engine. This bore fruit a year later with the launch of the company's first production V-twin, the Model D, essentially a doubled-up single with strengthened bottom-end.

The first such model became officially available on 15 February 1909, although the first working prototype appears to have been built as early as 1906. A press report from the time clearly mentions a 53in (869cc) Harley twin in April 1908, while a privately-owned Harley-Davidson twin won a hill climb event at Algonquin, Illinois, in July that same year.

Whatever its exact development history, the Model D twin was an inlet-over-exhaust valve design with a capacity of 53.7cu in (880cc), developing around six horsepower and capable

■ LEFT *By 1917 Olive Green had replaced Renault Gray as the factory colour, here on a Model J twin three-speed.*

of a top speed close to 62mph (100 kph). The cylinders were splayed apart at the trademark 45 degree angle.

The strength of the Model D twin was amply proven in June 1908 when Walter drove one of his bikes to its first "official" competition success, a two-day endurance run in New York's Catskill Mountains. The sole Harley scored a "perfect" 1,000 points, outstripping all the more fancied runners in a field of 61 machines. Surprisingly – and embarrassingly – the first production twins were beset by valve-gear problems, with production being suspended during 1910.

The factory resisted official racing for several years despite widespread success in competitions. The factory's reluctance continued even when a private owner took the new 61in (989cc) X8E twin (the first Harley with a clutch) to victory in the 1912 San José road race by no less than 17 miles (27km): Bill Harley established a works race department two years later.

■ A DEPENDABLE TWIN

When the V-engine reappeared as the "50-inch" (810cc) Model 7D of 1911, no expense had been spared and every effort made to produce a machine worthy of Harley-Davidson's reputation. Not only had proper mechanical valves replaced the hit-and-miss automatic inlets, an adjustable tensioner had been added to the slippage-prone belt final drive.

Another notable improvement to this model saw the revised powerplant housed in a new, much sturdier frame.

■ BELOW LEFT *Since opening in 1919, this Juneau Avenue factory has been the home of Harley-Davidson.*

■ BELOW RIGHT *William Ottaway, who was Harley's first race boss, sits astride a 1924 Model JDCA.*

■ RIGHT *Gordon, Walter Jnr. and Allan Davidson (sitting on bikes) in San Francisco after a cross-country ride in 1929.*

A year later, a 61cu in (989cc) version, the chain-drive Model X8E, reinforced these developments. With its second attempt, Harley hit the nail on the head, and the V-twin took its rightful place in Milwaukee history.

Production in the rapidly expanding company soared to 450 machines in 1908, housed in a new, brick-built factory of 2,380sq ft (221sq metres) and employing 18 people. New machinery arrived almost weekly and was set to work, according to legend, "as soon as the cement was dry", and in what must have seemed like an instant, became obsolete. Two years later, 149 staff were engaged in another new factory – a reinforced concrete structure of 9,520sq ft (885sq metres).

■ RIGHT *Harley-Davidson's first V-Twin engine, introduced in 1909. It displaced 49.5cu in (811cc).*

By the time the new 5hp, 35cu in single model (565cc 5–35) appeared in 1913, the company had established a reputation for producing machines that were dependable in both domestic and competitive use. The factory was hurtling ahead as well in this changing age and included a separate Parts and Accessories Department. More than 1,500 employees worked for a company whose manufacturing floor area had grown from nothing to almost 300,000sq ft (28,000sq metres) within a decade. Production rocketed from eight machines in 1905 to 1,149 in 1911 and 17,439 in 1916, the year prior to the United States' entry into the First World War.

Though not yet dominant in the industry, in 1913 Harley produced around 18 per cent of the 70,000 American-built motorcycles.

Very soon, however, all this would change, and much of this energy would be called to the service of Uncle Sam.

War and Peace

On 6 April 1917, the United States declared war on Germany. Harley's successful peace-time formula suddenly faced an entirely new set of demands for which, five years earlier, the company may have been ill-prepared. By 1917, however, this bullish, expanding company was ready to go to war for real.

Harley-Davidson supplied the best part of 20,000 motorcycles to the American military in total, the majority being 61-inch twins. Indeed, the war did little but good for the company's prospects. Rival European motorcycle manufacturers were preoccupied by hostilities for a much longer period (1914–18) than those in the United States. Consequently, Milwaukee was able to extend its markets and reputation overseas. By 1918, aided by a $3 million loan from the M&I bank, Harley-Davidson had become the world's largest manufacturer of motorcycles. Within a year, "Hap" Scherer had been appointed Harley-Davidson's first publicity manager. By 1921, machines were being sold through 2,000 dealers in 67 countries, with product catalogues printed in seven languages. As the dust settled on the carnage of the war, one-sixth of Milwaukee's production was destined for export.

■ ABOVE ***Harley was quick to develop its bikes for war, including mounting them with machine guns.***

■ BELOW ***Milwaukee-built sidecars proved to be extremely popular for both military and civilian use.***

■ RIGHT *Board racers were Harleys in their leanest form, stripped of even any semblance of brakes...*

The aftermath of war had other, less predictable side-effects. One of these was the retention of army green as the company colour in place of the pre-war pale grey. Another more enduring effect concerned training. To help military personnel keep Milwaukee's wares reliable, the Harley-Davidson Service School was established in 1917. Initially intended as a military measure and as concerned with riding instruction as mechanics, the Service School soon developed into a crucial arm of the factory's civilian service.

By the eve of the "Roaring Twenties", the Juneau Avenue factory had become a colossus. In 1919, close to 1,800 employees toiled on a floor area exceeding 400,000sq ft (37,000sq metres) to produce 22,685 motorcycles and over 16,000 sidecars. The Model J Sport Twin, unveiled that same year, was unique among Harleys, if not American motorcycles in general. Instead of the "V" layout, the 35.6cu in (584cc) twin adopted a horizontally opposed design, akin to today's BMWs. Instead of lying across the frame, the cylinders were orientated fore-and-aft. Although long and unwieldy, the layout offered a very low centre of gravity and a compact width, ideally suited to America's then-primitive road network.

■ RIGHT *...or silencing, as can clearly be seen on this handsome 1916 F-head twin.*

■ BELOW *Front brakes finally arrived in the late 1920s, as on this Model J Big Twin.*

There were other innovations, most of which would stand the test of time better than the model itself. The final drive was sensibly protected from dust in a metal enclosure, not unlike more recent MZ machines, lubricated by oil mist from the engine breather. It was also the first model to feature a full electrical

■ LEFT *Before 1927, only a rear brake was fitted onto bikes.*

system produced by the Harley factory. Although the Sport set many records – Canada to Mexico in less than 75 hours, no easy task even today – its six horsepower engine lacked the bottomless big-inch power America demanded, and was discontinued after 1922.

The 1920s didn't so much roar as whimper where motorcycles were concerned. Much of the blame for the Sport Twin's relative failure lay far beyond Milwaukee's control – 1920 witnessed a major trade recession with a massive over-supply of manufactured goods as global economies struggled to adjust to peace-time trade. One of the consequences was Henry Ford's slashing the price of his Model T car to $395, the same as the biggest Harley twin. The effects on motorcycle sales were inevitable. The trade slump was brief, but America's love affair with the car was not, and neither Harley nor any other bike manufacturer fully recovered their previous momentum.

Milwaukee's sales collapsed from over 28,000 in 1920 to 10,202 in 1921, with sales so poor during that spring that the factory, which had expanded 12 months before, shut down for a month. Sales would not return to 1920s levels for a further 21 years. Most of the machines that were sold during that time were 61-inch V-twins.

Although the Sport failed to make the impact Harley hoped, one of the next models quickly became a Milwaukee legend. In 1921, the V-twin was replaced by the JD and FD, the first 74-inch (actually 74.2cu in/1,216cc) models, with F-head, inlet-over-exhaust (ioe) valve layout. Each example was dubbed a "Superpowered Twin" in tribute to its 18-hp engine and both underwent rigorous pre-delivery testing: yet another Harley innovation.

■ BELOW *Inventiveness is apparent in this 1919 twin, fitted with stabilising skis for use in icy conditions.*

■ RIGHT *The 1920s was marked mostly by F-head machines like this 1922 61-inch twin. Flatheads began to appear from 1926, the same year as the first overhead valve engines.*

As for the rest of the range, the 30-inch single had been dropped after 1918. In 1926, a new single – the 21in (344cc) Model A – was introduced, joined four years later by a 30.5in (492cc) sister. In a radical move, Harley-Davidson pioneered the front brake in 1928, just as the company had pioneered kick-starts and three-speed transmissions more than a decade earlier. All models were sold in varied specifications of transmission, valve-gear and power, so that in 1928, for instance, three basic engine types accounted for no less than a dozen models. By this time, Harley's only surviving domestic competitors were Indian, Henderson, Cleveland and Super-X.

The last year of the decade introduced the machine that would become Milwaukee's bread and butter. The new WL was a 45in (742cc) side-valve V-twin which supposedly combined the single's agility with the power of the bigger twins. Capped by rakish twin "bullet" headlights, the new model was an instant success and constituted the lowest rung on a V-twin ladder made up of 45-, 61- and 74-inchers). Star billing in the 1929 Harley-Davidson catalogue went to the JDH Two-Cam, which housed a specially-prepared variant of the 74-inch engine that had been developed for the factory's all-conquering board racers.

Billed as "the fastest road model that Harley-Davidson has ever offered to the public", it could probably out-run any other two-wheeler on the American highway.

The WL may have been humbler but it proved its worth by keeping Milwaukee's head above water in the years ahead.

■ RIGHT *This stylish ohv "Peashooter" speedway machine dates from 1927.*

The 1930s

■ ABOVE *By the 1930s all Harleys were flatheads, such as this imposing 74-inch VL from 1933.*

The 1930s began in high spirits with arguably the most mouth-watering range to come out of Milwaukee for years. All models now had bigger brakes and tyres, improved ground clearance, lower saddles and – best of all – removable cylinder heads. These "Ricardo" heads were far more practical and efficient than the one-piece iron cylinders previously employed. Although plagued by early problems, the new high-compression 74.2cu in (1,216cc) VL offered fully 15 per cent more power than any previous Harley roadster. A nation-wide "open house" attracted customers by the thousands and, with sales quickly up 30 per cent on the previous year, the new decade appeared rich in promise.

There was one cloud on the horizon, however. In October 1929, a few weeks after the 1930 range was unveiled, the Wall Street stock market crashed, sending tremors throughout the American economy and the rest of the world. President Herbert Hoover's initial rapid intervention seemed to stem the tide but economic confidence continued to wilt. In 1930, 1,300 banks went to the wall. Manufacturers in every industry offered incentives to stimulate business, but to no avail. Within 12 months, the mighty Juneau Avenue factory was running at a mere 10 per cent of production capacity and would report a loss of more than $320,000 the following year. By 1933, one quarter of the United States workforce was unemployed. Few people had

■ LEFT *1932 saw the introduction of the enduring Servi-Car, which would continue in production for 40 years.*

■ ABOVE *The troubles of the Depression encouraged novel art-deco styling, such as the tank badge on this mammoth 80-inch VLH from 1936. The same motifs can be seen even on modern Harleys.*

money to spend on motorcycles. Of hundreds of American bike manufacturers, only Harley and Indian had the financial strength and acumen to survive. Industry-wide production fell from 32,000 to 6,000 units per year by 1933, by which time fewer than 100,000 motorcycles were registered in the whole of the United States. Of these new sales, Milwaukee's share was just 3,703 – its lowest in 23 years.

Desperately, Juneau Avenue wracked its brains for innovative sales ideas, ranging from savings plans to a medal scheme intended to turn every Harley owner into a salesman. One enduring response was the sale of branded clothing and accessories – a sideline now worth millions of dollars per year. A superficial but significant measure was the abandonment of dull green paint in 1933, in favour of more vivid colours and art-deco graphics which continue to brighten Harley-Davidsons today.

An altogether grittier response was the three-wheeled Servi-Car, a cheap delivery and police vehicle powered by the 45-inch (742cc) Model D engine. Surprisingly, given the fraught circumstances of the time, this three-wheeler was both a sound design and a solid piece of engineering – so tough and enduring, indeed, that it survived in production from late 1931 until 1974. The true hero of the Depression years was the side-valve twin: cheap to produce, economic to run and maintain, and easily repairable.

Almost on their own, the D and V models saw Harley through the Depression, along with the 30.5in (492cc) single-cylinder machine of 1929. As the financial vice tightened, no other significant new models were developed during those six years.

In many ways, the worst of the Depression also brought out the best in the company. By reducing the length of the working week, as many staff were kept on as possible, although this was less generous than it might appear, since it was partially mandated by the

government's National Recovery Administration, and every skilled hand would be needed when the slump finally abated. Prudent financial controls, police and military contracts, novel sales strategies and energetic pursuit of exports kept the company afloat, and by 1934, the books were back in the black.

■ KNUCKLING DOWN

Painfully slowly, President Roosevelt's "New Deal" began to take effect and, by 1936, the crippling Depression came to a close. New machines began to emerge from Milwaukee, whose 1935 model range had comprised a mere two basic models. These were the 45-inch (742cc) Model R (essentially the D model with light alloy pistons, soon to become the heroic W) and the 74-inch (1,216cc) Model V and its derivatives, now cured of its original and varied ills. Both were side-valve designs, slow and steady, whereas the American public increasingly craved more advanced machines.

■ ABOVE LEFT *A WLA in desert camouflage stands out against civilian chrome.*

ABOVE RIGHT AND BELOW *Drab green was more common. Almost 90,000 of these 45-inch (742cc) flathead twins were built for the military during the Second World War, and thousands served with the Soviet forces.*

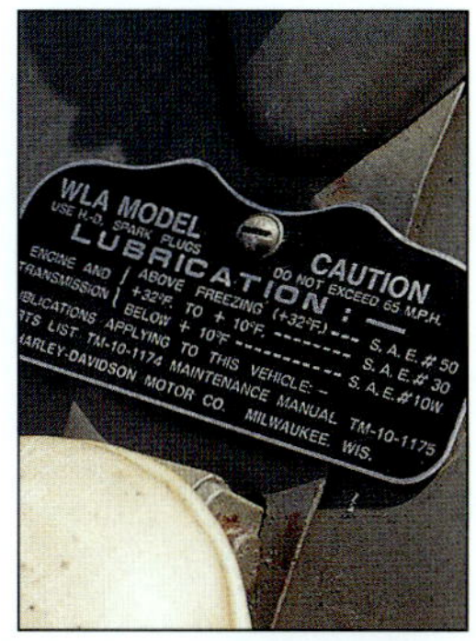

The biggest newcomer was the V-twin Model UL. Although still side-valve and visually similar to the proven DL45, it displaced a stupendous 78.9cu in (1,293cc), making it ideal for heavy sidecar use. It was to continue in production until 1945. Most important of all was a new generation of 61-inch (898cc) twin with overhead valves and twice the power of its predecessor. The legendary Model E – the Knucklehead – had arrived.

The 1936 Knuckle could have appeared in 1934 but for government restrictions aimed at reducing employment. For company and public alike, this was frustrating but certainly worth the wait. The Knuckle was a Juneau Avenue first in many respects – the first four (forward) speeder; the first overhead valve roadster twin; the first hemispherical heads. The engine was heavily influenced by the competition experience of the legendary Joe Petrali, Harley development rider and near-unbeatable racer. It announced its arrival by 136.183mph (219.16kph) on the sands of Daytona Beach, Florida. The rider, naturally, was Joe. His waterside speed record stands to this day.

■ **ABOVE LEFT AND RIGHT** ***The "A" in WLA stood for army, so naturally military rules came with the machines. Soldiers were warned not to exceed 65mph.***

■ **RIGHT AND BELOW** ***Even soldiers could be customizers: note the "Uncle Sam" on the fuel tank (right) and grenade-box lettering (below).***

With the new model as its flagship, Harley's fortunes rapidly improved. In 1937, sales exceeded 11,000 for the first time since 1930. The same year brought significant improvements elsewhere in the range: full roller bearing engines, chromolly fork tubes and interchangeable wheels.

As well as these technical advances, the lessons of the Depression had instilled in the company a faith in styling and cosmetics which stands them in good stead even today. The aftermarket and art-deco innovations of 1932 were continued. Balloon tyres appeared in 1940 (more striking, if less functional, than new aluminium alloy heads for the flathead side-valve models). In 1941, four-speed transmissions became standard across the big twin range. Eleven models were now on the books in four basic engine configurations: side-valves of 45-, 74- and 80-inch (742, 1,216 and 1,293cc), and Knuckleheads of 61-inch Model E (989cc) and 74-inch Model F (1,207cc).

■ LEFT *Civilian versions of the humble WL45 could be surprisingly handsome.*

■ BACK TO WAR

Motorcycle production in Milwaukee rose from a low of 3,703 in 1933 to more than 18,000 in 1941. Harley made it through the Depression by the narrowest of squeaks, emerging stronger than ever before. However, not long after this rocky period in Harley-Davidson's history, a catastrophe of an altogether more terrible kind occurred: the world once again went to war.

The United States entered the conflict after the bombing of Pearl Harbor on 7 December 1941.

As the country's largest motorcycle producer, it fell to Harley-Davidson to underpin the bulk of the country's two-wheeled war effort. Throughout the years of America's involvement in the war (1942–45), practically the entire output of the Milwaukee factory was turned over to military production – some 90,000 machines in total.

As with the First World War, the Second was fairly good to Milwaukee. In 1940, sales

■ LEFT *Astonishingly, the WL45 engine survived until the 1970s in the Servi-Car.*

■ LEFT *During the Second World War almost no machines were made for civilian use. This is one of the first post-war WL45 twins, in vibrant red.*

■ RIGHT *The noble Knucklehead, Milwaukee's first overhead valve roadster twin.*

totalled less than 11,000. These soared to 18,000 as the military build-up began in 1941, reaching more than 29,000 in each of the two years that followed before tailing off again as peace approached. However, since the military favoured Harley Davidson's robust side-valve plodders over the new Model E and Model F, this meant that Knucklehead production was practically zero during the same period.

HARLEY JAPAN

One little-known, highly ironic consequence of Milwaukee's quest for export markets in the 1920s and the economic slump of the 1930s was the creation of a Japanese big twin. During the 1920s, Arthur Davidson had pursued new sales openings with vigour, including the establishment of the Harley-Davidson Sales Company of Japan with a comprehensive network of dealers, agencies and spares distributors. Milwaukee's stock stood so high that Harleys soon became Japan's official police motorcycle.

Less worthily, in 1924 the Murata Iron Works began building copies of the 1922 Model J, but the quality was appalling. Murata would later build the Meguro, a distant precursor of modern Kawasakis. Harley exports to Japan all but ceased in the wake of the 1929 Wall Street crash, as the global economic slump crippled the yen. The story might have stopped there but for Alfred Childs, head of Harley's Japanese operation, who asked: "Why not build Harleys there?"

Juneau Avenue was sceptical at first, but such was Childs' persistence that Harley's first overseas factory soon began production at Shinagawa, near Tokyo. Built with tooling, plans, blueprints and expertise borrowed from Milwaukee, the factory was considered the most modern in the world. By 1935 Shinagawa was manufacturing complete motorcycles, mainly 74-inch V-series flathead twins. In 1930, these had become the official motorcycle of the Japanese Imperial Army. Later, when the army became the effective civil power, it declined the chance to convert production to the new ohv Knucklehead, preferring the proven durability of the side-valve twin. It was at this point that the Sankyo corporation took over control of the factory and began selling Japanese Harleys under the Rikuo name. The "74" twin became the Rikuo Model 97.

As an increasingly truculent Japan readied for war, Harley cut its losses and sold out. As military demand increased (especially after the invasion of China in 1937), Rikuo sub-licensed the product to Nihon Jidosha ("Japan Combustion Equipment Co."). Its "Harleys" were variants of the model 97s, entitled Kuro Hagane ("Black Iron").

Ominously, the factory had only a few more years to run. Nihon Jidosha was located in Hiroshima.

Back to Peace

■ BELOW *A 1946 FL Knucklehead, as handsome a motor as Milwaukee has built.*

Although the Second World War ended on 15 August 1945 following the Japanese surrender, it would be more than a year before the unveiling of any new revisions from Milwaukee. Even these – theoretically 1947 models – were no more than cosmetic updates of Harley's pre-war machines. Of all the changes, perhaps the best remembered is Brook Steven's design for new "streamlined" H-D tank badges. A revamped clothing and accessories catalogue appeared in the same model year, a harbinger of the direction the company would take three decades later.

For the time being, however, motorcycles were scarce as the industry readjusted to civilian production and the loss of military demand. In the aftermath of the War Department's cancellation of orders for over 11,000 machines in 1944, more than 500 Harley-Davidson workers were let go. The rest, limited to a shortened working week, went on strike in late 1945. Paradoxically, limits on civilian production remained in force, and things went from bad to worse when 15,000 war surplus WLs were offered for public sale. It would be two more years before motorcycle production regained its pre-war level.

■ BELOW *But by 1948 the Knucklehead was history as the era of the Panhead had begun, as with this HydraGlide.*

There was only one thing that had not changed in the forced interlude of war – Harley-Davidson's winning ways. In 1947, among other successes, seven of the first ten Daytona finishers rode Harleys. Over the next two years, 36 of 47 AMA championship events went to the Milwaukee marque.

Harley-Davidson took up residence in a second factory on Capitol Drive, Wauwatosa, in 1947. By 1948, production was at an all-time high and, more important to America's highways, the replacement for the noble Knucklehead made its first public appearance that same year. The Panhead as it became known, was a development of the Knuckle rather than an all-new concept. As well as a revised (and much more oil-tight) lubrication

■ LEFT *Before the appearance of the HydraGlide's telescopic forks, the first Panheads ran with the old girder-fork chassis, as with this magnificently restored 1948 example.*

system, the Pan featured aluminium alloy cylinder heads in place of the Knuckle's iron and hydraulic "lifters" rather than solid push-rods. The Pan, so named because its chrome-plated rocker covers resembled inverted baking pans, was built in both 74cu in (1,200cc) and 61cu in (1,000cc) sizes; the latter was discontinued in 1953. The larger version retained the "traditional" bore and stroke dimensions of 3⁷⁄₁₆ x 4in (87 x 101mm).

The first all-new model powered by the Panhead engine was the HydraGlide of 1949, so-called because it was the first Harley to incorporate hydraulically-damped, telescopic front forks. It was also, of course, the first model granted one of the most evocative titles in motorcycling: "Glide". The Panhead engine would do much to get the species on its famous way, propelling not only the DuoGlide of 1958 but the first of the ElectraGlides as well.

Though no-one knew it at the time, this first Glide was to set the visual cues for the "Retro-Tech" Harleys which would appear four decades later. From its deeply-valanced mudguards and its chromed fork shrouds to its stylized rear end, the style of modern Softails owes much to the HydraGlide.

■ INTO THE 1950S

Harley-Davidson styles of the 1950s were in many ways a contradiction of those with which the company is now synonymous. True, 1950s imagery rates high in current Harley design but the decade began under the cloud of the Hollister "riots" of 1947, which tarnished the

■ RIGHT *Another perfectly restored example of a 1948 Panhead.*

■ LEFT *Even the hottest side-valve Model K, the KHK, was unable to run with European overhead valve (ohv) sports machines which stole Harley's thunder during the 1950s.*

image of motorcycling and alarmed motorcycle manufacturers. The true creator of the riots, however, was the media (including *Life* magazine) which represented the gathering in Hollister as a major assault on small-town America. The world was just getting over the shock when the Hollister-inspired film *The Wild One* was released in 1953, reopening old wounds. Although the film's star, Marlon Brando, rode a Triumph Thunderbird on screen, many people still swear it was a Harley.

■ RIGHT AND BELOW *The Model K-derived KRTT fared better on the track, whilst on the street, their slowness made them popular with the insurers of Hollywood stars.*

Even if the typical Harley owner of the day could handle the tarnished image of the motorcycle he loved, he may have been less sanguine about another development: in 1947, the world's foremost manufacturer of big V-twins began the manufacture of two strokes.

This seemingly radical departure was an attempt to bring Milwaukee's appeal to a wider market, a move that was applauded at the time by many observers.

The line began with the 125cc Model S, a 1.7 horsepower machine based on the same German DKW RT125 design as the BSA Bantam, the rights to which both companies acquired as part of Germany's war reparations. More than 10,000 were built in the model's debut year, based on the expensive misconception that war veterans would buy almost anything with wheels, before production slipped to a more realistic 4,000 or so per annum. The engine grew to 165cc in 1954, powering the Models ST and Super Ten before increasing to 175cc for the Ranger/Pacer/Scat series in 1962. Perhaps Harley's best-known lightweights were the 125cc Model B Hummer, produced from 1955–59, and the 165cc Topper Scooter of the early 1960s.

■ ABOVE *The HydraGlide was special, but something was missing...*

■ BELOW *...this came with the DuoGlide, the first Harley big twin to feature real suspension at both ends.*

Unfortunately, other manufacturers were also intent on broadening their markets. Harley-Davidson had by now introduced dealer demonstrator models and was to lose one competitor with the demise of Indian in 1953, but Triumph's creation of a vibrant new American import network in 1951 was a major alarm.

Isolated by war and supported by military production, Harley had enjoyed easy pickings for too long. Triumph – along with other British marques such as BSA, Norton and Royal Enfield – had a range of cheaper yet much more exciting and technically sophisticated models than Harley-Davidson (whose flagship model persisted with hand-gear-change until 1952).

Harley's response was heavy-handed and ultimately counter-productive as they attempted to bully dealers into having no business with the British pretenders.

Milwaukee also went so far as to apply for federal trade protection in 1952, alleging that the British machines were being subsidized and "dumped" on the American market. They asked for a 40 per cent import tax and quotas on the number of machines that Triumph (and parent company BSA) could import.

Thirty years later, Harley would get the protection that it had wanted, this time against the Japanese. The first time around, however, the Government's Tariff Commission found that Triumph had no case to answer. Worse still, they told Harley to quit its restrictive trading practices – a ruling that was to have devastating echoes for the company in the decades ahead.

■ ABOVE *Not quite King of the Road: a Milwaukee two-stroke.*

■ **OLD, SLOW AND OBSOLETE**

No model summed up Harley's problem more than the Model K, introduced in 1952 to replace the WL. The K was a heavy 45.3cu in (742cc) side-valve design compared to the overhead valves, lightweight construction and good suspension offered by British twins (and, in the case of Norton, arguably the finest handling motorcycle in the world). Granted, the K included proper suspension at both ends – a first for Milwaukee – but in virtually every other respect it was woefully outclassed by the British-made bikes.

Harley claimed 30 horsepower for the Model K, which was only a little less than the contemporary Triumph Thunderbird. Whether or not this was true, the 85mph (137kph) V-twin was no match for the 103mph (166 kph) British model, although the KK version, which had hotter cams, was better. Early Model Ks also had serious mechanical problems, although quality and power was improved by a capacity increase to 883cc for the 55-inch KH model in 1954.

■ BELOW *The Shovelhead would replace the Panhead for the 1966 model year, as with this ElectraGlide.*

Remarkably, Paul Goldsmith took a K-based KR racer to victory by more than two miles (3km) in the Daytona 200 road race of 1953, a victory Harley-Davidsons were to repeat for the remainder of the decade. In 1954, the legendary Joe Leonard became first American national champion on KR and KR-TT racers. Although superficially impressive, these exploits owed much to the now familiar ploy of persuading the authorities to handicap the opposition. In this case, foreign ohv engines competing against 750cc Harley flatheads were limited to 500cc.

The K sold moderately well but overall sales figures show the full extent of Milwaukee's problem. In wheel-hungry 1948, Harley-Davidson produced more than 31,000 machines, the largest figure in its history. Yet by 1955, sales had plummeted to a low of less than 12,000. The problem could not be blamed on public disaffection with motorcycling, either – during the same period sales of imported machines went from strength to strength.

The machine which superseded the Model K in 1957 – the XL Sportster – was better in every way, eventually. The original Sportster's performance was lacklustre but by 1958 it benefited to the tune of 12 horsepower, due to lighter valve-gear, higher compression, larger ports and valves, and a legend was born.

■ RIGHT *What Harleys are best at: cruising the vastness of the good ol' US of A.*

Displacing 53.9cu in (883cc), as today, the XL boasted unit construction for the engine and gearbox. Swing-arm rear suspension with car-type dampers allowed early Sportsters to be sold for either on- or off-road use. The XL was an instant hit, accounting for almost 20 per cent of Harley's 1957 production of more than 13,000 machines. In 1958, the stock XL was joined by one of the most legendary Harleys ever produced, the XLCH – "Competition Hot". Other variations have included the low-riding Hugger (1979) and the limited-edition XR1000 (1983). The Sportster is also father to the remarkable XR750 dirt oval racer.

■ RIGHT *The Topper scooter was another of Milwaukee's attempts to diversify. At best, these achieved very limited success.*

■ GLIDING INTO THE 1960S

As the 1950s drew to a close, the HydraGlide finally got the rear suspension it deserved and the Model F DuoGlide was born in 1958. The Duo featured a hydraulic rear brake as well as handsome two-tone styling and a swinging-fork rear end. However, this was something of an indulgence as both wheels contained puny six-inch drum brakes which struggled to slow down the Glide's substantial bulk, whatever their means of operation. The Duo is perhaps better remembered for film stardom – Dennis Hopper rode one in the cult movie *Easy Rider*.

With a new heavyweight on the block and the Sportster selling moderately well, Harley-Davidson renewed its attention to expanding its market base. One of the more successful measures was a move into glass-fibre moulding – initially boats, but later golf carts and motorcycle accessories. The main goal was still a foothold in the global boom in motorcycle sales. At the time, this meant lightweight machines, a demand to which the existing two-strokes were proving unequal. Sales of the ST

■ BELOW *Harley would surely have done better to concentrate on its core business, big V-twins, than on other models.*

■ LEFT *Harley's purchase of Aermacchi broadened its range and even brought grand prix success.*

were roughly similar to those of the Sportster, yet profit margins were much lower. Juneau Avenue's Development Committee, responsible for future planning, decided that collaboration with an overseas company might be the most effective way forward.

Consequently, Harley became half-owner of the motorcycle division of Aermacchi, or Aeronautica Macchi SpA, for just under $250,000. Harley anticipated the partnership would generate sales of 6,000 lightweight bikes per year, to be produced in Varese, Italy.

The first Harley-Aermacchi appeared in September 1960, quickly announcing its pedigree with a 1-2-3 result at the Santa Fe AMA short track championship races. The 250 Sprint was based on a spine-framed, horizontal, single-cylinder, four-stroke design similar to that of the famous Aermacchi racers, although most subsequent "joint venture" models would be small two-strokes. The 250 was light, powerful (the company claimed 21 horsepower, growing to 25 by 1964), handled well and spawned a line of superb racing machines.

Yet the Sprint and its fellow Macchis – and indeed Milwaukee's home-grown lightweights – all failed to live up to Harley's commercial expectations, for a variety of reasons. Communications between the company's headquarters in the United States and Varese were often poor, causing continuous supply problems with bought-in components and incompatibility with American parts. Later, after the AMF take-over of Harley-Davidson in 1969, specifications were often changed erratically, without appropriate consultation or repricing. Most of all, the products were not wanted by a public being offered Japanese machines of ever-more sophisticated specification at lower prices (Honda had entered the American market in 1959). Nor were they wanted by dealers who had to carry new parts stock, retrain staff and relearn their business – all for a much smaller profit margin.

There were high-points, though – not least Walter Villa's consecutive world 250cc road-race titles in 1974 and 1975. The four-strokes got into the act: Roger Reiman took a Sprint-powered streamliner to a new world 250cc speed record of 156mph (251.05kph) in 1964, improved to 177mph (284.85kph) in 1965.

It was an unrewarding marriage and divorce came too late.

In June 1978, Harley closed its Italian factory. Juneau Avenue would never again aspire to a true mass market.

■ BELOW *ElectraGlide, possibly the most evocative badge in motorcycling.*

THE AMF YEARS

In 1964, Harley-Davidson not only unveiled its first new corporate logo in almost 60 years but also the model bearing possibly the most evocative name in the company's long history: ElectraGlide. Yet it was the following year that would be remembered as the more momentous. According to Harley lore, 1965 represented two climactic events. The first was the unveiling of a new generation of Shovelhead engines, replacing the venerable Panheads. Second, and ultimately more far-reaching, was the decision to list the company on the New York Stock Exchange – after more than 60 years as a family firm, its founding families were now to lose complete control.

More than 1.3 million Harley shares were sold in the four years that followed the original listing. They performed well and investors – and straightforward enthusiasts – felt good. Optimism was short-lived once again, however, as imported Japanese motorcycles made ever-increasing inroads in the American market. Initially, these machines were middleweights – light, fast, affordable and refined – but soon Honda would begin a full-frontal assault with the seminal four-cylinder CB750. The age of the high-performance "superbike" had arrived.

As Harley's fortunes ebbed and its shares dipped, it came under threat of takeover from an industrial conglomerate, Bangor Punta, which was busily accumulating Harley-Davidson stock. In 1968, fearful of the

■ ABOVE *Under AMF's ownership, sales improved but quality reputedly suffered, yet the Shovelhead soldiered on.*

■ LEFT *80-inch (1,340cc) versions of the Shovelhead first appeared in 1978, as with this FLH.*

■ ABOVE LEFT *The ohv Sportster was a vast improvement on the sidevalve Model K.*

■ ABOVE RIGHT *More prized still was the tuned XLH Sportster, such as this example from 1972.*

sweeping changes proposed, company president William H. Davidson resumed talks with American Machine and Foundry (AMF).

AMF was another industrial giant with designs on Harley but with less of a predatory reputation (chairman Rodney C. Gott was a keen motorcyclist). Harley recommended AMF's offer to shareholders, most of whom did well out of the subsequent $21 million deal. So it was that on 18 December 1968, Harley-Davidson voted to merge with AMF, a move ratified by shareholders on 7 January 1969. Thus the American icon became AMF property, with Gott as chairman, although it wasn't until 1971 that the new owner's logo would be seen on Harley-Davidson machines.

Today, it is fashionable to believe that AMF starved and milked Milwaukee's finest, that it didn't understand motorcycles or motorcyclists, that quality went to the dogs and that Harley/AMF never built a decent bike. Some of this is probably true, but AMF did sink millions of dollars into its new project. During its first three years in control, total sales more than doubled and, during its 12 years at the helm, sales of American-made machines more than tripled. In addition, the company diversified into such unlikely fields as snowmobiles and desert racers. Sales were reasonably strong but profits, unfortunately, were not.

Difficult labour relations at Capitol Drive were another concern. As a consequence of the

■ RIGHT *The look was still there, as with this flathead, but quality was declining as Harley struggled to keep pace with a changing market.*

tension, the bulk of production was moved to a vacant AMF plant in York, Pennsylvania (where it remains to this day, although Milwaukee has always made engines).

More exciting developments were afoot. 1970 brought a whole new kind of iron, the FX1200 SuperGlide. This was the first of a string of startling cosmetic innovations from the fertile mind of William G. Davidson. Just as crucial was AMF's marketing and promotion expertise, which certainly rubbed off on the future, independent Harley-Davidson company.

■ EXCITING IRON

If the 1970s was a commercially disastrous decade for Harley-Davidson, the hardware it produced at least paved the way for better times to come. Nowhere was this more evident than with the SuperGlide, the first major new twin launched by Harley after the takeover by

■ ABOVE ***"AMF" on the tank was not well received by many, but others still considered the ElectraGlide the king of the road.***

■ LEFT ***The King of the Road title actually referred to optional touring accessories. Bolt-on parts and other "goodies" would become huge business in later years.***

■ ABOVE *A 1972 ElectraGlide: no other motorcycle could get away with a white leather seat.*

AMF. The SuperGlide's hybrid philosophy – a little bit from one model, some from another and more parts from a third – became the essence of all the most memorable Harleys produced since. Despite the splash it made at the time – most road tests praised the SuperGlide expansively – early examples were distinctly under-specified for the new "superbike" age. Disc brakes arrived in 1973 and an electric start option, the FXE, in 1974.

By 1977, Willie G. launched another classic derivative: the FXS Low Rider, complete with standard highway pegs, Fat Bob two-piece petrol tank and a seat just 27in (685mm) above the ground. Later the same year, the XLCR Café Racer was launched. This sinister all-black device was too radical a statement to enjoy much sales success at the time, but is a highly-prized collector's piece today.

The range of options increased further with the introduction of the 80-inch (1,340cc) Shovelhead engine, initially on the ElectraGlide in 1978. This led to the FLH one year later, offered as standard with a complete set of touring extras, later to become the long-haul norm: saddlebags, luggage rack, fairing, running boards and additional lights. This in turn led to the FLT TourGlide of 1980, similar to the full-dress Glide but with better brakes and a larger, twin headlamp touring fairing. More significantly, the FLT featured Harley-Davidsons' first five-speed transmission and, not least, its first use of rubber-mounting to protect the rider from engine vibration.

■ RIGHT *Twin filler caps, tank-top speedometer and lashings of chrome: all Harley hallmarks.*

■ OPPOSITE *Willie G. Davidson (second left) pictured at Daytona with the Japanese-built Sundance racer.*

■ ABOVE *Willie G. Davidson's immortal "factory custom": the trend-setting SuperGlide.*

In fact, 1980 can be viewed as a vintage year all round. The Super Glide cruiser became the FXB Sturgis, named after the famous rally held annually in South Dakota. The "B" represented the first toothed-rubber belt drive – a clean, smooth and trouble-free system now standard across the range. For good measure, there was the FXWG Wide Glide and FXEF Fat Bob.

■ CHALLENGE FROM JAPAN

Nostalgia tells us that the 1970s produced a stream of classic Harley-Davidson models but, hardware aside, it was all an illusion. Even after shedding its Italian operation, the unpalatable truth was that, at the start of the 1980s, few people gave AMF Harley-Davidson very much chance of survival.

Who was to blame? It is tempting to point the finger at AMF, but whatever the company's shortcomings as custodians of the Milwaukee legend, Harley's biggest problem lay in a quite different direction. After all, it was scarcely AMF's fault that this period coincided so precisely with the rise to global domination of the Japanese motorcycle industry.

It is also a myth that Japan hijacked the American motorcycle market, either from Harley-Davidson or from the Europeans. Even after the British invasion of the mid-1950s, sales of new motorcycles in the United States stood at a paltry 60,000 units per year. By 1973, annual sales had soared to more than two million. This staggering increase was almost solely due to the inventiveness and enterprise of the Japanese, who produced reliable, fast and exciting machines far more advanced than any Harley, at a far lower price. Whatever "image" Harleys possessed was undersold, with few buyers prepared to pay the premium. The AMF years had seen turnover grow from $49 million to over $300 million but profits were going into reverse.

Milwaukee's response was to allege cut-price "dumping" of Japanese models, as with Triumph 20 years earlier. The American International Trade Commission agreed that dumping had taken place but that the effective subsidy was almost negligible. It concluded that the practice had not significantly harmed Milwaukee's sales and that the principal cause of Harley's difficulties was self-imposed: its model range was obsolete.

More than a decade earlier, William H. Davidson had remarked that AMF "thought Harley-Davidson could become another

■ BELOW *Another SuperGlide, this time fitted with optional pillion backrest.*

■ BELOW *The American – or is it Harley? – Eagle, proudly displayed in the Visitor Center lobby at Wauwatosa.*

Honda. That's ridiculous... we were never meant to be a high production company."

AMF had to some extent attempted to compete head-on with Japan rather than concentrating on the more specialized market that Harley suited best. Production figures for 1982 offer some measure of the hopelessness of such a strategy: Honda built more than 3.5 million bikes in the year; Harley built less than 50 thousand.

The situation was desperate. Just six short years after 1973, Harley's share of the rapidly growing American big-bike market had plunged from almost 100 per cent to less than 40 per cent.

Production in the United States plummeted from 75,000 motorcycles in 1975 to 41,000 in 1981. Dire labour relations had brought a 101-day strike in 1974 over cost-of-living wage increases. Some in the company saw this coming, despite an artificial boost in 1978 due to the company's 75th birthday celebrations. Vaughn Beals, company president since 1977, and chief engineer Jeff Bleustein alerted top managers to the unpalatable realities. Beals set up a quality control and inspection programme that began to eliminate the worst of the problems, but all these measures were at a prodigious cost.

New initiatives slowly began to put Harley-Davidson back on track. But what would be the first to give : the problem or the company?

■ BELOW *Another symphony in metal from Willie G., the XLCR Café Racer.*

"The Eagle Flies Alone"

The year 1981 brought what was probably the most momentous – and certainly the most audacious – episode in the long history of Harley-Davidson. With AMF losing interest and patience, chairman Vaughn Beals persuaded 12 other Harley executives to join him in an $81.5 million leveraged buyout from AMF control. The group included Charlie Thompson, appointed president the previous year, and Willie G. Davidson. A letter of intent was signed on 26 February and the bid went public five days later at Daytona Beach. The group found a willing lead lender in Citicorp Bank and after several months of tough bargaining with AMF, the newly-independent Harley-Davidson Motor Co. began business on 16 June 1981. The event, not surprisingly, was accompanied by widespread rejoicing and fanfares, under the slogan "The Eagle Flies Alone" – including a symbolic ride-out by the new owners, from Milwaukee to York, as well as a solid gold dipstick for the first bike built under the new regime. Harley-Davidson was

■ ABOVE *There's no mistaking the American roots of this early Evo FLH model.*

■ LEFT *One of the very first Evo engines in one of the very first Softail models, pictured here.*

finally owned and run by real motorcyclists, men who loved the big V-twins, men who really cared. They were heady days, but the euphoria counted for nothing on its own. The American market, and Harley-Davidson's part in particular, was about to cave in even further. The buy-out did not enhance the buyers' fortunes as much as had been hoped – the newly-independent company's share of the shrinking American big-bike cake had dropped to a mere 23 per cent by 1983.

Ownership may have changed but one fundamental truth had not: Harley-Davidson's competitors were still producing better bikes at lower cost.

Over-staffing was part of the problem, and almost 200 clerical jobs went almost at once, but there was much more to it. Put bluntly, Harley's – indeed, much of America's – manufacturing culture was antique. Beals and other managers had toured Japanese plants in 1980 but it wasn't until after the buyout, when they were given the opportunity to inspect the Honda assembly plant in Marysville, Ohio, that they began to understand fully.

■ ABOVE ***As quality suffered, many US police forces spurned Milwaukee machines.***

■ BELOW LEFT ***To confirmed Harley aficionados, nothing beat customizing, whether of an old Panhead...***

■ BELOW RIGHT ***...or perhaps something more recent... a Shovelhead.***

As chairman Vaughn Beals remarked: "We found it hard to believe we could be that bad – but we were. We were being wiped out by the Japanese because they were better managers. It wasn't robotics, or culture, or morning callisthenics and company songs – it was professional managers who understood their business and paid attention to detail."

Beal's message wasn't lost on the new team. With help from industrial fixers Andersen Consulting, within four months pilot programmes for "just-in-time" statistical process control (Harley called this "MAN" – Materials As Needed) and other up-to-date production systems were initiated and staff levels were slashed from 3,800 to 2,200. Tom

Gelb, in charge of production, explained the situation to Harley-Davidson staff as directly as possible: "We have to play the game the way the Japanese play it or we're dead."

Quality and efficiency was one thing, getting the message across to potential customers quite another. The company shifted its marketing focus, stopped trying to compete against Japanese mainstream motorcycles and threw all of its resources into developing what we now take for granted as its uniquely American big-bike niche. (Along the way, a little-known project inherited from AMF for an overhead camshaft V-four was quietly dropped after several working prototypes were produced.) Was it too little, too late? Despite new models such as the five-speed FXR SuperGlide II and a new Sportster, the lone-flying eagle reported a loss of $25 million in 1982. It was going to be a close-run thing.

■ THE PRESIDENT STEPS IN

In August 1982, another Harley delegation made the trip to Washington, again alleging illegal trading practices by Japanese motorcycle companies. Yet again, the ITC was told that cheap motorcycles were being illegally dumped on the market and that the Japanese were "virtually copying" Harley models, all of which was seriously undermining their sales. This time Harley had a case, as

■ ABOVE LEFT ***AMF did not realise how lucrative Harley lifestyle and hardware were to be in the future.***

■ ABOVE RIGHT ***The Evolution engine, as in this 95th Anniversary 'Glide transformed Harley's fortunes.***

■ BELOW ***Meanwhile, loading the heavyweights with goodies opened up a whole new field of Harley machines.***

massive over-supply in declining markets meant that many machines were sold at a loss. As Vaughn Beals put it, "We simply want the US government to restore order to a motorcycle market under siege by Japanese manufacturers who increased production in the face of sharp market decline."

As if to highlight the problem, the local Wisconsin police force bought Kawasaki motorcycles rather than Harleys, prompting a mass ride-out in protest from Capitol Drive.

The Commission duly found in Milwaukee's favour and recommended as much to President Ronald Reagan. On All Fools Day 1983, the White House confirmed that import tariffs were to be imposed on Japanese machines. The tariffs would apply to all imported models of

■ LEFT *The "CowGlide", Heritage Softail Nostalgia, coolest of all the Softails...*

■ ABOVE RIGHT *...although even this wasn't radical enough for some owners, as shown by this Springer Softail.*

more than 700cc, at the hefty rate of 45 per cent (in addition to the existing 4.4 per cent duty), decreasing year-by-year to 35, 20, 15 and 10 per cent until April 1988.

Although Japanese machines built in the United States, such as Honda Gold Wings, were exempt, the levy was inevitably a major asset to Harley-Davidson's regeneration. In the meantime, they had to continue to improve quality and efficiency. Perhaps most crucial of all, a credible replacement for the aged Shovelhead was long overdue. Short-term fixes such as the digital ignition introduced on the new FXRT in 1983 were no longer enough.

Harley threw $3 million into a "Super Ride" demonstration programme in 1984, to show that the company had solved its notorious quality-control problems. TV commercials invited bikers to visit any of its 600-plus dealers to road test a new Harley. Over three weekends, the company gave 90,000 rides to 40,000 people, half of whom owned other brands. At first, the venture didn't sell enough bikes to cover its cost, but it made the point.

Then there was HOG – the Harley Owners' Group. This was a major corporate effort to bring customers together in the Harley-Davidson lifestyle. Nothing so ambitious had ever been attempted by any motorcycle manufacturer, yet HOG proved uniquely suited to the Harley image. A runaway success, HOG now boasts almost half a million committed members worldwide and is a model for similar schemes by other motorcycle manufacturers.

The company also began to defend its name, copyrights and trademarks for the first time, and vigorously. In future, if anyone wanted a Harley-Davidson logo, Milwaukee would demand its rightful royalties. Over half a century after pioneering the sale of branded accessories, Harley was at last determined to cash in on the image it had taken eight decades to create. Slowly, Vaughn Beals and his team began to turn the near-disaster around. Thanks to improvements in quality and efficiency, and more aggressive marketing, Harley began steadily to catch up with mighty Honda in the heavyweight division.

At last, this very American company was beginning to make the most of its uniquely American image. 1982's loss became a small surplus in 1983.

A year later, in 1984, Harley reported a profit of $2.9 million on sales of $294 million. Even though there was still a very long way to go, the eagle was on its way.

■ BELOW *Meanwhile, out on the open highway, Milwaukee's long-legged punch counts for more than mere paint.*

EVOLUTION

The anxiously-awaited replacement for the Shovelhead finally arrived in 1984 – and Harley-Davidson's future balanced precariously on a knife's edge. The V2 Evolution engine certainly looked like the answer to everyone's prayers. Despite a bottom-end with origins dating back to the 61E of 1936, it was an altogether better powerplant than the Shovelhead it replaced.

As the name suggests, the "Evo" is a development of the Shovel rather than a totally new design, yet almost every component was different and improved. Its cylinders, splayed at the "classic" 45 degrees, displace 81.8cu in or 1,340cc (although badges round this down to 80in). Scaling 20lbs (9kgs) less but producing 15 per cent more torque than its predecessor, the Evo would prove to be all it was cracked up to be.

In 1983, Harley-Davidson made sure its new baby created an impact with a publicity stunt to mark the company's 80th birthday celebrations: 8,000 miles (12,875 km) at an average of 80mph (128.7kph) with none of the routine servicing a customer's machine would receive on standard FLT Tour Glides. At Talladega Speedway in July 1983, the Evolution-engined TourGlides thundered through the designated 8,000 miles, but slightly off the scheduled pace: allowing for mishaps that never occurred, they averaged 85mph (136.8kph).

A brand-new engine was cause enough for celebration (helped perhaps by the new H-D brand beer), but the first model powered by the Evo engine was a landmark in its own right. This was the 1984 FXST Softail, and with it came a whole new concept in motorcycle style and design. With its fake "hardtail" rear end, gleaming chrome and low, rounded lines, the Softail was a

■ ABOVE *Cruisin' through town can just look so cool.*

■ BELOW *Retro-Tech: the hardtail look of this Heritage Softail is clear. The system uses twin shock absorbers hidden beneath the engine.*

■ BELOW *The Springer Softail adopts a girder-style front end.*

strident echo of motorcycles of the 1950s: the age of Retro-Tech had dawned. Sportsters still cut a dash, especially with the launching of the new XR750-inspired XR1000. A year later, the Heritage Softail followed the basic FXST.

Almost overnight – or so it seemed – Harley-Davidson had a credible range and, after the gremlins of the Shovelhead years, a reputation for the dependability that had once been its hallmark. Again it had a product capable of meeting the demands of the California Highway Patrol (CHiPs) who, after a decade mounted on Kawasakis and Moto Guzzis, in 1984 ordered 155 FXRP Police Specials.

To Harley insiders, however, the "Evo year" was probably far more memorable for the financial strife which continued to undermine them. In 1984, Citicorp Bank, underwriter of the original buy-out, was becoming concerned that Harley's future might not be so rosy once the tariff on foreign competitors ended in 1988. Reasoning that the best time to get a good price for the company was when sales were still on the rise, they moved quickly, hitting Harley's directors with the bombshell: all credit facilities would be severely restricted from the following year.

This was a major blow to Harley's ambitious plans and the survival of the entire buy-out. Harley-Davidson was broke.

■ ABOVE *"Basic" Softails retain telescopic front forks.*

■ RIGHT *At the opposite extreme is this road-registered XR750 racer, as used in US dirt-track competition.*

■ LEFT *ElectraGlides and TourGlides evolved ever-more luxury features such as cruise control, CB radio and intercoms.*

■ TURNING BACK THE TIDE

"Hawking begging bowls around Wall Street" was how Vaughn Beals described his desperate response. Over the summer of 1985, Beals and chief financial officer Richard Teerlink (later to succeed Beals as H-D's head), chased in vain after new lenders. Then, with the situation looking hopeless and lawyers drafting bankruptcy plans, Dean Witter Reynolds put Beals and Teerlink in touch with the Heller Financial Corporation. Luckily for Beals, Heller's second-in-command, Bob Koe, was a long-time Harley buff and willing to listen. He was impressed by what he heard, and on 23 December 1985 a financial package was agreed – the best Christmas present for which Harley could have wished.

The rescue package turned out to be a good deal for everyone but Citicorp, who had badly underestimated the outlook for this vibrant new Harley-D. Including credits, the bank received $49 million for the deal, $2 million less than it had poured in. Harley received $49.5 million of working capital. In a supreme irony, Harley recovered the Number One spot from Honda a year after being abandoned by Citicorp, with 33 per cent of the over-850cc American market. The long struggle to improve production

■ LEFT *Detail of the striking Ultra Classic ElectraGlide.*

■ BELOW *In stark contrast was the Sportster series, of which this 1984 XR-1000 is surely the best looking and most prized.*

■ ABOVE *In Europe, as well as the United States, Evo Harley sales began to boom. This Heritage Softail Classic thunders across the Belgian Ardennes.*

and marketing, and regenerate the model range was beginning to pay dividends. 1986 profits were $4.3 million on sales of $295 million.

Harley's financial base was secured in June 1987 by floating the company on the New York Stock Exchange. The offer raised more than £30 million, allowing the company to reschedule its debts and buy the Holiday Rambler Corporation, a leading manufacturer of recreational vehicles. In October, the manufacturing rights to the military MT500 motorcycle were acquired from the British Armstrong company. Less comforting was the closure of the competition department, though it made sound financial sense. Production of XR750 dirt-track engines was unaffected, and racing continued in the famous livery through independent dealer teams.

The most impressive news of all came on 17 March. In what turned out to be a public-relations triumph, Harley had taken the unprecedented step of asking that trade protection be removed a year ahead of schedule. As Vaughn Beals explained at the time, Harley-Davidson "no longer need tariff relief to compete with the Japanese". The chairman highlighted "the strong message… to the international community: US workers… can become competitive in world markets." Harley was again "the pride of America".

This was brought home best of all by President Ronald Reagan. After touring the York factory in Pennsylvania in May 1987, he

■ RIGHT *In places such as Florida's Daytona Beach, Harleys inspire crowds of fans of American iron. Fittingly, this is the famous Iron Horse Saloon.*

■ BELOW *International Harley: an ElectraGlide Classic in the damp Welsh mountains.*

■ RIGHT *Flying the Stars and Stripes with pride: a 1200 Sportster about to be revealed.*

hailed the turnaround in Harley-Davidson's fortunes as "an American success story". And how right he was.

A major contribution to future success was tied up with the XLH 883 Sportster. With a price tag of just under $4,000 when introduced, the 883 was the type of entry-level machine so conspicuously absent from the Milwaukee stable in the past. In 1987, 883 owners got an even better deal with the announcement of Harley's innovative buy-back scheme: "Trade in your XLH against an FX or FL within two years and we'll guarantee $3,995 on your old machine."

Major new models included the stunning Heritage Softail Classic, ElectraGlide Sport and Low Rider Custom. By the end of 1987, Harley had 47 per cent of the American "super-heavyweight" market, a figure which would rise to 54 per cent just one year later. At last, Harley-Davidson was on its way.

■ SPRINGING AHEAD

1988 saw the debut of the largest-capacity Sportster ever – the 1100 grew to the full 1200cc of the XLH 1200. 1988 also brought a revamped FXRS Low Rider with improved forks and twin-cap Fat Bob fuel tank. Most striking of all was the model chosen to mark H-D's 85th birthday, the FXTS Springer Softail. The Springer was a radical step both forward and back. Looking like a 1950 classic, it dispensed with the telescopic front end in favour of gleaming, chromed, lookalike girders. For the first time, a Harley had Retro-Tech at both ends and, almost overnight, became the style king of the Milwaukee range.

Within a year, the Springer and new Low Rider were joined by "Ultra Classic" versions of the all-conquering TourGlide and Electra-Glide models. These luxurious machines came equipped with a host of extras as standard, including cruise control, cigar lighter, intercom, CB radio and a sophisticated stereo hi-fi system. These were, and remain, the best-equipped and most expensive models in the Harley-Davidson range.

Ironically, as standard equipment became even more comprehensive, there was counter demand for a model more like the stripped-down Glides of the 1970s, such as the handsome FLHS ElectraGlide Sport introduced two years earlier. The FLHR Road King of today is in much the same mould as its handsome predecessor.

■ BELOW *A big twin in the heat of New Mexico, south-west USA.*

In 1989, a revamped clothing division – "MotorClothes" – was launched. MotorClothes, allied with Harley-Davidson's flourishing aftermarket hardware accessories, accounts for a substantial portion of overall annual profits. It is now possible to buy anything from bowie knives to toiletries bearing the celebrated H-D motif. Since the early 1990s there have been "Harley" shops that sell no motorcycles at all. The company's image had been transformed from a sick joke to the height of fashion.

With this priceless image came a turnaround in overall fortunes, from near-broke leviathan to glorious sales success. The foundations were varied: much-improved manufacturing of a broader, better model range allied to shrewd financial management, as well as inspired marketing. Production methods had witnessed a revolution, with each worker both a vital part of the quality-control process and a partner in Harley-Davidson's affairs. The Evolution engine earned a deserved reputation for rugged durability, oil-tightness and general user-friendliness.

■ BELOW *During the 1990s' DynaGlides evolved from Low Riders to become one of the core elements of the Milwaukee line-up.*

■ ABOVE *The moody Road King was a stylish attempt to return to the leaner, cleaner lines of the earliest ElectraGlides.*

Not least was Harley-Davidson's good fortune in being located in the world's largest market for big-inch touring machines.

■ INTO THE 1990S

By the early 1990s, the tide had well and truly turned – indeed the boot was on the other foot. Annual production had reached more than 62,000 units, with 20 models accounting for 61 per cent of the American heavyweight market and more than 30 per cent of output exported to Milwaukee fans worldwide, double the figure of four years earlier. At the same time, sales of Japanese motorcycles were in steep decline, their dealers cutting margins or going out of business altogether.

New hardware continued to stream out of York. Many Harley fans rate the star of the 1990 catalogue as one of the most beautiful Harley-Davidsons ever created. "Fat Boy" was its unprepossessing title, yet the original FLSTF was an understated symphony in silver-grey. Later versions, in less restrained colours, never quite had the same class. The FXDB DynaGlide Sturgis, a mean and moody all-black cruiser unveiled for 1991, was the first of a new generation, and classy to boot.

If Milwaukee had any problems during the 1990s, one was encroaching noise and emissions regulations; the other the sheer difficulty of meeting soaring demand as customers waited up to a year for their new dream machines. A major victory for environmental concerns was the first fuel-injected Harley roadster, the FLHTC-I Ultra Classic ElectraGlide, in 1985. Injection made the twin smoother, cleaner and more powerful than any previous Harley-Davidson.

Then came the Twin Cam 88 powerplant for 1999, which promised to take the same qualities even further. After four years and more than 2.5 million test miles (4 million km) under development, Harley-Davidson's new Twin Cam offers new levels of performance, reliability and durability.

Solving the supply problem involved a whirlwind programme of capital investment, culminating in the opening in 1998 of an $85 million Sportster plant at Kansas City. The spending began with the opening of a huge new automated paint plant at York in 1992. This $23 million facility finally broke York's crippling production bottleneck, taking manufacturing capacity beyond 110,000 machines per year.

■ BELOW *By the mid-1990s, top of the range Glides had added fuel injection to their extensive repertoire of "goodies".*

■ RIGHT *For 1999, 15 years after the arrival of the redoubtable Evo, a new generation of Twin Cam 88 big twins hit the Harley scene.*

Accompanying this has been a hard-nosed commercial edge which began with the defence of trademarks – even including attempts to copyright the "Harley sound". To many die-hard fans, Harley's corporate clout sits uneasily alongside the image of easy-going, down-home virtues the company is at pains to present. Some might even prefer the mom-and-pop-corner-shop image of decades before – the one that almost went bust.

New Harleys might be objects of desire, but they are conceived and developed in an environment as implacably space-age as the bikes themselves are defiantly old-fashioned. The Willie G. Davidson Product Development Center was completed in 1997, at a cost of $40 million. Standing just a stone's throw from the existing Capitol Drive engine factory, it boasts a floor area of 213,000sq ft (20,000sq metres) under a graceful arc of concrete and glass, a structure befitting 21st-century ambitions. A new Big Twin powerline plant was also opened in 1997, located at nearby Menomonee Falls. Buell, now half-owned by Harley, assembles motorcycles in nearby East Troy, Wisconsin.

Harley-Davidson hasn't witnessed expansion like this since the years either side of the First World War. In fact, 1998 marked the thirteenth consecutive year in which Harley-Davidson had achieved record earnings. Sales topped $2,000 million for the first time, with output totalling 150,818 machines.

Thanks largely to the impetus provided by Kansas, production capacity is planned to reach 200,000 units.

For Harley-Davidson, the future of motorcycling at Milwaukee is looking good.

■ BELOW *The Deuce, introduced for the year 2000, sports the latest balance-shafted Twin Cam 88B engine.*

HARLEY
DAVIDSON
USA

Faces and Places

Harley-Davidson was founded on friendships, family and youthful enthusiasm. The single Harley (William S.) and the three Davidson brothers (Arthur, Walter and William) were practical men who would transform some garden shed engineering into an enduring motorcycle legend.

Although it is now more than 30 years since Harley-Davidson ceased to be a family company, it's a matter of pride to both the company itself and to its followers that at least one founder's name remains on the payroll. Willie G. Davidson is, of course, the man. As much as any other individual, his flair for expressing Harley-Davidson traditions in new and dramatic ways has been at the root of the success of the company his grandfather helped found.

The factories in which Harley dream-machines are now designed and built are a long way from the little wooden shed that was used in the early years. However, even though the Harley factories of today may in no way resemble the Harley factories of yesterday, the company has remained true to the ideal of building the ultimate motorcycle.

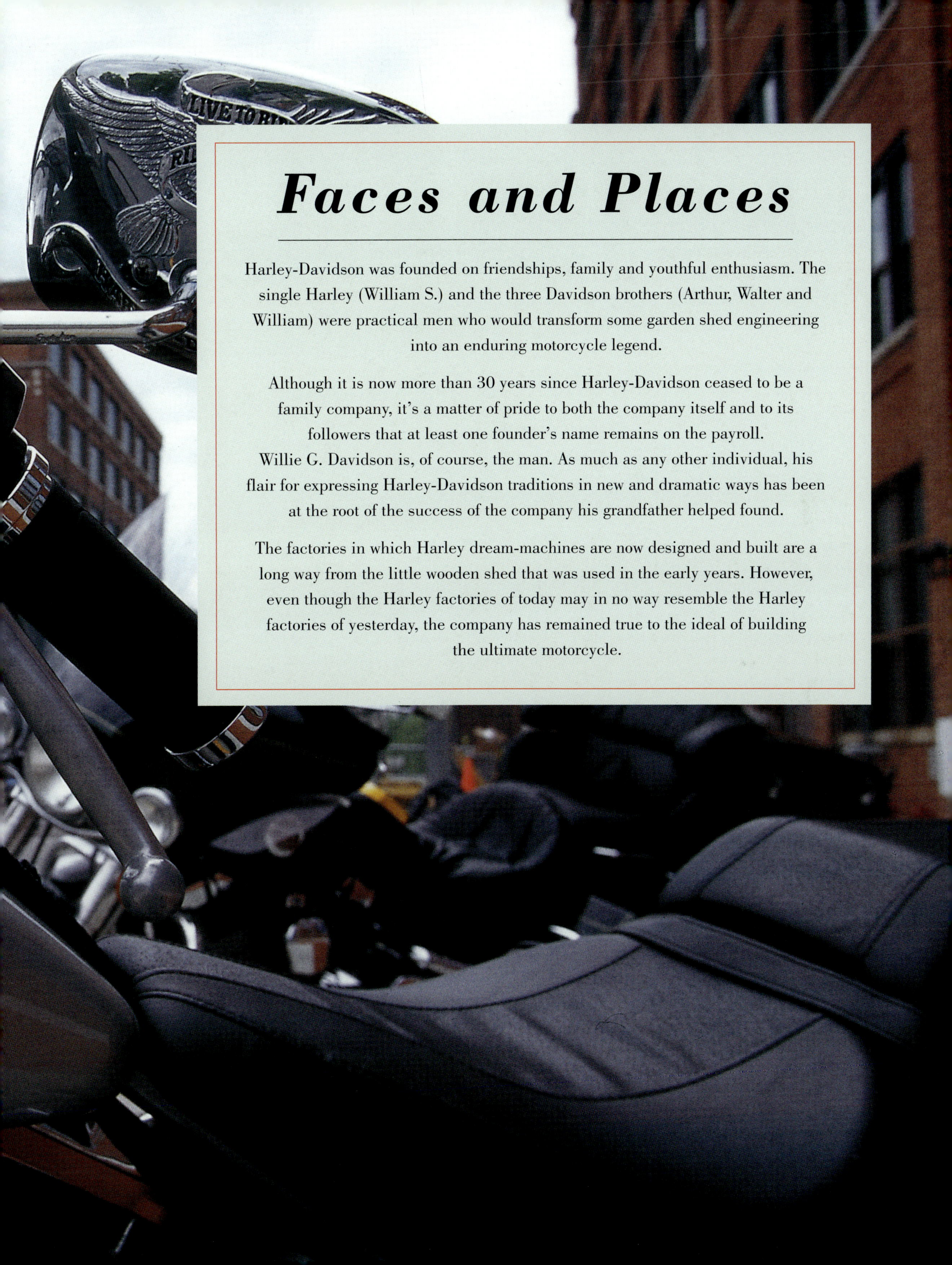

The Founders

■ **WILLIAM S. HARLEY**

"Young Bill" began work at the age of 15 in a Milwaukee bicycle factory, and even as an enthusiastic dabbler soon showed engineering skills. As able in the saddle as he was in the workshop, he later became Harley-Davidson's chief engineer and treasurer, positions he held until his death from heart failure on 18 September 1943.

On graduating from university in 1908, he had set about designing Harley's first successful V-twin, which appeared the following year, although it was 1911 before the design became as dependable as earlier singles.

Bill was later responsible for a host of classic Harleys, not to mention the first clutch, kick start and many other developments. In 1914, he established the factory's race shop, which scored 26 major wins in its first season. During both world wars, his contacts with the military were vital to the company's (and the nation's) success. Active in the governing body of American bike racing, the American Motorcycle Association (AMA), he was also a keen wildlife photographer in private life.

■ **ARTHUR DAVIDSON**

A pattern-maker by trade, Arthur had the reputation of being the most outgoing of the founders, his energetic temperament making him particularly suited to sales. Arthur became the company's secretary and general sales manager, roles he discharged with distinction until his death in a car accident on 30 December 1950, at the age of 69. His own son, James, and James' wife, were also to die in a road accident 16 years later.

Perhaps Arthur's most lasting legacy was the establishment of Harley-Davidson's nationwide and international dealer networks. Beginning in 1910, he had no fewer than 200 American outlets by 1912, later expanding to include official Harley-Davidson dealerships as far away as Australia and New Zealand. In the early years he practically ran the AMA "because there was no-one else around". After the Second World War, he spent an increasing amount of time at his farm in Waukesha County where he raised prize-winning Guernsey cattle.

■ ABOVE *The founders, left to right: William A. Davidson, Walter Davidson, Arthur Davidson and William S. Harley.*

■ **WALTER S. DAVIDSON**

Trained as a mechanic and machinist, Walter was a naturally gifted rider who brought the emergent Harley-Davidson company its first competition success. In June 1908, he entered a Harley-Davidson single in a two-day endurance run in New York's Catskill Mountains. The sole Harley in a field of 61, he scored a "perfect" 1,000 points, outstripping all of the preferred bikes. One month later, Walter was at it again, winning a Long Island economy run at no less than 188mpg (66km/litre) over 50 miles (80.5 kilometres).

Walter is best remembered, however, as Harley-Davidson's first president. Generous and scrupulously honest, he also became a

■ RIGHT *Harley-Davidson's first "factory", a 15 x 10ft wooden shed.*

director of First Wisconsin, the state's biggest bank. Walter died on 7 February 1942, still in charge at Juneau Avenue.

■ WILLIAM A. DAVIDSON

If Walter was the head of the company, "Old Bill" Davidson was regarded as its heart and driving force. Perhaps the least able rider of the foursome, Bill quickly found his niche as works manager, a vital position in a company expanding as quickly as Harley-Davidson. A big, burly character equally at home hunting and fishing as on the factory floor, he had a generous but paternalistic attitude to Harley's employees. Despite his bitter opposition, the factory first became unionized in April 1937. Within two years, Old Bill was gone, the victim of diabetic complications and the first of the founders to die. His son, William H., believed the stress of losing the battle to the unions hastened his father's death.

■ SECOND GENERATION

In the late 1920s, the founders' sons began to join the company. William H. Davidson joined in 1928, although he had worked on the shop floor while a student at the University of Wisconsin. A year later, he was joined by Gordon and Walter C. (both sons of Walter S.)

■ RIGHT *The famous Juneau Avenue factory, which was a large step up from the wooden shed.*

■ ABOVE *The Founders inspect the first Knucklehead to roll off the Juneau Avenue production line for the 1936 model year.*

Davidson, William J. Harley and, later, John E. Harley. Of the other sons, Allan Davidson, son of William A., worked only briefly for the company and died young; Arthur Davidson Jr. made a successful business career in his own right. Four of these "first generation founders" were to make major contributions to the American icon the company would become.

William J. Harley succeeded his father as the company's chief engineer. He became vice president in charge of engineering in 1957, a position he held until his death in 1971. A connoisseur of fine wines and cheeses, he evidently needed little encouragement to visit the Harley-Davidson factory in Varese, Italy, after the take-over of Aermacchi.

John E. Harley, younger brother to William J., was elected to the board in 1949 and ran the Harley parts and accessories business, today one of Milwaukee's major profit centres. He rose to the rank of major during the Second World War, including a spell instructing army motorcyclists.

Walter C. Davidson ultimately followed his uncle Arthur as vice president of sales, earning a reputation during the Second World War as the man who could somehow get materials other companies could not. After the war, he fought Harley's increasingly rebellious dealer network, as Triumph and BSA in particular began offering cheaper and faster products in the American market. Harley's efforts to hold the fort not only backfired at the time but were to lead to legislation which would later open the door for the Japanese. When AMF took over the company in 1968, Walter saw the writing on the wall and took early retirement.

William H. Davidson, the son of William A., made the most lasting mark of all. A skilled rider (he won the prestigious Jack Pine Enduro in 1930 riding a Model 30DLD), he was later described as "the mortar that cemented the company". He joined Harley-Davidson full-time in 1928, was elected to the board in 1931 and became vice president six years later. For the next five years, he was the driving force behind Harley-Davidson's vital government contract work. When Walter S. died, William H. was the obvious candidate to lead the company, becoming president "by common consent" 16 days later, on 23 February 1942.

William H. had no doubts about where the company's future lay: "We tried for a long time to convince people that motorcycles had some

■ RIGHT *During the Second World War John E. Harley, younger brother of William J., was responsible for training army motorcyclists on bikes such as the one pictured.*

■ LEFT *The famous "Silent Gray Fellow" of 1914.*

■ RIGHT *The 2000 Harley model: the Deuce.*

utility value," he once presciently observed, "[but they] have never been anything but pleasure." In 1971, three years after the AMF takeover, he was appointed chairman of Harley-Davidson, but felt that the new company had "pulled my teeth" and soon resigned. Nor did he fully share AMF's ambitions, observing with typical foresight that AMF "thought Harley-Davidson could become another Honda. That's ridiculous... we were never meant to be a high production company."

■ WILLIE G. DAVIDSON

Willie G. is a remarkable man from a family of remarkable men. Yet it's perhaps surprising that he began his working life not with Harley-Davidson, but cutting his teeth with Ford and Excalibur cars. By the time he joined his grandpa's company in 1963, he had a broad schooling in industrial design – although he had also found time to design a new Harley-Davidson tank logo in 1957. He has spent most of the intervening years as vice president of styling – arguably the single most important role in such an image-conscious company. In another quirk of fate in which Harley seems to specialize, the model that made Willie G.'s name, the FX Super Glide of 1971, was the first major new model produced by the much-maligned AMF. A decade later, he was one of the prime movers of the buy-out from AMF orchestrated by chairman Vaughn Beals.

AMF's hold on Harley-Davidson may not have lasted but Willie G.'s has. During the week, his domain is the Willie G. Davidson Product Development Center, a space-age structure of steel and glass tucked behind the Sportster Engine Plant on Wauwatosa's Capitol Drive. Yet to the biking world he's the man in the trade-mark black beret at gatherings such as Sturgis and Daytona Bike Week, ogling hardware just like any other Harley fan.

Willie G. has an uncommonly successful stylist's touch, yet he also has the common touch. To many he *is* Harley Davidson, and when he finally hangs up his leathers, there are two Davidsons waiting in the wings. Son Bill, who joined the firm in 1984, runs HOG, while daughter Karen runs the MotorClothes division. Harley-Davidson is truly a family affair.

■ BELOW *Willie G. Davidson, grandson of the founder, and a great guiding spirit of Harley.*

HARLEY-DAVIDSON FACTORIES

William S. Harley and the Davidson brothers first went into production in 1904 in a shed hastily thrown up in the Davidson backyard, bearing the grand legend "Harley Davidson Motor Co." on its humble wooden door. These days, the location of the famous shed, 38th and Highland Boulevard, is owned by a company producing something else for which Milwaukee is famous – the huge Miller Brewing Company.

■ **JUNEAU AVENUE**

The founders took on their first employee in 1905, and moved into their first building on the present Juneau Avenue site twelve months later (although the road was then called Chestnut Street). In that year another five workers joined the Harley bandwagon as production soared to 50 motorcycles. Progress was relentless – and punishing. Walter Davidson later described how "we worked

■ ABOVE *3700 Juneau Avenue, possibly the most famous address in motorcycling.*

■ LEFT *Like it says, "motorcycles only".*

■ ABOVE *On Juneau Avenue, even the water is branded Harley-Davidson.*

■ LEFT *Now more than 80 years old, the former main factory is a protected historical site.*

■ LEFT AND BELOW *The Juneau Avenue factory now houses only management and administrative personnel, but echoes to almost a century of Harley's history.*

every day Sunday included, until at least 10:00. I remember it was an event when we quit work on Christmas night at 8:00 to attend a family reunion."

So it continued: 1907 – around 150 machines built, including the first police Harleys; 1908 – 18 employees and production tripled again to 450 units. By this time, manufacturing was in Harley-Davidson's first brick building, with a floor area of 2,380sq ft (220sq metres).

Such was the pressure to grow and get new bikes through the door that workers recall "putting machinery in place and starting production before the cement was dry". From 1907 to 1914, the Harley facility at least doubled in size every single year. At the outbreak of war in Europe, 1,574 employees built more than 16,000 machines in a factory of almost 300,000sq ft (28,000sq metres). With no exaggeration, the Milwaukee Journal described the company's breakneck progress as a "modern miracle".

Wartime pressure for space became so intense that the company once threw up a 2,400sq ft (220sq metre) brick building, only to tear it down and build something even bigger six months later. Buildings were leased on a temporary basis all over Milwaukee. Even Prohibition came to the company's aid, in a manner far more benign than Al Capone's. When breweries became idle, Harley-Davidson stepped in to rent the Pabst Brewing Company as storage space for Harley parts.

The post-war boom helped Harley-Davidson become, briefly at least, the largest motorcycle manufacturer in the world, pumping machines out of its huge, six-storey plant on Juneau Avenue, offering more than half a million square feet (50,000sq metres) of floor space on its completion in April 1919. The distinction

■ BELOW *The Harley "bar and shield" is as recognizable in Morocco as here in Milwaukee.*

■ LEFT AND RIGHT *High-tech computerized machining is now part of the Harley way (left), but testing (right) is still hands-on. And could this man work for anyone else?*

lasted only until the Depression of 1920, when annual sales collapsed from more than 28,000 to just 10,202. America's economy recovered from this slump but motorcycle sales somehow did not. It was 1942 before Harley sales again exceeded 1920 levels. Under these circumstances, the last thing Milwaukee needed was more plant. Since its conversion to offices and warehousing in 1973, there has been no manufacturing at Harley's most evocative address: 3700 West Juneau Avenue, Milwaukee. Instead, the old site – and the grand old building – houses H-D's corporate headquarters and training departments.

■ BELOW LEFT *Sportster engines awaiting shipment from Capitol Drive to Kansas.*

■ BELOW RIGHT *Heavyweight engines are now made at Pilgrim Road before shipment to York for their final assembly.*

■ CAPITOL DRIVE

No sooner had Harley sales begun to recover from the Depression of the 1930s (sales slid to a pitiful 3,703 bikes in 1933) than Pearl Harbor was bombed and the United States entered the war. Towards the end of the 1940s, the company was looking to expand again as markets recovered. At the end of 1948, Harley moved into its first new address for 42 years, in the Milwaukee suburb of Wauwatosa.

■ RIGHT *For finishing items such as mudguards, no machine can match a craftsman, as here at the factory in York, Pennsylvania.*

Thus, Capitol Drive, a single-story building of more than 260,000sq ft (24,000sq metres) which had previously housed the A. O. Smith propeller plant, became Harley-Davidson's second manufacturing centre. In anticipation of a boom in post-war demand for motorcycles (and the opposite for aircraft propellers), the factory had been bought for $1.5 million two years earlier. Harley dealers – introduced to the new facility in a night-time "mystery tour" – weren't the only ones impressed.

Within a year, production was at an all-time high, although tougher times lay ahead. Also, less auspiciously (for V-twin die-hards, at least), November 1947 marked the debut of the 1.7 horsepower Model S 125cc single – a two-stroke Harley, heaven forbid. This was based on the same German DKW RT125 design as the BSA Bantam (and later Yamaha's very first model, the YA1 "Red Dragonfly") – and not least on the expectation that demobbed GI's would buy almost anything with wheels.

It was to be decades before the potential of Capitol Drive was fully realized, however. From today's viewpoint, it's difficult to envisage the trials cash-starved Harley-Davidson faced after that first burst of post-war optimism. During the 1950s, Harley sales were totally outstripped by British imports. From 31,000 units in 1948, sales never exceeded 17,250

■ RIGHT *Capitol Drive, home of Sportster engines and the official Harley Visitor Center.*

■ ABOVE *"Heavy powertrains" – Evo engines – awaiting shipment to York.*

again until 1965 – and for most of that time they were nearer 12,000. Paradoxically, matters only began to improve when the mass arrival of Japanese motorcycles stimulated wider interest in two-wheelers. Sales averaged around 30,000 for the remainder of the 1960s, rising to 70,000 by the mid-1970s.

This latter upturn in sales was due largely to AMF's heavy investment in manufacturing space, much of which is still in use today. The biggest single purchase was a $4.5 million monster for machining five-speed cases. Prior to this, Juneau Avenue had been a model of inefficiency, with part-assembled machines wheeled about and moved from shop to shop in lifts. Engine assembly moved from Juneau Avenue to Capitol Drive in 1971, although Harley-Davidson headquarters continued to undertake engine painting and the assembly of XR race engines for some years, the last actual manufacturing at the original site.

The addition of a modern facade means the Capitol Drive site no longer looks like a war-time propeller plant, but behind the facade the old factory now makes "small powertrains" for final assembly at Buell and the new Sportster plant in Kansas City. The facility also houses Harley's official Visitor Center, as well as a new customer engine reconditioning plant which is quite unique among volume motorcycle manufacturers.

■ RIGHT *Chrome and glass: a Springer guards The Willie G. Davidson Product Development Center (PDC), where the dreams of the future are generated.*

■ RIGHT *The PDC is located to the rear of the "small powertrains" plant on Capitol Drive.*

■ **VARESE**

With the exception of the original wooden sheds, Harley-Davidson has never abandoned one of its permanent sites on American soil. Overseas, however, it is a different story.

Milwaukee's Italian connection arose out of a desire to diversify into smaller, cheaper models, in order to hoist itself out of the financial mire of the 1950s. In 1960, Harley bought half of Aermacchi's two-wheeler division, based in Varese, Italy. The purchase was seen as a more sensible means of expanding the Harley-Davidson range than actually trying to develop new, cheaper models from scratch. In September 1960, the first Italian Harley emerged. This was the 250cc four-stroke Sprint, although two-strokes later predominated. (Although a stinkwheel Harley may sound like an offence against nature, lightweight two-strokes were produced in Milwaukee from 1947 until 1965.)

The joint venture didn't quite work out as hoped, but it did give Milwaukee its first and only world road race titles, with Walter Villa taking three 250cc and one 350cc crowns between 1974 and 1976, all on two-stroke twins. Roadster production was dogged by such absurdities as fitting American-made cables and controls to bikes built in Italy (where they made such things quite well).

Fundamentally, however, Varese couldn't compete with Japan. In June 1978, John A Davidson announced the closure of the project. The factory was bought by Cagiva which was producing 40,000 machines per year within less than three years.

■ BELOW *Many Harley employees favour motorcycles, but winter in Milwaukee is no place to be riding them.*

■ **YORK**

In 1972, AMF's massive plant in York, Pennsylvania, lay almost idle. This coincided, after two decades in the doldrums, with Harley-Davidson's dire need for more manufacturing capacity and, not least, with one of

■ RIGHT *"The Tool", a 70 year-old monster which presses fuel tanks at York.*

Milwaukee's periodic upsurges in union militancy. York was refurbished and motorcycle final assembly took over. The first "York" Harley rolled off the lines in February 1973. Capitol Drive would now build only engines and transmissions. York remains Harley's largest production facility, although production is less diverse than it once was. After buy-out, York continued to manufacture military hardware – the casings on some of the bombs dropped over Iraq during the Gulf War were made at York – as well as IBM circuit boards. These peripheral activities have now ceased.

■ BELOW *Capitol Drive now reconditions customer engines.*

In common with the rest of the company, the plant at York has received massive investment in recent years – not the least of which was a new paint shop to unplug what was once the biggest production bottleneck.

With the transfer of Sportster production to Kansas, York now concentrates on building Big Twins on four lines – three for customs and one for heavyweight tourers.

■ **TOMAHAWK, WISCONSIN**

About 250 miles (402 km) north-west of Milwaukee lies the old Tomahawk boat company plant, of which Harley-Davidson bought a 60 per cent share in 1962. The 35,000sq ft (3,250sq metre) plant was purchased principally to make Servi-Car three-wheeler and golf-cart bodies (for which Harley-Davidson once controlled a third of the American market). It has since specialized in the manufacture of fairings, saddlebags, windshields and sidecars.

Like pretty much everywhere else in the Harley-Davidson empire, Tomahawk was

■ RIGHT *This plant on Pilgrim Road, Menomonee Falls was once the home of Briggs and Stratton engines, but has produced Harley "heavy powertrains" since 1997.*

recently expanded after an extension of 14,250sq ft (1,300sq metres) was completed in 1997.

■ **KANSAS CITY, MISSOURI**

The brand-new $85 million plant in Kansas City is the jewel in Harley's manufacturing crown. The first machines rolled off the line at the 330,000sq ft (30,000sq metre) factory in 1998. Kansas builds all Sportster models.

Kansas is the nearest Hog-building comes to state-of-the art. Expressions like "evolutionary turning point" and "ergonomically-friendly production lines" roll off corporate tongues as easily as "unique labour-management joint leadership philosophy".

■ **MILWAUKEE**

There was a time when "Milwaukee" meant just one thing – Juneau Avenue. Capitol Drive then opened to confuse the issue. Now there are six facilities in the Milwaukee area.

The Product Development Center (PDC) is where future H-D models are created. It is immediately behind the Capitol Drive engine factory measuring 213,000sq ft (20,000sq metres), and was completed in 1997 at a cost of $40 million.

■ BELOW *Pilgrim Road is where the latest Twin Cam 88 and 88B engines are built.*

In 1997, a new Big Twin powerline plant was opened in nearby Menomonee Falls, and a new P&A Distribution Centre at Franklin, outside Milwaukee.

Pilgrim Road now produces all Evo and Twin Cam engines, before final assembly at York. Buells are built a half-hour's drive to the south-west, in East Troy, Wisconsin.

Harley-Davidson hasn't witnessed such expansion since the First World War. Production for 1998 totalled 148,000 machines compared to just 62,000 at the start of the 1990s. Thanks to the impetus provided by Kansas, production is planned to increase even further in the near future.

All of this is a very long way away from that little wooden shed where it all began.

HARLEY-DAVIDSON
95
HORN
LO
95

The Hardware

Wild innovation has never been the Milwaukee way. Neither young Bill Harley nor the Davidsons had a taste for the radical or the extreme. Almost from the outset, their target was dependability. That's not to say that Juneau Avenue was opposed to progress. In the pre-First World War years, Harley maintained a steady stream of technical novelties. By 1912, Harley-Davidson offered a choice of all-chain drive and a primitive clutch on the X8E model. The 1914 models boasted carburettor chokes, internally-expanding rear drum brakes and two-speed transmission. The first three-speed Harley appeared the following year, with a proper engine clutch.

Bill Harley was quick to understand the importance of heat-treatment and metallurgy, and quick to employ this new, unseen technology in his designs. Exotic alloy steels appeared inside even the first Milwaukee V-twins; similar developments occurred with frame construction and lubrication.

This tradition of rugged simplicity and steady improvement can be traced to the present day, through seven generations of classic V-twin engine. First came the inlet-over-exhaust and side-valve designs, followed by the revered Knucklehead, Panhead, Shovelhead and Evolution motors. By 1998, the latest in 90 years of big-inch V-twins, the Twin Cam, had graced the Milwaukee stage.

F-HEADS & FLATHEADS

■ LEFT *The F-head. The long push-rods to the overhead inlet valves and the "under head" exhaust valves are clear on the 1915 twin shown here.*

■ F-HEADS

A halfway house between flathead and overhead valve design was the inlet-over-exhaust (ioe) layout. Also called the "F-head", as the name suggests, this configuration combined an overhead inlet valve with a side exhaust valve.

All early Harleys followed this design, with one important additional characteristic. For reasons of simplicity, the inlet valve was of the "automatic" or induction type, in which the descending piston simply "sucks" the valve open only for it to be returned to its seat by a conventional spring. This spring was of necessity light, which precluded high engine revs. One major advantage of the system was that by removing the inlet valve housing, both valves could be removed easily for servicing – a considerable advantage on these relatively primitive engines. It was also found that since the valves directly faced each other, the incoming fuel charge helped cool the exhaust valve, extending its life. As well as the early singles, the first V-engines adopted the same layout – to their cost, for it proved an untimely failure with the twin cylinder design.

Both the revised twin and the 5–35 series singles of 1913–18 moved to a far more positive ioe arrangement with a conventional, mechanically-operated overhead inlet valve. The same design was grafted on to the 74-inch Model J of 1922, also known as the "Super-powered Twin". This 18 horsepower engine was also the first Milwaukee twin to feature lightweight aluminium pistons. When Model J

■ LEFT *Inlet-over-exhaust layout was the norm on singles, such as this 1914 example.*

production ended in 1929, Harley twins remained exclusively side-valvers for the next six years.

■ **FLATHEADS**

"Flathead" was the unflattering generic title given to any side-valve engine, whether made by Harley-Davidson or not. The reason for the nickname is obvious: with all the valve gear, including the valves themselves, located below the level of the piston at the top of its stroke, the heads were flat. The first side-valve Harleys were the Series A and B singles of 1926. All roadster twins from the end of the 1920s until the arrival of the Knucklehead in 1936 were flatheads as well. Milwaukee's catalogues continued to feature side-valve models until 1951 and even into the 1970s.

Side-valve engines were popular because they were relatively cheap to make and maintain, as well as much more compact than F-head and overhead valve designs. Although valve control was usually quite good – the camshaft and valves were in close proximity – the side-valve layout inevitably produced an elongated combustion chamber with tortuous gas-flow characteristics and poor valve cooling. This placed a severe limitation on the power such designs could produce. Side-valvers were renowned as dependable plodders, such as the seemingly unstoppable WL45.

■ ABOVE LEFT ***By the late 1920s, side-valve engines were the norm.***

■ ABOVE RIGHT ***Sidevalve engines formed the backbone of the Harley range into the 1950s, as with this WL45.***

■ BELOW ***This angle clearly shows the utter simplicity of the basic side-valve V-twin.***

Harley's side-valve years threw up one notable exception, however – the overhead valve 21-inch (346cc) single, produced from 1926 until the eve of the Knuckle in 1935. Designed with the help of Harry Ricardo, this single was not only successful in its own right but gave rise to the celebrated "Peashooter" racer. Five years earlier, Ricardo created the Model R, Triumph's first four-valve engine. His company contributed to the development of the latest Triumph triples and Aprilia's new V-twin, the RSV Mille.

Knucklehead, 1936–47

The Knucklehead's chunky looks make it the quintessential Harley-Davidson. To many motorcyclists its debut in 1936 announced the end of years of crippling economic depression survived by only two American motorcycle manufacturers – Harley and Indian. Sales were so poor that, only one year earlier, Harley's entire range comprised just two models. With the new model – formally designated the Model E – as its flagship, Harley's fortunes rapidly improved. Sales in 1937 exceeded 11,000 for the first time in the decade.

Development of what would become the Knuckle effectively began in the late 1920s, first with specials comprising single-cylinder Peashooter top-ends grafted on to existing V-twin JDH crankcases, then with the factory DAH racers. Although substantially new, the DAH utilized heads derived from the Peashooter's. Board approval for the "official" Knuckle project was granted in 1931 – a bold move at a time when the factory was running at just ten per cent capacity. The engine would probably have been in production by 1934 but for government restrictions intended to reduce unemployment which effectively barred overtime in the engine development shop. It was a long haul but certainly worth the wait.

■ ABOVE *The Knucklehead, Harley's first production overhead valve twin.*

■ BELOW *Developed from the ohv Peashooter single, the Knuckle was a direct ancestor to the Evo engine of 1984.*

The Knuckle was a Juneau Avenue "first" in many respects – the first four (forward) speeder, the first engine with hemispherical (hemi) heads and the first overhead valve roadster twin. The engine was heavily influenced by the competition experience of the legendary Joe Petrali, Harley-Davidson development rider and near-unbeatable racer. The Knuckle announced its arrival with a resounding flourish by posting 136.183mph on the sands of Daytona Beach, Florida. This speed record still stands.

The 61-inch – actually 60.32cu in (989cc) – Knuckle was initially available in three specifications: E (standard), ES (sidecar) and EL (high compression sport, with 6.5:1 pistons). Petrali's influence was clear. With more than 40 horsepower at 4,800rpm, the EL

in particular offered a huge increase in performance over the sluggish side-valvers. Despite its leisurely route to production – and not for the first time – there were initial reliability problems.

The worst of these concerned its new dry-sump lubrication. Some parts got too little oil while others – including the road underneath – got too much. A partial fix came in 1937 but the problem was not solved fully until the arrival of the 73.7cu in (1,207cc) Model F Knuckle in 1941, with its centrifugally-controlled oil pump by-pass. Although notorious for oil leaks through its many external seals and separate primary drive oiling, in very hot conditions many riders would prefer the big Knuckle's oil system to that of the later, "improved" Panhead.

■ ABOVE ***But for the Depression, the Knucklehead would almost certainly have reached production before 1937.***

■ BELOW LEFT AND RIGHT ***The numbers of Knucklehead models built were severely curtailed by the Second World War, three years after which it was succeeded by the Panhead.***

The bigger Knucklehead had come about largely in response to competition from large-capacity Indian V-twins. The larger engine's extra torque demanded a new seven-plate clutch in place of the old five-plate device, giving 65 per cent greater friction area. In addition, there was a bigger rear brake, an "airplane-style" speedometer and a larger, more efficient air-cleaner.

For a variety of reasons, the Knuckle never quite made the impact it deserved. It would certainly have reached production earlier, but for the Depression. No sooner had the Model F reached the street than the Japanese attacked Pearl Harbor in December 1941. The outbreak of war obliged the factory to divert most of its attention to military production.

Milwaukee lore has it that the best of the big Knuckles were those built in that final pre-war year, but hostilities meant that relatively few 74-inch (1,207cc) Knuckles reached the road until 1947.

By 1948, a new boss at Harley meant that the Knuckle was consigned to the annals of company history.

PANHEAD, 1948–65

■ RIGHT *The Panhead powered Harley-Davidson's big twins from 1948 until 1965.*

In 1945, Harley resumed civilian motorcycle production, although sales would not return to pre-war levels (partly due to industrial action) until 1947. In 1948, the replacement for the noble Knucklehead made its first public appearance.

In the Milwaukee tradition of steady evolution, the "Panhead", as it was dubbed, was a development of the Knuckle rather than an all-new concept. So-named because its chromed steel rocker covers (stainless steel from 1949) resembled inverted baking pans, the Pan was built in both 74-inch – actually 73.66cu in or 1,207cc – and 61-inch (989cc) sizes, although the latter was discontinued in 1953. The larger version retained the "traditional" bore and stroke dimensions of $3\frac{7}{16}$ x $3\frac{31}{32}$in (or 87.3 x 100.8mm).

The Pan featured aluminium alloy cylinder heads in place of the Knuckle's cast iron ones, new rocker gear and hydraulic tappets (or "lifters" as they're known in the United States) rather than noisier solid push-rods, as well as a revised and less leaky lubrication system. The camshaft was also new. Although the bottom-end was substantially like the Knuckle's, the oil system benefited from a larger capacity oil pump and the main oil feeds were now internal rather than untidy external lines.

The new aluminium heads not only improved engine cooling but contributed to an engine weight 8lbs (3.6kg) lighter than before. To ensure durability, the spark plugs and cylinder bolts threaded into steel inserts rather than the

■ BELOW LEFT *Since 1948 Pans have powered everything from the first Glide, the HydraGlide...*

■ BELOW RIGHT *...to crazy dirt racers, as pictured here.*

■ RIGHT *The very first ElectraGlide was Panhead-powered.*

■ ABOVE FAR RIGHT *The DuoGlide had also been Panhead-powered.*

relatively soft aluminium of the head itself. Despite these improvements, the power output of early Pans was about the same as the Knuckle's – around 50bhp at 4,800rpm for the 74-inch motor. The valve lifters were relocated from the top of the push-rods in 1953, to lie between cam lobe and push-rod in the timing case. At the same time, both crankcase halves were heavily modified, with particular emphasis on oil control. In 1956, Harley-Davidson introduced even more of the same. By now, a freer-breathing air cleaner and high-lift "Victory" camshaft had brought a gain of around 5bhp on the Pan's original power output. Near the end of its life in 1963, the Panhead reverted to the Knucklehead's external top-end oil feeds to prevent overheating, a particular problem in the scorching deserts of the American south-west.

At least as enduring as the Panhead itself was the name given to the first new model to bear such an engine.

The HydraGlide of 1949 was the first Harley-Davidson to employ hydraulically-damped telescopic front forks.
It was also the first model granted one of the enduring names in motorcycling: "Glide".

The Panhead engine would do much to get the famous species on its way, propelling not only the DuoGlide of 1958 but the very first of the ElectraGlides as well.

■ BELOW *One of the first Panhead Harleys, a 1948 girder-forked Model F.*

SHOVELHEAD, 1966–84

■ LEFT *Early Shovelheads used an all-new light alloy top end on what were essentially Panhead crankcases.*

According to Harley lore, 1965 is notable for two things. The first was the unveiling of a new generation of Shovelhead engines, replacing the venerable Pans. Second and ultimately far more momentous was the decision to list the company on the stock market. What no doubt seemed a good idea at the time would ultimately lead to takeover by American Machine and Foundry (AMF).

Popular opinion now says that AMF neglected the company, that it didn't understand motorcycles and that quality went rapidly downhill. Much of this criticism has an element of truth to it but AMF actually sank millions of dollars into its new project and actually tripled annual sales.

If Harley had a problem it was probably as much to do with being part of America as being part of AMF for, like many other sectors of American industry, it was overwhelmed by the tidal wave of sophisticated new products pouring in from Japan. As the British motorcycle industry learned to even greater cost, the 1960s and 1970s were no place for leisurely updates of a 1930s design. Put simply, the Shovelhead never had a chance.

■ FAR LEFT *This is a "generator" Shovelhead, produced up to 1970.*

First seen on the 1966 ElectraGlide, the Shovelhead followed the usual Harley practice of bolting a new top-end on to the tried-and-tested crankcases developed during the course of the previous generation of engines. There were minor revisions to the right crankcase half and a fin-less timing cover, but the bottom-end was essentially that of a 1965 Panhead, including the external oil feeds reintroduced in 1964.

An all-new top-end included aluminium alloy cylinder heads and iron cylinder barrels. Light alloy was also used for the rocker boxes in place of the Panhead's pressed steel. These were derived from the XL Sportster engine and enclosed redesigned rockers and exhaust valves. Although this rendered the Shovel top-end slightly reminiscent of the Sportster range, the latter was a quite separate family of unit-construction engines. Equally striking was the Shovel's "Ham-can" air cleaner cover, mated to a constant velocity Tillotson diaphragm carb from late 1966 onwards. The "Power Pac" head

■ LEFT *Harleys managed to be both practical and stylish.*

design gave around 60bhp in FLH specification, 5bhp more than an equivalent Panhead. The standard FL developed 54bhp. Observers described the new heads as resembling the backs of coal shovels, hence the nickname.

Like all Harley Vs, the ohv engine runs forked con-rods with both cylinders in the same plane to eliminate rocking couple. Primary drive is via chain to a four-speed box (with a sidecar option up to 1980, of three forward and one reverse). The Shovel received its new bottom-end in 1970, in which a crankshaft-mounted alternator replaced the previous generator (and made the engine even wider) – hence "generator" and "alternator" Shovels. The later type, also called "cone motors", are recognized by their cone-shaped, right-side engine cover. The ignition points assembly was moved from its original external position inside the timing case and the timing gears simplified.

Originally produced in 74cu in (1,207cc) form, Shovels grew to 80cu in (1,340cc) with the FLH-80 of 1978, when electronic ignition was added. Two years later, the first five-speed gearbox appeared, firstly on the FLT Tour-Glide, and was also the first of Harley's rubber-mounted engines.

■ BELOW *"Alternator" Shovelheads are recognizable by the conical housing on the end of the crankshaft, here marked with AMF's Number One logo.*

V2 Evolution, 1984–present

Perhaps the biggest fault of the next in Milwaukee's noble line of big twins is the lack of an attractive nickname. Its official title is "V2 Evolution" which, in common with most Milwaukee monikers, is a registered trademark. It is also profoundly fitting, since like the Shovel and Panhead before, it evolved from its predecessor rather than representing an all-new design.

Appropriate as the name might be, it is not evocative at all. After decades of Flatheads, Knuckles, Pans and Shovels, it has to be said that "Evo" lacks the same gritty authentic ring. Happily for its creators, an unkind early suggestion of "Blockhead" failed to stick.

It's a curious Milwaukee fact that all major Harley-Davidson ohv engines have been born in the midst of strife. The Knuckle was a child of the Depression, the Pan arrived surrounded by strikes and post-war rebuilding, and the Shovel heralded years of decline. As the long-awaited replacement for the Shovel arrived in 1984, Harley-Davidson was effectively broke. The story of how the company got out of perhaps the biggest crisis in its history is

■ LEFT *The Evolution engine was developed from the Shovelhead twin, but soon proved itself stronger, cleaner and more dependable. It saved Harley's fortunes just in time.*

■ LEFT *By 1985, Evolution engines powered the entire big twin range, with Sportsters getting similar treatment one year later. It eventually gave way to the Twin Cam.*

■ RIGHT *The Fat Boy is one of the most stylish examples of the Softail family.*

related elsewhere, but never was Milwaukee in greater need of an engine that would deliver the goods for them.

Fortunately for Harley-Davidson fans everywhere, the Evo was – and remains – everything they and Milwaukee had hoped for. Compared to the venerable Shovel which began life 18 years before, the Evo is 20lbs (9kgs) lighter and generates 10 per cent more horsepower and 15 per cent more torque. Its cylinders retain the "classic" dimensions of 3⁷⁄₁₆ x 4¼in (88.8 x 108mm), giving an actual displacement of 81.8cu in or 1,340cc (not 80in as it is nominally called). As with the evolution of Pan to Shovel, the Evo uses a bottom-end derived from its (alternator-type) predecessor but with improved con-rods and a new all-alloy top end. Efforts were made to improve oil-tightness and reliability, and decrease maintenance chores, with great success.

The extra power (around 70bhp at 5,000rpm) comes mainly from steeper, straighter ports feeding into redesigned combustion chambers, a new ignition, revised valve timing and higher compression ratios. During the seven years of the new engine's development, much effort also went into redesigning the lubrication system to prevent the Shovel's notoriously leaky nature. All but a handful of Evos sport five-speed transmission and, from later 1984, a much-improved diaphragm clutch. By 1986, the 1340 Evo had been joined by V2 Sportster cousins offering 883cc and 1100cc, the latter growing to become the first 1200cc Sportster two years later. Unlike the 1340s, Sportster Evos are of unit construction in which the crankcases and gearbox form a single unit.

So much for metal. As far as the vibrant, imaginative management team running the newly-independent company was concerned, the Evo had one other priceless asset the much-derided Shovelhead lacked. Milwaukee now seemed to have its finger on the pulse of motorcycle culture, and most importantly, seemed to understand its market.

Those at the helm now reached out to their customers in a way that the remote, faceless AMF never could, in stark contrast to the Shovelhead era. They sold their new product as if Harley's life depended on it – which, make no mistake, it did.

Twin Cam 88

■ RIGHT *Known as plain P22 during development, the Twin Cam has yet to attract a pet name, despite unkind suggestions that "Fat head" might fit the bill.*

The Twin Cam was unveiled in 1998 and billed as "the biggest change in engine design since the Knuckle". First seen on the 1999 SuperGlides, DynaGlides, Road Kings, RoadGlide and ElectraGlide, the Twin Cam offers more power and torque in a smoother, more refined package. Yet despite the name, this is still an overhead valve engine – the cams in question are downstairs. Unlike the gear-driven camshafts of previous big twins, these are chain-driven and far less costly to produce. Considerable savings are also made in crankcase machining, which required 37 distinct operations on the Evo but only three on the Twin Cam.

One area which received particular attention was the oil circulation. Surprising though it may seem, as they set out to create the Twin Cam, Milwaukee's engineers had very little idea what the lubricating oil in the Evo engine actually did – except that it didn't always go where it ought and that pressure could fall dangerously under very hot conditions. After 18 months of painstaking work on engines littered with Plexiglass "windows", the engineers believed they had the new engine figured out at last. In fact, the actual hardware – a high-capacity "gerotor" pump and two distinct scavenge systems – is less crucial than the engine's internal detailing. This was simple compared to the project's biggest problem, which had nothing to do with hardware, but with people. After the lay-offs of the 1980s, Harley simply didn't have a team capable of developing a new engine. One had to be created almost from scratch before work on the Twin Cam could begin.

■ BELOW *The Twin Cam brought a new dimension of power and refinement, first to heavyweight Glides, then the Softail range.*

■ ABOVE *Faster, cleaner, easier to service – any Harley rider's delight.*

Depending on the state of tune, Harley claims a 14–22 per cent power increase (to 87bhp on the DynaGlides) compared to the previous Evolution design. This is achieved partly through higher compression ratios, improved combustion-chamber shape and induction plumbing, as well as a new ignition pack.

Last but not least is a ten per cent increase in capacity to 88.4cu in (1,449cc), making this the largest stock engine Milwaukee has ever built. To achieve the extra volume, the stroke has decreased from 4¼ to 4in (108 to 101.6mm) while the bore has risen substantially from 3⁷⁄₁₆ to 3¹³⁄₁₆ (88.8 to 95.3mm). Traditionalists may bemoan the departure from the hallowed 88.8 x 108mm (3⁷⁄₁₆ x 4¼in) dimensions which have endured since the Shovel.

They will certainly not bemoan, however, the Twin Cam's prodigious peak torque: 86lb/ft (116Nm) at a mere 3,500rpm. Riders needing more can take heart: the Twin Cam was designed to allow an increase in displacement as high as 1550cc, adding another six to eight horsepower.

Compared to the bolted-up crankshafts of previous ohv twins, the Twin Cam has a pressed-up crankshaft. With its shorter stroke, it is capable of higher revs. Although the 5,500rpm redline is only 300rpm higher than before, development engines have been safely tested at up to 7,000rpm.

Harley surprised everyone by dropping the Evo and unveiling the Twin Cam 88B for the year 2000, a unit-construction engine specifically tailored for the Softail range.

It represents another Harley first – twin balance-shafts to smooth out engine vibrations. Softails will no longer be able to lay claim to being the "judderers" of the range.

■ RIGHT *Twin Cam power reached the Softail range with the balance-shafted Twin Cam 88B for year-2000 models.*

Retro-Tech

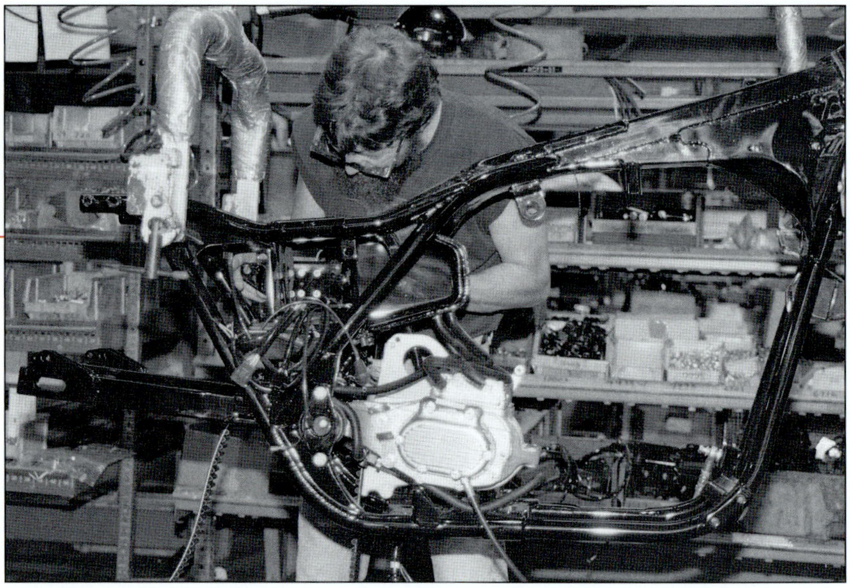

Harley-Davidson, like any ambitious pioneer motorcycle company in its early years, introduced scores of new ideas and technologies as its motorized bicycles evolved into true motorcycles. With running gear, as with engines, change was based on a trial-and-error philosophy, in which good practice prospered and bad quickly failed and fell into disuse. It was soon clear to Harley-Davidson's founders, however, that their interests lay foremost in making things that worked – and dependably. Unfamiliar ground was broached only in response to some specific need or shortcoming, and then with a thoroughness that often escaped their rivals. To this extent, the company has changed little.

It's perhaps surprising, then, that Juneau Avenue occasionally lapsed into dubious claims of motorcycling "firsts". The "step-start" and front brake, introduced in 1914 and 1927 respectively, are cases in point. British Scotts had kick-starts much earlier and front brakes were already commonplace on European machines by the 1920s. In 1923, for instance, Douglas racers were sporting quite modern-looking front-disc brakes. When Harley-Davidson claimed a "first", what it really meant was an American first.

Milwaukee makes little pretence at space-age technological innovation these days, although it might claim its machines are state-

■ ABOVE *Even today, all Harleys use variations of twin-loop steel frames, as on this one on the York assembly line.*

■ FAR LEFT AND LEFT *Two of Milwaukee's major innovations: belt final drive, as on this five-speed 883 Sportster (far left) and the "Retro-Tech" Springer front end (left).*

of-the-art – with the emphasis very much on "art". In sheer performance terms, novel engineering is usually introduced slowly: its first five-speed gearbox in 1980; fuel injection in 1995 (to clean up emissions more than to enhance power); and the long-awaited and still anticipated overhead cams (other than on the high-tech VR1000 Superbike racer). The two fields in which Harley-Davidson has taken a lead are in toothed-belt final drive – a relatively simple but truly wonderful development first seen on the 1980 FXB Sturgis – and, most strikingly, the concept of "Retro-Tech".

Retro-Tech grew out of the imaginations of Willie G. Davidson and his colleagues at the Product Development Center as well as the ingenuity of Harley's engineers. It is the means by which modern engineering receives a post-modern styling twist which is uniquely Harley-Davidson, which can contrive to make a 1999 model look for all the world like a 1949 HydraGlide but function far better. Willie G. coined the phrase, the "New Nostalgia".

Its chief elements are the Springer and Softail front and rear ends, respectively. The Softail system, designed by consulting engineer Bill Davis and much imitated by competitors, comprises a cantilever suspension system using two underslung shock absorbers cunningly persuaded to look like the rigid rear end of bygone days. Hence the name – Softail, a play on the "hard tail" nickname of custom machines whose rear suspension has been removed in favour of lines that are cleaner, if distinctly less comfortable.

■ ABOVE *Another view of the Springer front forks, inspired by the girder forks of Harleys of the 1940s.*

■ BELOW *Detail of the revolutionary Sturgis of 1991.*

■ LEFT *This deceptively simple-looking rubberized mounting transformed the ride of the 1993 WideGlide and subsequent Dyna-Glide models.*

Springer front forks are highly-stylized facsimiles of the girder forks used on Harleys prior to the HydraGlide. Despite the 1940s looks created by their exposed springs and brilliant chrome blades, Springer forks benefited from more computer-aided design than any previous piece of Harley-Davidson hardware had done.

Almost any other make of motorcycle you can mention boasts "more" than any Harley-Davidson – more cylinders, valves and camshafts, more gears, more revs, more power – but with Milwaukee's finest, as the cognoscenti well understand, less is more.

If a Harley is about anything, it's about getting back to motorcycling's roots. As styling vice president Willie G. himself observed a few years ago, owners "rank the Harley look right up there with motherhood and God and they don't want us to screw around with it." Like that other American icon, the Zippo cigarette lighter, "It Works".

And, as the saying goes, "if it ain't broke, don't try to fix it."

ODDBALLS

Harley-Davidson began as a company with lofty aspirations, but some developments must have surprised even the founders. In 1924, a Harley-engined (18hp) plane built by Harvey Mummert won the speed and efficiency contest at an air race at Dayton, Ohio.

Four years later, Flying and Glider Manual published plans for crafting a propeller for a 74-inch Harley twin. By the mid-1930s, several hundred light planes were powered by Harlequin engines, using Harley-Davidson cylinders on special, horizontally-opposed crankcases. The resulting boxer twin produced 30 horsepower and could be built for less than $100. At the opposite end of the spectrum was the bicycle built for Harley by the Davis Sewing Machine Co. from 1918–24 – a "Hog" with no engine at all.

Milwaukee twins have also been used in boats and as all manner of stationary engines. Contrary to popular belief, it has not been a single, seamless tide of thundering big twins from almost the dawn of the 20th century into the 21st. Other than the early singles, perhaps

■ LEFT *The TourGlide certainly wasn't strange, but for a while motorcycles towing trailers were. Now they are commonplace.*

■ ABOVE *Harley-Davidson golf clubs?*

■ LEFT *Well, Milwaukee did make golf carts for a while.*

■ ABOVE *Another variation on Harley wheels, this time used as paddock transport by the factory race squad.*

■ LEFT *One American icon mutates into another: the Harley hamburger.*

the best-known variation from the V-twin theme was the Sport Twin of 1919–22, using a 37in (584cc) horizontally-opposed engine, similar to contemporary Douglas motorcycles. A generation later, the military XA appeared during the Second World War, powered by a transverse, horizontally-opposed, flathead twin.

Even the oddball XA might not have made it had other military prototypes reached production. These included a three-wheeler for use over rough ground, an armoured machine-gun carrier and a small tank powerplant consisting of a linked pair of Shovelheads. By then, one Milwaukee three-wheeler was an everyday part of American civilian life.

They called it "Servi-Car" when introduced in 1932. Although the front end – "borrowed" from the Model D side-valve V-twin – was fairly conventional, what lay behind caused surprise. Above a two-wheel rear axle sat a metal-framed "boot" (trunk): this ungainly-looking device was a cheap delivery vehicle which found a ready market in Depression-torn America. For many Harley fans worse was to come, beginning with the 1947 Model S and ending with the Topper Scooter.

■ LEFT ***Odd, but the Servi-Car worked, from 1932 until the 1970s.***

■ ABOVE RIGHT ***Harley was one of the world's biggest sidecar manufacturers, as with this WL45 outfit.***

■ BELOW LEFT ***This Evo-engined prototype of a Servi-Car successor failed to reach production.***

■ BELOW ***The little-known XA was a boxer twin.***

One of the strangest ventures was a Harley two-stroke actually manufactured in the United States – without wheels. The Harley Snowmobile, powered by either 400 or 430cc engines, was built for four years until 1975.

Another quest for diversity saw the company branching out to build military bomb casings, computer circuit boards and "Holiday Rambler" recreational vehicles.

If nothing else, this demonstrates just how far the company had strayed from what it now regards as its essential roots.

Legislation permitting, in the future, all Harley-Davidsons will be air-cooled, 45-degree V-twins with both cylinders precisely in line. You can bet your house on it.

Harley-Davidson

Work and War

Almost as soon as the first model rolled off the Milwaukee production lines, Harley-Davidsons have been involved in all kinds of work.

In 1909, Harley provided motorcycles for the fledgling Rural Mail Carriers of America, but it is their association with police forces across the United States that is most well-known. 1908 was the year when the first Harley became involved with law enforcement; since then they have gone on to be an integral part of police forces' transportation worldwide.

Fire engines, delivery vans, golf carts: Milwaukee-built engines have driven them all. And if they were indispensable as civilian workhorses, as a tool for the military they were unsurpassed. The First World War was the first time a Harley had been used in a major conflict and, having established themselves as "Uncle Sam's choice", they went on to be even more invaluable during the Second World War.

Whether with a side-valve V-twin Model D for the police, a Servi-Car for deliveries or military 45-inch WLA, Harley-Davidson has always been able to come up with the goods.

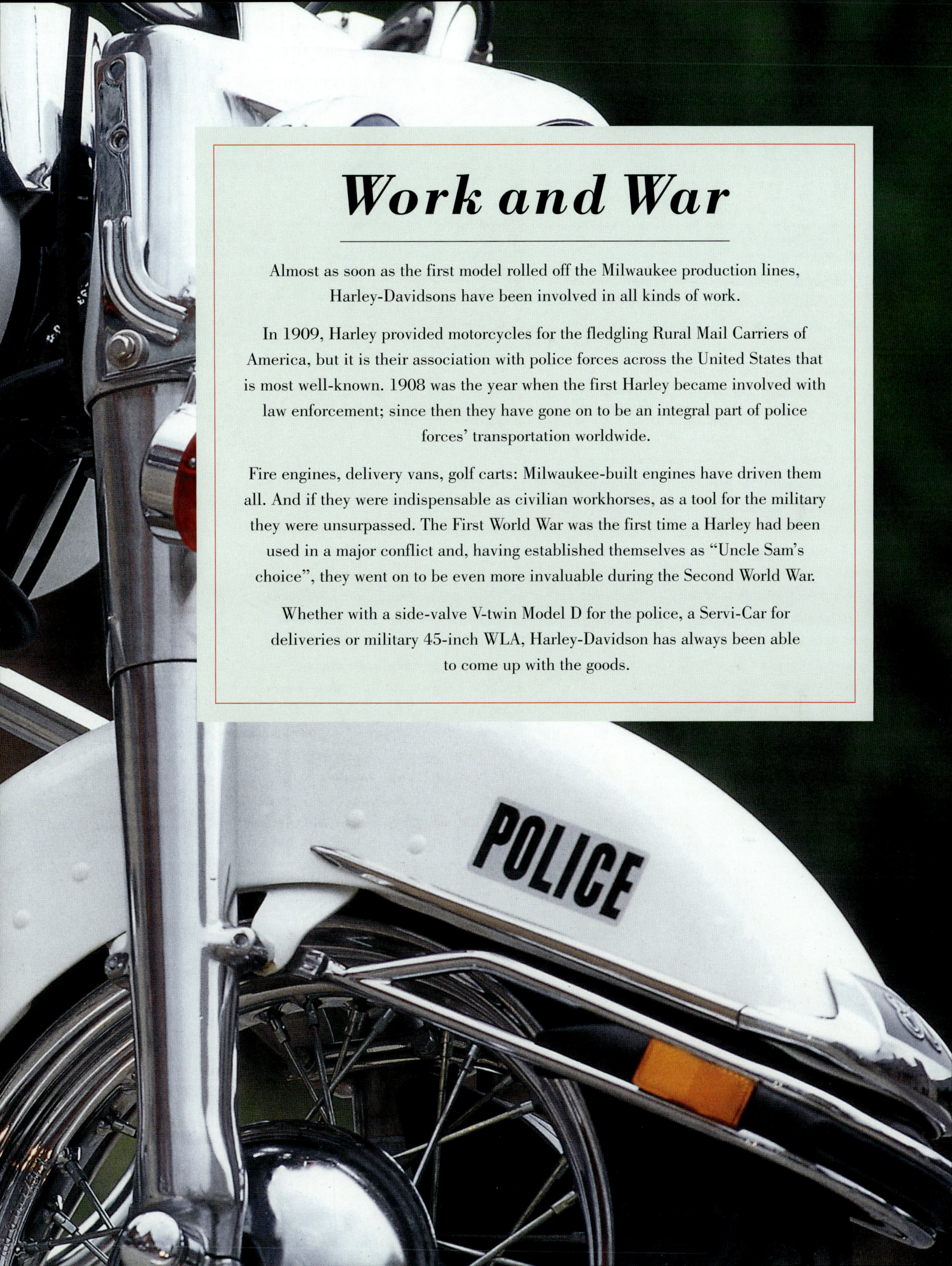

WORK AND WAR

■ **WORK**

Throughout the 1920s and 1930s, the words "Harley-Davidson" and "workhorse" were almost synonymous. Surprising though it may seem now, much of America's road network scarcely existed until President Roosevelt's job-creation programmes of the Depression years. Even the celebrated Route 66 dates from only 1926 (and was almost obliterated by Interstate 40 after 1985). Any affordable, rugged machine able to cope with rough terrain had something going for it, and Milwaukee's finest certainly met that bill. Harleys have offered mobility in every walk of American life, from painters to policemen. The company saw this potential early – Arthur Davidson attended the annual meeting of the Rural Mail Carriers of America as early as 1909, coming away with a pocketful of sales. It is with the police, however, especially the Highway Patrol, that Milwaukee twins are best associated.

Literally thousands of Harleys have joined America's police forces since they first went into uniform in 1908. Until recently, it was believed that the first police Harley went to Pittsburgh in 1909, although the distinction actually goes to Detroit one year earlier. Indeed, Harley-Davidsons have been popular across the globe, and Milwaukee twins have often been prominent in newsreel footage of presidential cavalcades in countries as far-flung as Burma and Guatemala. By 1915, Juneau Avenue was also producing "rapid response" sidecar outfits equipped with fire extinguishers and first-aid kits. A decade later, Harley motorcycles were in use by more than 2,500 American police forces, some of which quickly saw the public-relations benefits of organizing their riders into display teams. By the 1930s, police-model special equipment

■ ABOVE ***Police officers on 1944 UL models patrol Minneapolis, Minnesota. Harleys have been involved in law enforcement since 1908.***

■ BELOW LEFT ***The Servi-Car three-wheeler did much to allow Harley to endure the Depression.***

■ BELOW RIGHT ***A police Panhead, one of thousands of machines to have served US law-enforcement.***

■ ABOVE *An impressive line-up of police Harleys outside the Juneau Avenue factory.*

included radios (initially only one-way; two-way arrived 1948), although some squads made riders buy their own police lights and sirens.

The same period also welcomed two definitive Harley-Davidson workhorses. The archetypal side-valve V-twin Model D, introduced in 1929, became the Model W in 1937 and continued in production until 1951. Although crude and slow – its 22-or-so-bhp, 45-inch engine generated around 65mph (105kph) – it was rugged, dependable and easy to fix – ideal for cash-strapped Depression America. The American military version, known as the WLA – the "A" stood for "Army" – represented the bulk of Milwaukee's contribution to the Second World War. Though the majority of WL production during the war years was earmarked for military use, some also went to police forces and other strategic or security operations.

The Servi-Car, introduced for 1932, was the Model D's three-wheeled sister ship, and enjoyed an even longer production run – until 1974. The model's capacious boot (trunk) made it as popular with trade and delivery men as it was with local police forces. This unique three-wheeler remained in service, even in metropolitan San Francisco, into the 1990s. One clever and user-friendly Servi-Car touch

■ RIGHT AND BELOW *This immaculately restored Flathead served with the Daytona Beach Fire Department.*

was the adoption of the same 42in (1,070mm) wheelbase as the typical car – so inexperienced riders would not need to forge their own ruts in mud and snow.

So enduring was the Servi-Car's appeal that for a period during the late 1970s and early 1980s it was the only Milwaukee machine serving many American police forces.

The later Shovelhead years were not happy ones for Harley-Davidson's law-enforcing pretensions. Quality-control problems and general performance issues caused many forces to look elsewhere. For around a decade, even the California Highway Patrol (CHiPs) found itself powered by Italian Moto Guzzi V-twin and Japanese Kawasaki four-cylinder machines. It was not until the arrival of the Evolution engine in 1984 that Harley could again supply machinery that met CHiPs' requirements. Since then, Harley's principal police models have been the FLHT-P Electra-Glide and FXRP PursuitGlide.

■ THE FIRST WORLD WAR

By the time the United States entered the First World War in 1917, H-D machines had already seen action in skirmishes against the forces of Pancho Villa, the Mexican revolutionary. Under General "Black Jack" Pershing, machine-gun-toting Harley-Davidsons proved themselves ideal for border patrols in rough terrain.

In the process, Juneau Avenue proved itself adept at meeting military demands. An order for additional machines was placed by a War Department telegraph on 16 March 1916. A

■ ABOVE LEFT *Fancy being paid to ride a Harley at Sturgis: a local cop.*

■ ABOVE RIGHT *Busted for good taste? Harley catches Harley.*

■ LEFT *An Evo serving with Volusia County Police, one of several forces in the Daytona Beach area.*

■ LEFT *Since the first police Harley of 1908 there have been literally thousands, most of which have travelled further than this.*

dozen motorcycles equipped with William Harley's design for a sidecar gun carriage duly arrived at the border – more than 1,000 miles (1,610km) distant – two days later. Nine days later still, a second order for six machines reached Milwaukee. This one was filled in just 33 hours. Needless to say, the factory was not slow to advertise its efficiency in meeting "Uncle Sam's Choice".

Harley was just as quick to recognize the contribution it might make to the war in Europe. Within four months of the United States' entry into the war, Arthur Davidson was telling a sales meeting where the country's – and perhaps the company's – destiny lay: "The time is coming when no man can be in the middle of the road. He must be either for America or against America, and the sooner we get together on this question, the better able we will be to win the war."

During the first year of America's war, roughly half of all motorcycle production went to military service. By the end of the conflict, every motorcycle Milwaukee made was built for Uncle Sam. Along the way, William Harley, a member of the Motorcycle War Service Board, was instrumental in giving motorcycles a "B-4" classification, which gave them essential production status with priority for raw materials. Some 312 Harley-Davidson employees also enlisted, of whom all but three survived the experience.

As to hardware, in all some 20,000 motorcycles became American "conscripts" in the First World War, the vast majority of which were Harley-Davidsons. This success finally

■ ABOVE *Daytona: Sun, sea and Harleys.*

■ RIGHT *William Harley oversees the testing of specially equipped Harley twins during the early years of the First World War.*

■ ABOVE *A Second World War WLA45 assigned to the US military police.*

leap-frogged Harley ahead of its main rival, Indian, a position it was never to relinquish. Military Harleys were mainly 61-inch (989cc) twins of conventional F-head design, producing almost nine horsepower. They were employed mainly for dispatch and scout duty. One became a cause célèbre.

Its rider was Corporal Roy Holtz of Chippewa Falls, Wisconsin, little more than 200 miles (320 km) from downtown Milwaukee. On 8 November 1918, with the German army in chaotic retreat, Holtz was assigned to take his company captain on a reconnaissance mission. At night and in foul weather, the captain became disorientated and, over Holtz's objections, directed him across enemy lines where the duo eventually stumbled across a German field headquarters at which Holtz was instructed to ask directions. They were taken prisoner but released with the Armistice three days later. Holtz – and his Harley V-twin – thus became the first American serviceman on German soil.

■ THE SECOND WORLD WAR

No sooner had Harley sales begun to recover from the Depression of the 1930s than Pearl Harbor was bombed and the United States entered the Second World War. Milwaukee had begun planning in anticipation of military needs as early as the autumn of 1939, shortly after the outbreak of war in Europe. Early work, in competition with Indian and Delco, focused on a flat twin Servi-Car to meet army proposals for a three-wheeler for rough terrain. Other unfinished projects were even stranger, including an armoured machine-gun carrier and a prototype powerplant for a small tank comprising paired overhead valve engines.

With civilian motorcycle production suspended, by far the bulk of Harley-Davidson's war effort was the production of military versions of the WL side-valve V-twins, the WLA. The equivalent 74-inch (1,207cc) military UA and USA (sidecar) models were built in much smaller numbers. Of almost 90,000 military Harley-Davidsons, around 88,000 were 45-inch WLAs, of which one third served with Soviet forces. The same attributes of rugged simplicity that had brought the side-valve twin such a dependable peacetime reputation made it ideally suited to the harsher demands of war.

With very few Knuckleheads "enlisting" (although a special ELC model was built for the Canadian army), Milwaukee's other major contribution was the oddball Model XA, powered by a horizontally-opposed flathead twin displacing 45cu in (739cc). The XA was

■ RIGHT *A particularly war-torn WLA, but they were remarkably sturdy machines.*

■ RIGHT *The horizontally-opposed XA twin looked more like a German BMW or Zundapp, but served in small numbers during the Second World War.*

expressly designed for use in the North African desert, with its shaft final drive and plunger rear suspension. There was also an XS variant, with sidecar. Less well known was a mission for American intelligence, the stripping and assessment of a Russian motorcycle.

Harley-Davidson's contribution was not confined to hardware. John E. Harley, later in charge of the parts and accessories division, rose to the rank of major in the Second World War. Among his various tasks, and one to which he was eminently suited, was the training of army motorcyclists at Fort Knox, Kentucky. WLAs in the hands of raw recruits must have tested Harley's talents to the limit. Even setting off on such a machine was a knack, thanks to its hand gear-change and foot-operated "suicide" clutch.

From late 1941 until the armistice in 1945, Juneau Avenue burned the midnight oil to meet the escalating demands of the forces as almost the whole of American industry was turned over to the war effort. Fittingly, Harley-Davidson's special contribution was recognized by the award of three coveted Army-Navy "E" awards for excellence in wartime production. Milwaukee's factory workers couldn't necessarily go to war with the enemy but they could certainly help those who did.

Some might believe Harley's military career ended with the Second World War but there are two surprising post-scripts.

The first was the 1987 purchase of the rights to the military MT500 motorcycle from the British Armstrong company.

The second was a legacy of the AMF takeover: one "sideline" at the former AMF plant in York, Pennsylvania – where Harleys are still assembled – was the manufacture of bomb casings, a practice which continued well into the 1990s. It is likely that some of these found their way into the Gulf War.

■ RIGHT *Although intended primarily for service in the North African desert – hence this colour scheme – the XA suffered badly from all the sand which would collect in its wheel bearings.*

Live to Ride... Ride to Live

To aficionados, a Harley-Davidson is as much an emotion as a lump of metal, and certainly much more than a mere motorcycle. Precisely what the "more" constitutes isn't easy to explain, except that Milwaukee iron can be almost anything you want it to be: wheels, plaything, lifestyle accessory, fashion statement, membership card or any of a hundred other things. To many owners, their Hog is almost as crucial as life itself. Transport is often the last thing on a Harley owner's mind.

STYLE

The image forged from steel in the American Midwest travels across frontiers and media. It's as instantly recognizable in Bangkok as it is in Brooklyn, as rich with associations in Clackmannanshire as it is in Cincinnati. Advertisers know this and use it as shorthand for youth, freedom, rebellion and freewheeling affluence. It is almost impossible to watch a commercial for anything from cars and pensions to jeans and toiletries without a Harley-Davidson cropping up sooner or later in a mood-setting role. In other words, Harleys may be motorcycles – but they're also stars.

Some of this rubs off on the people who ride them. Owning a Harley isn't about speed or performance, or about imitating your favourite racer or impressing friends. It's about individuality but also brotherhood, retro-cool and happening places, latter-day cowboys or folk who just want to get away from it all.

When they move, Harley-Davidsons cruise. To the ear, they also thunder rather than rev. You can cruise around the block, along the beach or down to the bar; equally you can cruise from New York to San Francisco if that's your thing. They work equally well on the long-haul because of where they evolved – in a land of empty spaces and almost no corners at all.

■ ABOVE ***Poster of Peter Fonda and Dennis Hopper cruising to New Orleans in* Easy Rider.**

■ LEFT ***Christian Slater and Harley in* Heathers.**

■ BELOW LEFT ***"Captain America" and helmet, as ridden by Peter Fonda.***

■ BELOW ***"Harley-Davidstones" – one Stones fan wears his heart on his Harley.***

■ LEFT *Mickey Rourke cuts loose on a Harley in* **The Marlboro Man.**

■ ABOVE ***You will find Hogs everywhere!***

■ BEAUTIFUL PEOPLE

"God rides a Harley", according to some. The King certainly rode one. As well as Elvis Presley, celebrity hoggers have included Muhammad Ali, Bob Dylan, Clint Eastwood, Sly Stallone, Mickey Rourke, Dan Ackroyd, Malcolm Forbes, Cher, Whoopie Goldberg and dozens more. You're as likely to see a film star in Hollywood riding a Harley-Davidson today as lounging in a stretch limousine. Often, the stars want something out of the ordinary. Custom builders can easily charge $40,000 for bespoke machines and, in the process, become minor celebrities themselves.

The phenomenon is far from new, especially in Tinseltown. Photographs from Hollywood's golden years show everyone from *Gone with the Wind*'s Clark Gable to Marlene Dietrich astride Milwaukee machines. In some cases, the pictures were pure publicity stunts, but even Roy Rogers rode a Harley when he wasn't riding Trigger. Hollywood even had its own Harley group once – the Three Point Motorcycle Club.

Harleys themselves have become film stars, notably Robert Blake's mount in *Electra Glide in Blue* and, of course, in the hugely successful *Easy Rider* starring Dennis Hopper. Hopper's co-star in the film, Peter Fonda, remains a committed Harley-Davidson fan to this day.

■ ABOVE ***"Made in the USA" – and long before Springsteen sang it.***

■ RIGHT ***Nothing else out there: just you, your Harley and the open road.***

RALLIES: STURGIS

■ ABOVE *At Sturgis, you don't necessarily need a lot of clothes, but they have to be the right ones.*

Sturgis is an unremarkable little farming community in South Dakota. For most of the year very little happens until, in mid-August, this sleepy little hamlet goes motorcycle crazy as the famous Sturgis Rally lets rip.

The monster that Sturgis has become was born way back in 1938 when the Jackpine Gypsies Motorcycle Club organized the first Black Hills Rally and Races, with a $300 purse to the winner. Almost every year since, bikers by the thousand have cruised in along Interstates 85 and 90 to renew old friendships or make new ones. Being conveniently located in middle America – if 900 miles (1,450 km) from Chicago and 1,500 miles (2,410 km) from San Francisco can be considered convenient – attendance tends to be huge. Any old Sturgis Rally attracts 50,000 of the faithful. For the 50th anniversary in 1990, somewhere between 250,000 and 300,000 turned up.

Sturgis is not specifically a Harley rally – not that you'd notice if you were there for all the Harley bikes on site. It lasts for a week – a week of swap meets, hog roasts (pigs, not bikes), drag-bike racing at the Sturgis Dragway, tours, gawking at fancy Harley hardware and generally having a good time. Bikers hang out at joints like the Bear Butte Café. Main Street is air-cleaner to wheel-spindle full of Hogs. If you need a break, there are tours to the nearby Dakota Badlands, Devil's Tower (featured in the movie *Close Encounters of the Third Kind*) or Mount Rushmore.

There's strangeness, as well. One year, a guy rode a buffalo into town, moseyed down Main Street and hung a left on to Junction Avenue. Another year, the nearby US Air Force base

■ BELOW LEFT *Usually the action lasts right through the night.*

■ BELOW RIGHT *And some people say all Harley owners are alike.*

■ RIGHT *Ladies are welcome, too.*

reputedly laid on a rather special kind of fireworks display when a couple of their jets dipped low over town, hit their afterburners and drowned out even the noise of a thousand V-twins.

The whole town joins in (Sturgis is usually quite lucrative, although the town is so outnumbered by bikers it has little choice) from the women of the United Presbyterian to the Grace Lutherans. There have been occasional troubles with biker gangs, notably in 1982, but on the whole Sturgis is comparatively peaceful (if far from tranquil). These gangs are actively encouraged by the Sturgis city fathers, who clearly know a good deal when they see one.

According to Jackpine founder, former Indian dealer J.C. "Pappy" Hoel, there's never been a serious problem with outlaw biker groups: "We have their co-operation as long as we don't hassle them."

Mainly, it's a week-long party. Behaviour has been known to be on the excessive side, but it's usually harmless and only takes place once a year. Besides, it's legendary.

■ BELOW *Main Street in Sturgis, as can be seen, is a car-free zone.*

RALLIES: DAYTONA CYCLE WEEK

■ BELOW *Like it says: "Daytona Beach Welcomes Bikers".*

Outside the Rat's Hole custom shop, Main Street reverberates to the rumble of big-bore Vs on open pipes. Heavy-looking bikers in wraparound shades stand beergut-to-beergut, shoulder-to-tattooed-shoulder on every inch of sidewalk. It's March and almost 200,000 bikers have Daytona Beach under siege.

Like Sturgis, this is a week-long party. For the most part, the siege is friendly. As the barmaid at La Playa Hotel put it, "Bike Week's the best because they're all really nice. You don't see manners like this any other time. Wannanother beer?"

■ BADASS BIKERS?

Like Sturgis, Daytona's Cycle Week is one of those mammoth events that didn't begin as a celebration of all that is Harley-Davidson but somehow became one. Cycle Week takes place each year during March's Spring Break in the Florida coastal city of Daytona Beach. Its focal point is ostensibly the races at nearby Daytona International Speedway, a spectacular banked oval which also hosts the famous Daytona Nascar races.

■ ABOVE LEFT *At Daytona you can cruise or watch others cruising...*

■ ABOVE RIGHT *...or you can just chill and chew the fat.*

It's yet another of those Harley enigmas that, as the factory's twins' interest in the races has declined, its profile in Cycle Week as a whole has risen dramatically. Milwaukee's official XR750 road racer last competed there in 1973 (although the VR1000 has competed in recent years) and hasn't had a win since Cal Rayborn's in 1969, but this hasn't spoiled the party one bit. Quite the reverse – not having to ride the few miles out to the Speedway seems to leave more time for downtown fun. Daytona has become pure festival.

Sturgis, a small town, is understandably overwhelmed by bikes. Daytona Beach is big, yet the effect is much the same. The scene centres on the junction of Atlantic and Main Street, where bikes and bodies are crammed sidewalk to sidewalk. Harley-Davidson – wise to the public relations coup Daytona has handed them – takes over the city's Hilton Hotel to strut its corporate stuff and show the latest models. However most Daytona life goes on in the street, in the bars, on the beach and in nearby campgrounds.

Cycle Week has custom shows and impromptu drag races. During the day, bikes cruise along Daytona's beaches. There's official racing at the local quarter-mile dirt track and the main event at the International Speedway. There are swap meets in which enthusiasts sell or search for bike parts, notably at the Volusia County Fairgrounds.

Mainly it's lots of partyin', posin' and cruisin', and if you can't wait 12 months for your next Daytona fix, you can show up at the HOG "Biketoberfest" in October.

■ OPPOSITE BELOW LEFT *Spot the Honda.*

■ OPPOSITE BELOW RIGHT *If you can find a standard bike, you can keep it.*

■ RIGHT *If you can't paint your Hog, paint your clothes...*

■ FAR RIGHT *...if there's anything left to paint, that is.*

Bad Boys

Mention Harley-Davidson to anyone in the street and they'll probably mutter back something about "Hell's Angels". The original Angels were a California bike gang of Second World War veterans sensationalized by magazines such as Life and author Hunter S. Thompson in his book *The Hell's Angels: A Strange and Terrible Saga of the Outlaw Motor Cycle Gangs*. Almost overnight, the Angels became a role model for "outlaw" groups across the globe.

According to many observers, such groups revelled in their new-found celebrity status and, in living up to their reputation, became even more shocking and antisocial than before. Inevitably, bikers in general and Harley-Davidson riders in particular were tarred with the same unsavoury brush. Some stereotypes persist, but the bad old days of negative biker images have largely passed. In the United States, Harley owners have been growing older, wealthier and better educated. In 1984, the average age of a Harley buyer was 34; today it is almost 40, around one third of whom enjoyed a college education. Indeed, the modern stereotype is more of the well-off professional cruising any city's more fashionable streets rather than the grime-ridden outlaw of the past.

These days Harleys are the weekend wheels of lawyers, mayors and bankers: respectability, with an edge. This is all in motorcycle manufacturers' interests, for minority groups,

■ ABOVE *The original Hell's Angels were a group of Californian war veterans. Note Willie G., standing, facing the camera, third from the left.*

■ FAR LEFT *Imitators of the original Angels have since evolved as far apart as New Zealand...*

■ LEFT *...and Germany.*

■ RIGHT *Although "Hell's Angels" has become a cliche, Satan's Slaves is another well-known group of affiliated biker gangs.*

apart from tarring the rest, inevitably buy in minority numbers. One of the secondary purposes of HOG – the factory-sponsored Harley Owners' Group – was to broaden both the marque's appeal and its respectability, a service from which all bike producers benefit.

Hell's Angels and other so-called "outlaw" groups survive, and occasionally their activities hit the headlines. Perhaps the most notorious was a wave of knifings, bombings and shootings between rival Canadian gangs in the early 1990s, which left around 40 dead yet only attracted serious police attention when an innocent bystander became a victim. In the late 1970s, Australia was the scene of a shoot-out in a supermarket parking lot between rival gangs. More recently, Denmark witnessed a spate of murders and even anti-tank missile attacks arising from a long-standing feud between the Angels and Bandidos for control of drugs interests. Crime – particularly the sale of stolen goods – and later the manufacture and dealing of hard drugs has long been a source of income for some outlaw bands which, in Europe in particular, are also associated with neo-Nazi activities. Even the FBI has shown an

■ RIGHT *"Many are called... few are chosen" and even fewer care.*

■ FAR RIGHT *Sometimes known as "One Per Centers", although this veteran Angel begs to differ.*

A DAY OF INFAMY

One of the most notorious episodes in American motorcycling history concerned the so-called Hollister riots of 1947. Events unfolded around the first Hollister Memorial Day races to be held since the Second World War, a focal point for recently demobbed biking GIs. As with the Isle of Man Tourist Trophy ("TT") today, the races were welcomed by residents of the little Californian town for the business and prosperity they brought.

Thousands arrived for the races, including bike clubs such as the "Booze Fighters" from Los Angeles and San Francisco. Main Street was crowded "like sardines" and undoubtedly rowdy. The press loved it: "Riots... Cyclists Take Over Town" and "Havoc in Hollister" cried the *San Francisco Chronicle*. Other papers and magazines quickly jumped on to exploit the bandwagon. Six years later, the "riots" would be commemorated on celluloid in the film *The Wild One*, starring Marlon Brando and Lee Marvin. In the film, Johnny – angrily and effectively played by Brando – is asked what it is he's rebelling against. "Whaddya got?" he replies, one of Hollywood's most memorable lines. Although Harley-Davidsons feature heavily in the film, Brando is actually portrayed riding a Triumph. Nonetheless, the American Motorcycle Association saw fit to picket the movie on its release.

It was one thing for the movie to portray fiction, quite another for the contemporary press to do the same. For the truth was that the Hollister riots were largely fabricated. Some people were arrested for drunkenness but this was certainly nothing resembling a riot. As local hotelier Catherine Dabo later recalled to journalist Mark Gardiner, "I didn't even know anything had happened until I read the San Francisco papers."

Other Hollister residents were equally baffled: "It was a mess but there was no real evidence of physical damage," said Harry Hill, of the American Air Force.

"I brought my two daughters along... it never occurred to me to be worried about their safety," remembered local pharmacist Marylou Williams.

Finally and perhaps more to the point was the observation made by car mechanic Bert Lanning: "Some people don't like motorcycles, I guess."

According to one witness, cinema projectionist Gus Deserpa, a famous *Life* magazine photograph of a drunken biker sitting on his Harley surrounded by bottles, was faked. The drunk was real but it wasn't even his bike and the bottles had been gathered expressly to "improve" the picture.

Yes, Hollister was a weekend of infamy: for the media.

avid interest in them and certainly not because the G-men have an innate love of motorcycling. These self-styled "One Percenters" mostly exist on the fringes of Harley-Davidson culture and of motorcycling in general. Ironically, much of HOG's paraphernalia – its insignia, colours and organisation into "chapters" – echoes the ways of the outlaw gangs. Beards, badges and leather are part of many everyday Harley riders' uniforms but the trappings don't always say much about the person underneath. Sometimes the individual in the street must be hard-pressed to tell the difference. Perhaps Milwaukee likes it that way.

■ LEFT *These guys are probably discussing needlework.*

Harley and its Public

Harley-Davidson has a long and imaginative tradition of embracing the interests of its customers. As early as 1916, Juneau Avenue was producing its own magazine, *The Enthusiast*, to encourage pride of ownership and fellowship among Harley owners – and to do no harm to sales. Within three years, sales of the nickel magazine had reached 50,000. A trade equivalent, *Dealer News*, began in 1912 and a Spanish-language manual and catalogue, *Los Entusiastas Latinos*, appeared briefly the following year. *The Enthusiast* carried tales of racing, travels and other daring Harley deeds.

In the dark days of the 1930s Depression, the Harley "medal system" was born in which bonuses were offered to owners generating a motorcycle sale. January 1951 brought the Harley-Davidson Mileage Club which offered recognition for riding achievements. Harley riders could earn a pin badge and membership card for clocking up 25,000, 50,000 and 100,000 miles. By the end of 1954, no fewer than 73 Mileage Club members had logged 100,000 miles (160,930 kilometres).

The same concept of customer involvement – and a certain degree of desperation – lay behind the creation of the Harley Owners' Group (HOG). It was founded in 1983 (a year after Carl Wick's less phonetic HDOA – the Harley-Davidson Owners' Association).

Today, HOG is run by its own vice president (Bill, son of Willie G. Davidson). Under the factory's guidance and auspices, many Harley dealerships worldwide now run HOG groups, arranging everything from hog roasts to ride-aways, dances and charity events.

With the creation of HOG it was no longer enough to sell a customer a motorcycle – dealers had to be able to offer the lifestyle to go with it. A shrewd and prescient move, it anticipated the way motorcycling was going before any other manufacturer really took note. HOG now boasts more than 450,000 members in over 1,000 local chapters world-wide and has its own website, www.hog.com. On almost any summer weekend, it offers a choice of half a dozen rallies in the United States – plus others as far flung as Tunis, Darwin or Argentina. Like the motorcycles themselves, it is often imitated but never equalled.

If this portrays the company as only interested in the bottom line, it is also true that many of Harley's employees – at every level – are also committed motorcyclists. Harley-Davidson is fiercely protective of its interests, but also seeks to understand its customers. As the official company policy statement suggests: "It's one thing to have people buy your products. It's another for them to tattoo your name on their bodies." Sentiments such as that have brought Harley-Davidson a very long way.

■ ABOVE ***Years of effort and imagination have made HOG the envy of other manufacturers.***

■ BELOW ***You need long sleeves to be a lifetime HOG devotee.***

CRUISING

Harley-Davidsons may be sold, cherished and owned in every corner of the globe but there isn't a hogger alive who doesn't fantasize about cruising a Hog across the good ol' US of A. Epic American journeys are the stuff of Milwaukee dreams: thundering across the wide-open Midwest prairies or the baking deserts of Utah and the south-west; soaring over the Rocky Mountains or gliding down California's coast-hugging Highway 1. There is simply nowhere else where Harleys feel so resolutely, resoundingly right.

Harleys suit the United States perfectly because they're part of the cultural landscape you find yourself riding through. In the United States, Harleys open doors, start conversations and bring smiles to passing faces, but best of all is the way they glide over the staggering panoply of scenery that is the American West.

■ **CRUISING**

From the saddle of an ElectraGlide or Low Rider, America passes by at a pace your senses can get a hook on; horizons rise in waves, roll

■ ABOVE *The author heading north on Route 95 in Utah, with the Colorado River in the background.*

■ LEFT *Dream come true: a group on a Harley package tour cruises through Baja, Mexico.*

■ OPPOSITE LEFT *What Hogs do best: thundering towards distant horizons in the American south-west.*

■ OPPOSITE RIGHT *A Fat Boy swings through the bends under the towering cliffs of Zion National Park, Utah, USA.*

■ LEFT *A group of German riders on hired Harleys near Monument Valley on the Arizona/Utah border.*

in like a gentle swell and gently recede under your wheels. It demands a different sort of tempo – more relaxed, less preoccupied with destinations – than riding in Europe. As it thumps over hills and plains, the big, lazy V-twin engine seems attuned to the environment in a way that other machines never could be. Then, with a jolt, you encounter somewhere like Utah – scenic America at its most extraordinary.

Utah is Mother Nature under hallucinogenic influence. Utah has National Parks in profusion, all with something spectacular and different: Arches, Canyonlands, Bryce, Capitol Reef and glorious Zion, to name but a few. Next door to Utah are Arizona and the Grand Canyon, Colorado and the Rockies, Nevada's sweeping high desert basins and the red rocks and white sands of New Mexico.

From magical, mystical Moab, it's just a short ride up Highway 191 to Canyonlands. Hang a left and let the Harley thunder up the

■ LEFT *Hoggers on a traditional ride-out from the Sturgis Rally to Dakota's Devil's Tower.*

■ BELOW *Baja California, the sea of Cortez beyond, and what better way to enjoy them?*

endless grades until suddenly the road stops and the world simply disappears. Gone. In its place, space – a void as big as the Alps. Half a mile (800 metres) below, the Colorado River surges noiselessly, framed by a rocky never-never-land that might be awe-inspiring if it were real. It takes a while to get your head around the fact that it is.

There's more. There always is in Utah. Shater Canyon, Grand View Point, and then the daddy of them all, the Green River Overlook on the "Island in the Sky". From here, the western horizon is 100 miles (160km) away, about the distance from London to Bristol. Around where Berkshire ought to be is the baking wilderness of the Soda Springs Basin, through which Stillwater Canyon carves a distant trench which looks tiny but is fully 1,000ft (300 metres) deep. But for the shadows of passing clouds, creeping as though in awe of the landscape, it could be the dark side of the Moon.

If the landscape is dramatic, the sheer scale is extraordinary. Take Route 41 – cresting a rise north of Montezuma Creek,

■ BELOW *108°F (42°C) in the shade, and there is no shade. Must be time for a cold beer.*

■ LEFT *Dead Horse Point, near Moab, just one of the scenic jewels of dazzling Utah.*

a view 200 miles (320 km) leaps into sight. Seventy-five miles (120km) away in Arizona, the orange spires of Monument Valley guard the western horizon; to the east, the snow-capped Colorado Rockies are fully 125 miles (200 km) distant. This a scene that is far larger than many countries in Europe, and yet it's a single, sweeping view – or a panoramic day's ride on a Harley-Davidson. For the great, mythic emptiness of the United States, nothing else comes close to experiencing it all – and more – as from the seat of a Harley-Davidson V-twin that has been made in Milwaukee.

■ BELOW *This man emigrated to the United States just to be able to do this.*

LEGEND
LIVES ON

The Custom Scene

The identity of the first Harley-Davidson custom isn't recorded but it's surely almost as old as the company itself. It's in the nature of motorcycles that owners seek to "improve" them – not because there's necessarily anything wrong with the way they came out of the crate, but to add that extra touch of individuality.

Over the years, this "extra touch" turned from a trend into a craze and finally into a phenomenon. Today you'd be hard-pressed to find a Harley that has not been altered in some manner from the original that Milwaukee intended. Indeed, to judge by the amount of customizing that goes on, a Harley certainly isn't finished when it leaves the factory, if ever. Far from being discouraged by this slight on its judgement, the company actively encourages it. It's no coincidence that Harley-Davidson produces three catalogues crammed full of official "goodies", while the bikes themselves warrant only one. Custom Hogs are booming.

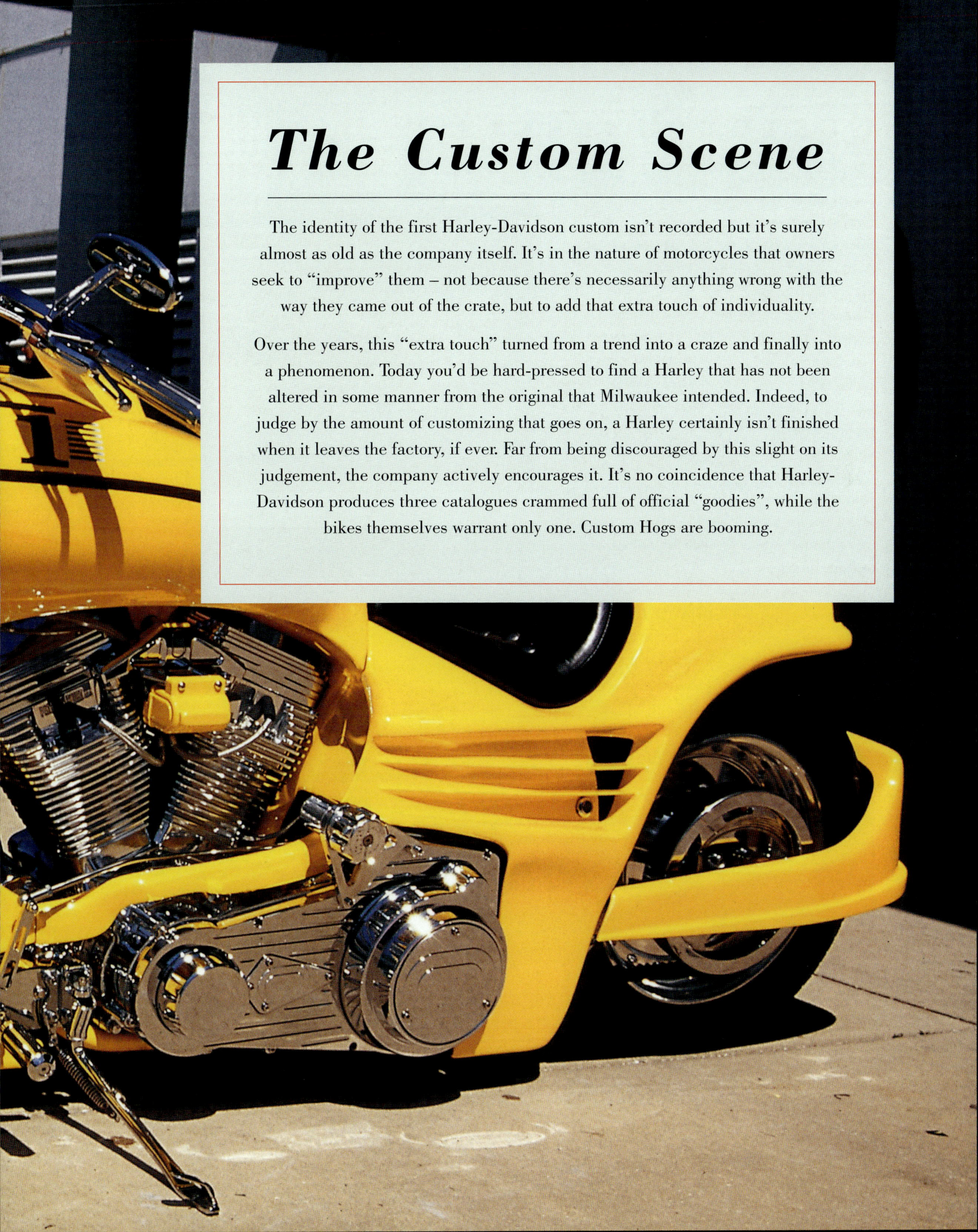

CUSTOM HARLEYS

A customized Harley today can be anything from a Sportster pared down to the barest essentials to a Glide decked out with almost anything you'd expect to find in a deluxe motorhome. Perhaps in the very early days, changes were functional: one carburettor worked better than another, this mudguard kept you cleaner than that. And, since America fell in love with horsepower almost as soon as there was such a thing, engine tuning quickly became a growth industry: in almost every state of the union, someone was willing to sell you high-lift camshafts, high-compression pistons or any of the other goodies that make an engine even stronger. In the racing field in particular, many tuners became legends for their prowess at extracting more power.

Extravagant cosmetic "tuning" came later. More than with any other make of motorcycle, Harley-Davidson customizing is an oddly circular process. First came Harley-Davidsons, which owners either lived with as they stood or adjusted to their tastes. Many of these creations were attractive in the extreme, a fact that was not lost on the people back at base in Milwaukee. Styling ideas which had first appeared as owners' one-offs fed back into the melting pot of Juneau Avenue design. Eventually, the wheel came full circle as the echoes reverberated through standard "factory custom" machines, beginning in 1970 with the FX1200 SuperGlide – although, at the time, the FX was resented by many in the custom scene for doing their job for them. Let's not forget that Buells – now an integral part of the Milwaukee range – began life as specials.

As far as graphics and paint are concerned, the inspiration reaches back farther still, to the art-deco designs with which the company

■ BELOW *Bob Lowe's custom creation "Evil Twin".*

■ ABOVE *Not surprisingly, this one goes by the name of "Full Metal Jacket".*

■ LEFT *This level of detail can take months to achieve.*

■ ABOVE *Custom can be three wheels...*

■ ABOVE RIGHT *...or designer grunge!*

attempted to sell bikes during the hardships of the 1930s. At the time, Harley was already marketing aftermarket parts such as mirrors and racks, but most were more functional than decorative. The true custom scene arrived in the California of the 1950s, with men such as Von Dutch and Ed Roth prominent. Often, 1930s art-deco was their inspiration in creating "blend" bikes – machines built from parts of several different models, as well as one-off components. Today, stylistic cues sometimes come from the Harley-Davidsons of the past, as demonstrated by the whole concept of "Retro-Tech". Harley brochures today speak about machines of the 1950s inspiring several of their Softail models, although the Springer looks more like a child of the 1940s.

The 1960s and 1970s, of course, were the heyday of the chopper, with its radically extended forks, limited lock and lousy handling. These days, customizers and riders alike look for either something more functional or something that is very much more art than motorcycle – such as the creations of the doyen of customizers, Arlen Ness. Other celebrated custom artists include Dave Perewitz, Ricki

■ RIGHT *Presence, yes, but if you want ground clearance and rear suspension, look elsewhere.*

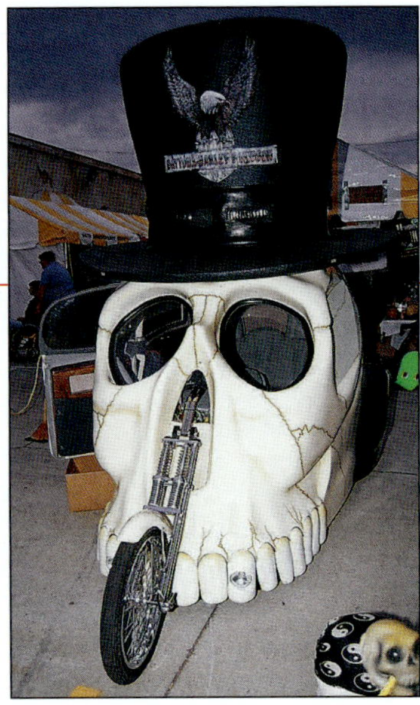

■ RIGHT *Sometimes practicality comes a very poor second to effect.*

■ ABOVE *"Choppers" like this are now passé in the US, but live on in parts of Europe.*

Battistini and Donnie Smith, but almost anyone with a Hog can join the scene in their own small way.

Mechanically as well as cosmetically, Harley-Davidson gladly promotes change, chiefly through its range of "Screaming Eagle" accessories, and they tacitly acknowledge that, even at 1450cc, the new Twin Cam engine can be further enhanced with a factory kit, increasing displacement to a mammoth 1550cc. Other suppliers, such as California's Custom Chrome, feed the fertile ground of Harley customs.

■ ARLEN NESS

The most revered of all Harley special builders is Arlen Ness, a slight, grey-haired Californian who doesn't so much customize Harleys as transform them into works of rolling art. Like so many others in the custom field, Arlen Ness' interest started as a hobby, growing and growing as people took note of his creations and begged him to craft something equally extraordinary for them.

Beginning with a 1937 Knucklehead bought for $300 in 1967, he now designs and manufactures everything from the tiniest, most exquisite chrome-plated detail to his own overhead-cam "Harley" twin, the engine that powers the gleaming Light-Ness machine. "I started out painting motorcycles in my garage," he explains, "but it got so busy with people coming and going that I couldn't get any work done, so I ended up renting a little store. This meant people would go there instead so I could work at home in the daytime and kept the shop open at night."

From paint jobs and custom handlebars, he now runs a huge mail-order business from a 70,000sq ft (6,500sq metre) building in San Francisco's Bay area. He actually builds just a handful of specials each year, at prices ranging from $25,000 to $50,000, but turns away far more customers than that. Sometimes the problem is sheer pressure of work (would "Busy-Ness" make a good project?), sometimes it's aesthetic.

■ BELOW *Sometimes, Milwaukee must wonder why it bothers at all.*

■ LEFT *Light-Ness (closest), Antique-Ness and Smooth-Ness, three of Arlen Ness' most famous creations.*

■ BELOW *Arlen Ness (left) with Hank, president of the Chopper Club.*

"We turn away quite a few people if we don't like a style they want or if we don't think they would be real happy… and others can't seem to make up their mind," he explains.

"There isn't a lot of money in building bikes. I just do it for fun." Or maybe Arlen just hates the one he hasn't built yet: Idle-Ness.

■ THE BIKES

The silver machine – "Light-Ness" – is powered by Ness' 100-inch (1,639cc) ohc "lightweight" motor housed in a special aluminium frame. Following the same theme, tank, fenders, mufflers and most other components are also highly-polished aluminium. Arlen values the bike at some $40,000.

The yellow bike is "Antique-Ness", Ness' first sidecar outfit. Based around a 1200cc Harley Sportster engine, it was created over a period of nine months by Arlen and fellow American customizers, Mun and Jimmy Rose. Built for Ness' wife, Bev, it was styled along the lines (if not the colour) of Harleys of the 1920s. Similar machines can be bought in kit form for around $27,000.

Although to some eyes it resembles half of a 1959 Cadillac, "Smooth-Ness" was inspired by the sleek, flowing lines of a classic Bugatti motor car. The all-aluminium body houses a rubber-mounted Harley "Evo" V-twin in a prototype Softail-type chassis. It took a year to build and is valued at $100,000.

■ BELOW *An earlier and slightly less radical Ness special.*

agv
AMA
103

Competition

Although Harley-Davidson is not always automatically associated with the white heat of competition, it is part of the deep-seated American tradition of racing pretty much anything on wheels. The first mention of a Harley racing dates from 1904. Perry Mack (possibly the company's first employee) set a speed record on a local Milwaukee track as early as 1905. The first recorded "factory" win in actual competition came in 1908, with Walter Davidson at the controls.

Company presidents don't figure among the results any more, but Harley-Davidson has won since on tarmac, dirt, boards, ice, grass and just about any other medium possible. Much of this success has been in the spectacular field of American dirt-track racing, 130mph (210kph) speedway, with huge fields of 16 riders competing like fury for millimetres of space. On the grand prix front, Harley's Italian connection Aermacchi brought Walter Villa four world crowns between 1974 and 1976. The factory has recently been striving towards a competitive presence in world superbike action with the VR1000 twin ridden by former AMA Number Ones Chris Carr and Thomas Wilson, and more recently by former World Superbike champion Scott Russell.

RACING

■ ABOVE *Harley-Davidsons board racing in Los Angeles, 1912.*

Harley-Davidson's early years were marked by racing successes too numerous to mention. The earliest of note came in 1908 when one of the first V-twins, ridden by company president Walter Davidson claimed victory in the FAM (Federation of American Motorcyclists) seventh annual endurance event in New York's Catskill Mountains. The 365-mile (587km) course was dauntingly rugged, yet "so strong was my confidence," Davidson later said, "that I carried with me no additional parts." This was in marked contrast to several other manufacturers, whose machines were followed by car-loads of spares.

In July of the same year, the Chicago Motorcycle Club sponsored a hill climb in nearby Algonquin, Illinois. Fastest time of the day went to Harvey Bernard riding a Harley-Davidson. Mysteriously, contemporary photographs clearly show Bernard aboard a V-twin machine, yet the model did not officially appear until early the following year.

The succeeding years were distinguished by numerous, similar Harley-Davidson successes, yet they almost exclusively involved machines which were privately owned and run. A company advertisement from September 1911 bragged, "We don't believe in racing and we don't make a practice of it, but when Harley-Davidson owners with their own stock machines win hundreds of miles from the factory, we can't help crowing about it."

This boast was nowhere more graphically demonstrated than in the San José road race of 1912, in which a 61-inch Model X8E triumphed by the small matter of 17 miles

■ LEFT *Harley had major success in racing from the outset.*

(27 kilometres). That same year, Harley-Davidson twins won at Bakersfield and the following year took first, second and third place in a 225-mile (362km) dash from Harrisburg to Pennsylvania and back, but these were private machines contesting relatively obscure races.

In 1914 – four years after Indian had won the prestigious Isle of Man TT – Milwaukee bowed to the inevitable when Bill Harley established a works race department which was to continue its winning ways into the 1970s. Some reports refer to instant success in taking that year's Dodge City 300-mile (480km) race, when in fact only two Harleys finished, well off the pace, in a race dominated by Indian. Clearly, the battle-hardened Springfield eight-valve twin was a formidable foe, but under the direction of the Bills Harley and Ottaway, Harley's progress was rapid. By 1915, Milwaukee twins were the bikes to beat.

■ ABOVE *One of the legendary "Peashooter" racers of the 1920s, in this case prepared for hill-climbing.*

■ BELOW RIGHT *From 1920, a board-track racer.*

The step from factory racers to racer production was a short and logical one. By 1916, $250 would buy any aspiring racer a special stripped-down competition version of the Harley twin, producing 11 horsepower and capable of around 75mph (120kph).

As well as speed, Harley iron chased many endurance records during the same period. In 1917, a Harley-Davidson ridden by Alan Bedell covered 1,000 miles (1,610km) non-stop at Ascot Park, taking almost 21 hours and averaging a remarkable 48.3mph (77.7kph).

In the same year, another Harley set a similar mark fitted with a sidecar.

RACE BOSSES

It's a remarkable fact that, once it finally got around to racing officially, Harley-Davidson needed a mere three race-team managers in all its many decades of competition – Bill Ottaway, Hank Syvertson and Dick O'Brien. They, too, became legends.

The factory crew's early successes were overseen by the cool gaze of Bill Ottaway. Described as "a wizard" by William Davidson, Ottaway began his career at Thor, manufacturer of proprietary motorcycle engines, leaving for Juneau Avenue in 1913. A talented engineer and a shrewd manager, he saw the factory squad through its formative years and into the glory days of the 1920s before Hank Syvertson took over as director of racing.

Dick O'Brien began a lifetime of working on Harley engines at Puckett's in Orlando, Florida. Apart from a period of military service as a senior aircraft mechanic during the Second World War, he continued as a Harley service-shop manager, with a special talent for tuning racing machines – Daytona Speedway was, after all, only a couple of hours distant. In June 1957, he joined the factory race squad as Syvertson's assistant. Three months later Syvertson retired and O'Brien took the helm, a position he held until his retirement in 1983.

■ LEFT *Wrecking Crew at Dodge City in 1920. From left: race boss Bill Ottaway, Maldwyn Jones, Ralph Hepburn, Fred Ludlow, Otto Walker, Ray Weishaar, Jim Davis and mechanic Hank Syvertsen.*

■ THE WRECKING CREW

During the buoyant 1920s, Harley-Davidson's competitive exploits were even more remarkable than the salvos of new models roaring out of Milwaukee. In 1920, a Harley became the first powered vehicle to top California's 10,000ft (3,050 metre) "Old Baldy" hill-climb. In February 1921, at Fresno, a Harley became the first bike to win a race at an average of more than 100mph (160kph).

Many of the factory's innumerable successes came courtesy of the legendary Harley-Davidson "Wrecking Crew". The Crew was almost unbeatable on the dirt and boards of America from the days before the First World War until the factory briefly pulled out of racing following the 1920 slump. Board racing, on banked ovals of raw wood, was uniquely – and spectacularly – American.

The Crew included barnstorming individuals: Eddie Brinck, Otto Walker, Jim Davis, Leslie "Red" Parkhurst and many more. Walker marked the factory's withdrawal by taking a 61cu in, eight-valve machine to victory in a 50-mile (80km) race at San Joaquin, California, at the sensational average speed of 101.43mph (163.23kph). The crew began 1920 by taking the first four places in the Ascot 100-miler (160.93km) race on America's fastest track. In February, Harleys set 23 records, including four by Parker at the kilometre, mile – both at more than 103mph (165kph) – two mile and five mile marks.

■ LEFT *Scott Parker, the most successful dirt-track rider in AMA history.*

■ ABOVE *The legendary Cal Rayborn on the XR750, Brands Hatch, 1972.*

These men, riding in little more than cloth caps, sweatshirts and jodhpurs, were tough little heroes in the same mould that was later to produce stars such as Cal Rayborn, Jay Springsteen and Scott Parker. The racing life was hard and cruel. Eddie Brinck himself was killed when a tyre blew out in a race at Springfield, Massachusetts.

As America's road system developed, it was only natural that men would create some form of contest on it. As early as 1920, Hap Sherer took a Sport Twin (584cc boxer) from Denver to Chicago in 48 hours – no easy feat even today. Meanwhile, Walter Hadfield made a habit of lowering the "Three Flags Run" record from Vancouver (Canada) to Tijuana (Mexico), a route on which Fred Deeley later averaged more than 104mpg (36km/litre). Perhaps most impressive of all was the remarkable Earl Hadfield, who covered more than 3,000-plus miles (4,800-plus km) between New York and Los Angeles in less than 78 hours. At around the same time, the immortal Windy Lindstrom was king of America's booming hill-climb scene, on specially-modified Milwaukee iron.

Harley victories were by no means confined to the United States. Harley-Davidson found willing, winning pilots as far apart as Scandinavia and Australia, notching up successes in fields as diverse as ice speedway and grass track. At the legendary banked Brooklands track in Surrey, England, Doug Davidson (no relation) took a factory 1000cc ioe twin to a record-breaking average of 100.76mph (162.15kph) over a flying kilometre. Within a few months, a similar machine ridden by Claude Temple had taken records in the hour, five mile, flying mile and kilometre.

Yet even these efforts paled when compared to those of the mercurial Englishman, Freddy Dixon, riding a special twin with four pipes and eight overhead valves. Dixon was nearly unbeatable in all forms of competition from hill-climbs to long-distance events around the daunting Brooklands circuit. On 9 September 1923 at Arpajon, near Paris, Dixon set a new world speed mark of 106.8mph/171.8kph (a record Harley-Davidson would not hold again until 1970). Ten months later he was at it again, flying through the half-mile at the Clipstone Speed Trials at 103.44mph (166.47kph). In 1925 he averaged 100.1mph (161kph) winning the Brooklands 1000cc championship – possibly the noisiest victory ever, for the machine had no exhaust pipes.

■ BELOW *Jay Springsteen is one in a long line of champions that stem from the legacy of the Wrecking Crew of the early part of the 20th century.*

■ LEFT *The Knucklehead streamliner on which Joe Petrali set record speeds at Florida's Daytona Beach.*

■ JOE PETRALI

If Freddy Dixon had a counterpart on Harley's home turf, it was surely the legendary Joe Petrali. More than perhaps any other man, Petrali single-handedly made Harley-Davidson an unbeatable force during the late 1920s and throughout the 1930s. Born in Sacramento, California in 1904, he owned his first bike at 13 years of age and was racing – and winning – on boards by the time he was 16. Petrali first hit the big time when he showed up bike-less at Altoona, Pennsylvania, in 1925. Luckily for him, former Wrecking Crew man Ralph Hepburn had broken a hand. Petrali took over the factory Harley-Davidson instead. He was practically unknown at the time.

Less than an hour later (59 minutes and 47.2 seconds later to be exact), Petrali was a legend. He left the entire field of hardened pros in a cloud of dust, averaging 100.32mph (161.45kph) in the 100-mile (160.93-km) race over Altoona's lightning-fast boards. Earlier that same day, Jim Davis won the five-mile "sprint" at over 110mph (177kph) – at a time when the Indianapolis car race was being won at less than 101mph (163kph). From then on, there was no stopping Joe Petrali. He became so dominant that, for more than a decade, the rest were effectively riding for second place. In 1935, he won every single event of the National season, including five wins in a single day at Syracuse, New York. In 1937, he took a Knucklehead streamliner through the timing strip on the sands of Daytona Beach at 136.183mph (219.159kph), a record that still stands.

■ THE MICHIGAN MEN

Flint, Michigan, must be a remarkable place. Jay Springsteen is from Flint, where they build Chevrolets out of the same hard stuff. So is Scott Parker. So, too, is "Black" Bart Markel.

■ BELOW *Scott Parker rockets the XR750 around the Del Mar track.*

■ ABOVE LEFT ***Scott Parker (left) and Jay Springsteen (right), both chips off the same Flint block.***

■ ABOVE RIGHT ***During the 1950s, the flathead KRTT needed a capacity edge to compete with European ohv twins.***

During a dirt-track career that began in 1957 and spanned 23 years, Markel was the original Michigan hard man. He won three national titles (in 1962, 1965 and 1966) but it was his style that caught the eye. Old boys still whistle in awe at the memory of Markel bouncing off guard rails, bales and other bikes – whatever it would take him to get to the finish line first.

Like the rest, he had to race on tarmac as well as dirt to take those titles. He crashed an awful lot, for the simple reason that "he refused to slow down for the turns," according to Harley-Davidson race boss Dick O'Brien. Instead, he just threw the bike sideways and slid round the turn – or slid off.

For the past decade and perhaps for all time, Parker has been "The Man" on the ovals, picking up titles most years and smashing every record in the books. Like his buddy Jay Springsteen (who was champion from 1976 to 1978), he's also from Flint, Michigan.

Born in 1962, Parker started riding at the age of six and racing at 13. He picked up his first Number One plate in 1988, posting four consecutive titles before Harley-Davidson team-mate Chris Carr took the crown in 1992. Ricky Graham won in 1993, but Parker struck back with five consecutive crowns since. His nine titles make him far and away the most successful rider in AMA dirt-track history.

THE HOLE IN THE WALL GANG

In the Depression years of the 1930s, people would try almost anything to turn a buck. If Evel Knievel enlivened the 1970s, the 1930s shone for an assorted bunch of desperadoes who might be called the "Hole in the Wall Gang". These weren't Butch and Sundance but a fellowship of maniacs who believed that if you hurtled a bike fast enough at a solid timber wall, you could punch clean through it. The first recorded case of a Harley-Davidson attempting the stunt came in Texas in 1932 when Daisy May Hendrich thudded repeatedly through inch-thick boards. (Daisy May, incidentally, was a man.) J.R. Bruce of Wooster, Ohio, went one better by setting the wall ablaze before the stunt. Wall stunts, burning or not, were a common feature of American county fairs in the 1930s.

■ BELOW ***As well as his prowess on dirt, Springsteen was an able road racer, as here with the Sundance twin.***

■ RIGHT *Quarter-mile action at Daytona. The bikes are Rotax-engined single-cylinder "Harleys".*

■ DIRT TRACK

Dirt track "oval" racing spans the decades and is the essence of American motorcycle sport. This is the craziest and meanest of them all – chasing the prized "Number One" plate of the AMA champion. Although superficially similar to speedway, oval racing is held on tracks a mile or half-mile long where 750cc machines reach speeds in excess of 130mph(210kph).

Dirt track grew up on the county fairgrounds of middle America, a sort of rodeo on two wheels. In the early years, it was barely organized and, even during times when it was, it often wasn't: an "outlaw" series flourished in the 1940s. In 1946, the AMA founded the national championship which has been keenly contested ever since.

■ LEFT *Scott Parker leads the field into turn one during the Sacramento Mile.*

■ BELOW *The start of the "Dash for Cash" race at Daytona. Winner takes all.*

■ LEFT *Sideways at 100mph (160kph) – not for the faint-hearted.*

The pre-eminence of Americans in 500 road-racing grands prix has been ascribed to the special skills honed by dirt-track experience. Champion riders, including the likes of Kenny Roberts, Wayne Rainey, Eddie Lawson and most of the rest cut their teeth learning how to control bucking, sliding motorcycles on dirt.

The early Harley-Davidson heroes were men like Jimmy Chann, Joe Leonard and Carroll Resweber, who took ten titles between them from 1947 to 1961. In those days and until 1986, the champion's cherished "Number One" was decided in a series which included quarter-, half- and mile flat-track racing, TT Steeplechase (a cross between dirt track and motocross) and European-style road-racing. These days, there's a separate road-race series, and the days of the great all-rounders are over – Bubba Shobert was the last, with three consecutive AMA titles. Shobert held the record for mile wins with 25, until eclipsed by current champ Scott Parker in 1991. The famed Harley-Davidson "Number One" logo, incidentally, was designed in 1970 to celebrate Mert Lawwill's AMA Grand National title.

■ ABOVE *What it's all about: the coveted Number One plate.*

■ BELOW *The all-conquering XR750, brutal and elegant at the same time.*

Done well – and the top exponents do it very well – dirt track is oddly balletic, almost poetry on wheels. But it can go wrong with sickening suddenness, ending in a maelstrom of muck, blood and machinery. Catch the motorcycle film *On Any Sunday* and you'll see men thrown through four-inch fence posts, clamber to their feet, dust off the dirt and the straw and climb right back on their bikes. You'll see men who can't walk drifting both wheels at three figure speeds. You'll see Dick Mann saw off a plaster cast – "I'm a fast healer" – just to chase that Number One plate.

■ ABOVE *Springsteen's XR750, sponsored by Bartels of California.*

DRAG RACING

If all Harley-Davidsons thunder, none thunder with quite such a clap as fire-breathing drag machines. Like so much else in motorcycle sport, drag racing lies deep in the soul of America. Naturally, Harley-Davidsons have always been there when the lights go out at the start of the quarter mile. Men like Marion Owens, Leo Payne and Danny Johnson, with his celebrated double-engine Harley, continued to show that big-twin power was a force to be reckoned with long after multi-cylinder machines and two-strokes had dominated in other fields.

■ ABOVE, LEFT AND RIGHT ***The idea is to expend as much money and effort in the shortest possible time. Strange, but thousands are addicted to this power-mad sport.***

■ CAL RAYBORN

The great Cal Rayborn never won the coveted Number One plate but that didn't stop him being the best. Rayborn was the consummate road racer, a true natural and arguably the man who opened the door to Kenny Roberts, Wayne Rainey and other Americans who have since made their mark in grand prix competition. From Spring Valley, California, Rayborn won Daytona twice, as well as nine other major AMA road-race wins. Yet his career almost never began at all – in 1958, at only 18 years of age, he broke his back at California's Riverside circuit.

Never truly at home on dirt, Rayborn compensated with absolute mastery on tarmac. In 1968, he became the first man to average 100mph (160.93kph) winning the then world-renowned Daytona 200-miler (321.86km) – and comfortably: he recorded 101.29mph (163kph). In the process, his XR750 Harley-Davidson lapped the entire field. He won again in 1969, in what would prove to be the last Daytona triumph for Milwaukee. British fans will remember him for trouncing the field in the Easter Match Races in 1972, also on a factory XR750. The big V-twin had almost

■ BELOW ***The late, great Cal Rayborn pictured at Oulton Park, England, at the Easter Match Races, 1972.***

■ ABOVE *Evel Knievel, the ultimate showman – especially for Milwaukee. The tank says "Harley-Davidson" but the engine's a Triumph twin.*

been dismissed in favour of factory Triumphs, Nortons and Japanese machines, but Rayborn made them eat their words.

Rayborn also found time for a succession of speed record attempts, in his case on Utah's Bonneville salt flats. In 1970, he took a pencil-thin, 19ft (6-metre), streamlined 1480cc Sportster to a staggering 254.84mph (410.11kph), a figure he later improved to 265.49mph (427.25kph).

Rayborn was killed tragically in 1973 while riding in Australia, ironically on a two-stroke which seized and threw him into a trackside barrier.

■ EVEL KNIEVEL

If Harley-Davidson's earlier successes had been in racing, Evel Knievel had a better idea: he'd make them fly. A pure showman, Knievel chased women and long-jump records in roughly equal measure. Beginning in 1970, his crazy schemes ran on Harley-Davidson power, mainly with a succession of XR750 machines.

Knievel's bikes had to be tough – if not quite as tough as the man himself. He jumped cars (21 at Ontario Speedway on 28 February 1971), trucks, buses and even the fountain at Caesar's Palace in Las Vegas. Evel's problem was that he was effectively on piece-rate – his fees rose with the number of obstacles cleared. And he liked money: the jumps got bigger and the litany of crashes grew longer. In the process, he broke most of his important bones and a lot of smaller ones. When you went to watch Evel Knievel, you knew that you were in for a show. The Las Vegas leap resulted in one of his more spectacular crashes when he

■ RIGHT *The Sport-engined streamliner which took the 250cc land speed record in 1965, driven by George Roeder, pictured here.*

■ FAR RIGHT *Here the Knievel flying machine is pictured astride the genuine Harley article.*

bounced off cars, cartwheeling through the Caesar's Palace parking lot.

By 1978, Knievel had run out of conventional things to jump and crash into, and announced he would leap the Grand Canyon instead. The Canyon is over a mile wide and almost as deep, so the local Native American tribe probably did him a favour when they vetoed the plan. Undeterred, Knievel turned his sights to the Snake River Canyon, abandoning his beloved Harley-Davidson for a rocket-powered projectile. However, the rocket only fizzed, and the attempt was a failure.

In 1999, Knievel's son put the record straight when he, finally and triumphantly, leapt over the Grand Canyon.

■ GRANDS PRIX

Whatever disappointments the arrangement brought in terms of sales, Harley's ties to Aermacchi produced resounding success on the world stage during the mid-1970s. Factory RR-250 and RR-350 twins ridden by Italy's Walter Villa won three consecutive 250cc world titles and one 350cc title between 1974 and 1976.

Producing 58bhp at 12,000rpm and 70bhp at 11,400rpm respectively, these were unlike traditional Harley-Davidson twins.

The engines were two-stroke, initially air-cooled but later with full liquid cooling. The gearboxes housed six ratios, due to the RR's narrow, peaky powerband. These two-stroke

■ ABOVE LEFT *Based on the XR1000 roadster engine, Lucifer's Hammer surprised many onlookers by its speed in Battle of the Twins competition during the 1980s.*

■ ABOVE RIGHT *Walter Villa contesting the 250cc Belgian grand prix at Spa-Francorchamps in 1977 on an RR250. Despite carrying the number 10, he was world champion at the time.*

■ LEFT *An Aermacchi 350 charges round the Brands Hatch circuit.*

■ ABOVE *A Harley superbike – the factory VR1000.*

■ ABOVE RIGHT *Harley's inspired 883 Sportster series even attracted stars such as Jay Springsteen.*

twins were also raced with some success in the United States by championship-winning riders such as Cal Rayborn and Gary Scott.

■ LUCIFER'S HAMMER

Perhaps the single most celebrated Harley racer of recent times, Lucifer's Hammer began its racing life with a win at Daytona in 1983 with the great Jay Springsteen on the saddle. The same bike went on to dominate American Battle of the Twins racing (under Harley Owners' Group sponsorship) during much of the 1980s, taking Gene Church to three consecutive American titles.

Powered by a highly-tuned XR1000 engine generating 104bhp at 7,000rpm, the Hammer was timed at no less than 158mph (254kph) at Daytona. The XR750 road race frame, albeit heavily reworked, had debuted at Daytona fully ten years before Springsteen's epic win, showing that at Milwaukee, they build 'em to last.

■ 883 SPORT TWINS SERIES

The Sport Twins series, launched in the United States in 1989, quickly became a worldwide phenomenon. A "one-make" competition for modified 883cc Harley twins, the series' instant success saw it exported to race tracks all around the world, where spectators would flock to hear the thunder of a grid-full of Milwaukee twins. When Harley created the series, it probably expected it to be an all-American affair. If so, they were mistaken. That very first American Sports Twins series title was won by an Englishman, Nigel Gale.

■ VR1000

The factory has recently been striving towards a competitive presence in world superbike action. This has been achieved with the VR1000 twin ridden by former AMA Number Ones Chris Carr and Thomas Wilson and, latterly, by the former World Superbike champion, Scott Russell.

■ BELOW *Using double overhead cams in each head, four valves per cylinder and fuel injection, the VR1000 is unlike any Harley ever seen on the street.*

The Models

The section that follows is a guide to the major models produced by Harley-Davidson, from the first primitive single of 1903 to the style kings and lavishly-equipped cruisers of today. It is not an attempt to cover every Harley-Davidson model, but all the most important and significant examples are included.

In reviewing machines spanning Harley-Davidson's history, the reader might become aware of one overriding enigma. The company is certainly the most enduring of all the world's motorcycle marques and is currently enjoying an almost unparalleled period of success. Yet, while other motorcycle manufacturers leap headlong into increased technical complexity, Harley-Davidson is as dedicated as ever to its original convictions of sound design and solid simplicity, remaining faithful to its dependable, thoroughbred V-twins.

What Harley-Davidson has in abundance is that indefinable quality called "character" – an attribute no specification panel can reveal. Harley-Davidsons are visceral. They have guts and charisma. Only by riding one can you really begin to understand.

HARLEY-
DAVIDSON

The Singles

Harley-Davidson's future was forged not out of the rumble of V-twins, but with the thump of simple, single-cylinder engines. The very first examples differed little from the 1903 prototype, and the engines conformed to the same basic "F-head" design housed in a primitive chassis only slightly removed from bicycle practice.

It was inevitably plain and basic, but this humble single showed a ruggedness that was to become a Milwaukee hallmark. Only ten years after the debut of the first Harley-Davidson model, the company was advertising that one of its machines had travelled 100,000 miles (160,930km) on its original bearings. In those days of dirt roads, mud, dust and potholes, bikes had to be tough.

These attributes of durability, simplicity and economy ensured that singles figured somewhere in the Harley-Davidson range well into the 1930s. It was during the era of the singles that Harley's credo was first expressed: "Experience has shown that it is preferable to use a comparatively large motor running at moderate speed in preference to a small motor running at high speed." Those words appeared in a publicity brochure printed in 1905 but could almost have been written today.

FIRST SINGLE, 1903–11

■ BELOW AND BOTTOM *One of the first De Dion-Bouton-inspired singles. Pedal assistance was essential on hills. The belt final drive with its crude de-clutching mechanism is clearly seen in the lower photograph. The 1910 "Silent Gray Fellow" is altogether more sophisticated but retains pedals and belt final drive.*

Harley-Davidson's first motorcycle, though nominally a single-cylinder model, evolved with the company over a production span of eight years. During that time, annual production figures soared from fewer than a handful to over 4,000 as demand – and know-how – grew in leaps and bounds. One thing that changed relatively little was the price: $200 in 1904, yet only $25 more by the time production ceased in 1911.

The heart of the engine was a bolted-up crankshaft running car-type, plain, big-end bearings in cast aluminium crankcases. Above this sat a one-piece iron cylinder head and cylinder barrel housing an iron piston. To allow for differential expansion – its top generated far more heat than its bottom – each piston was tapered, a considerable machining achievement for the time. Valve layout was inlet-over-exhaust, the "automatic" or "vacuum" inlet valve controlled – crudely – via pressure created by the rise and fall of the piston. Removable housing permitted the extrication of both valves for servicing: no method of valve-lash adjustment was available until 1908.

SPECIFICATIONS (1909)

Engine	single cylinder ioe with automatic inlet valve
Capacity	30.16cu in (495cc)
Transmission	single speed, leather belt drive
Power	around 3.5bhp
Weight	185lb (84kg)
Wheelbase	51in
Top speed	around 45mph (72kph)

The initial cylinder dimensions of 3 x 3½in (76.2 x 88.9mm) gave a displacement of 24.74cu in (405cc). In 1905, the bore increased to 3⅛in (79.4mm), giving 26.84cu in (440cc). At the same time, the single loop frame was redesigned, as all previous examples

showed a tendency to crack at the headstock. Capacity was further increased to 30.16cu in (495cc) in 1909 by a 1⁄16in (1.6mm) increase in bore, by which time the exhaust port had also migrated from the side towards the front of the cylinder. Until 1910, all the motors had used horizontal "beehive" finning for both barrel and head; in 1911 this changed to distinctive vertical cylinder head finning.

Lubrication, like almost all engines of the time, was "total-loss" – a gravity feed dripping oil into the engine from a half-gallon (1.9 litre) tank, good for around 750 miles (1,200km). Transmission was of the simplest possible type with a 1¼in-wide (32mm), two-ply leather belt driving the rear wheel directly. There was no gearbox or clutch, although belt tension could be adjusted on the move by 1911.

The starting technique was straightforward, if energetic – run alongside then jump on board and pedal like mad until the motor fired.

A hand-crank starter became available in 1906 for an additional cost, and was standardized the following year, although neither method of starting was notably elegant.

Like modern motorcycles, power was governed by a twist-grip on the right-hand handlebar and a simple "coaster" brake in the rear hub slowed things down. Lighting of any kind was only made available with the introduction of acetylene lights in the final year of production. Initially, suspension consisted entirely of springs under the leather saddle – and whatever the rider could suffer – but, in 1907, a crude but remarkably effective Sager front fork was added to ease the pain.

As well as standard, conservative "piano" black, by 1906 the single was also available – at an extra cost – in "Renault" pale grey with red pin-striping. This model thus became known from then on as "The Silent Gray Fellow", partly in tribute to its unusually effective silencing. Unpainted metal parts were nickel-plated and the aluminium engine covers were brightly polished to a high shine.

■ ABOVE LEFT ***By 1907, the single had grown to 26.84cu in (440cc), was looking more sophisticated and had changed hue: "The Silent Gray Fellow".***

■ ABOVE RIGHT ***A 1905 24.74cu in (405cc) single, which cost $200 when new.***

■ ABOVE ***A very original 1907 single undergoing restoration work.***

HIDDEN TREASURE

The very first production Harley-Davidson may currently enjoy pride of place behind a bullet-proof glass screen in the Juneau Avenue lobby, but it hasn't always been quite so treasured.

The bike was originally retained by the company and sent to the Pan American Exposition in California in 1915 (since which time Harley has kept at least one example from each year of production). Upon its return, however, the company somehow "forgot" this bike was Number One. During the 1970s, it was damaged in transit to the Rodney C. Gott Museum in York, but its true identity remained unrealized, even while it was being repaired.

It was only when it underwent a recent comprehensive restoration at the hands of Harley Archives craftsman, Ray Schlee, that the machine's true pedigree was disclosed – by internal parts bearing the legend "Number 1." It is believed to have been raced in 1904 but is now housed in a 1905 frame, as all the earlier examples broke at the headstock.

This unique machine has now been insured for $2 million.

Model 5-35 Singles, 1913–18

The second-generation single-cylinder machine, produced from 1913 to 1918, housed a refinement of the earlier engine rather than an all-new design. Although the bore remained unchanged at 3 5/16in (84.1mm), the stroke increased from 3½ to 4in (88.9 to 101.6mm), giving a capacity of 34.47cu in (565cc). The new engine was known generically as the 5-35, signifying 5 horsepower and 35 cu in.

Many lessons learned during the troubled development of the first twin were incorporated in the new single's design. Valve layout was still inlet-over-exhaust, although now the inlet valve followed the revised V-twin practice of mechanical operation via a long push rod on the motor's right-hand side. The camshafts – one exhaust, one inlet – were driven by a chain of gears, ending with the Bosch magneto (replaced by a Remy instrument from 1915) which provided the sparks.

■ ABOVE AND BELOW ***By the time this Model 9-B was built in 1913, chain drive was a factory option on single-cylinder machines and twins. Both the chain-drive and belt-drive singles cost the same: $290, $60 less than the twin.***

SPECIFICATIONS	
Engine	ioe single
Capacity	34.47cu in (565cc)
Transmission	1-, 2- and 3-speed
Wheelbase	55in (1,400mm)
Top speed	around 54mph (87kph) (side-valve) or 65mph (105kph) (ohv)

As before, the iron cylinder head and barrel were one-piece, accommodating a steel three-ring piston. The crankcases were of aluminium, in which a high-grade steel crankshaft ran on phosphor-bronze main bearings, with the whole crank assembly balanced. Lubrication was still total-loss, engine oil being metered by hand from its own compartment in the tank slung beneath the frame's top rail. A sight-glass below the tank gave the rider some idea how frequently to deliver drops of oil. As well as manipulating this, the rider was required to adjust the degree of ignition advance (in other words, the precise point at which the spark plug ignited the mixture), by means of yet another control lever. In those days, getting the best out of an engine was not a simple business. It demanded considerable awareness from the operator.

Perhaps the most obvious difference between these early singles was the replacement of belt with chain as the drive medium, eliminating the wet-weather slip that plagued all leather belt drives. On early examples, the drive was taken direct, via roller chain, from a sprocket on the left-hand end of the crankshaft to another on the rear hub. The same hub also contained a type of rudimentary clutch operated by a long lever on the left side of the machine. Starting involved placing the machine on its stand, which lifted the rear wheel off the ground, then vigorously rotating the bicycle-type pedals. These same

■ BELOW *All three images show a two-speed Model 10-C from 1914. The single-speed Model 10-B proved far more popular.*

■ BOTTOM LEFT *Harley's astonishingly complex two-speed rear hub is clearly visible in this view. The hub employed a ring of interlocking bevel gears to vary the final drive ratio.*

pedals, when rotated backwards, engaged the "coaster-type" rear brake via a chain on the right-hand side. Lever-operated brakes did not appear until 1918.

A "step-starter" and Harley's first two-speed rear hub arrived in 1914 (also in the V-twin), offering increased flexibility with maximum speeds of around 54 and 65mph (87 and 105kph) in the two ratios. Within a year, this deceptively intricate device had given way to three-speed transmission with a true sliding-pinion gearbox on better-specified models. Nonetheless, single-speed and even belt-drive models continued to be built for some years.

Chassis refinements included a more robust front suspension offering around 2in (50mm) of travel. The rear, of course, would remain rigid for many years. However, a degree of consolation was provided by Harley's patented "Full Floteing" seat.

As well as the paired springs common on other motorcycles, this seat featured a hinge at the front and a coil spring inside the seat post to cushion the rider from the worst of the bumps.

■ BELOW *Although it retained pedals, the two-speeder offered footboards for the first time. Note the ignition magneto which is below the carburettor.*

Models A & B Single, 1926–34

Although single-cylinder machines were as much a hallmark of Harley-Davidson's formative years as the big V-twins with which they are now associated, Juneau Avenue produced almost no such models from 1919 until 1926. The sole exception was the Model CD, a 37.1cu in (608cc) machine created by the simple expedient of removing one pot from the 74-inch twin. It was built in very small numbers from 1921 to 1922 and was intended for commercial use only. When singles did reappear, they were considerably smaller than before, displacing just 21.1cu in (346cc) compared to the earlier 30-inchers.

Somewhat confusingly, the single was known simultaneously as both Model A and Model B. The former denoted a magneto version, the latter that the machine was fitted with a generator and coil ignition. This was further refined into Models AA and BA Sport Solos, where the second letter indicated that the engine had overhead valves. The more basic model, designated by a simple A or B was of straightforward "flathead" design, with valves side-by-side and operated by short push-rods.

SPECIFICATIONS

Engine	side-valve or overhead valve single
Capacity	21.1cu in (346cc)
Transmission	3-speed
Power	8bhp (side-valve) or 12bhp (ohv)
Wheelbase	55in (1,400mm)
Top speed	around 50mph (80kph) (side-valve) or 60mph (96kph) (ohv)

The overhead-valve model was an altogether more potent piece of machinery that would achieve considerable competition success as the legendary Peashooter racer. It was inevitably less aggressive in roadster trim, yet still capable of what was then a giddy 4,800rpm and close to 65mph (105kph). Its side-valve sibling, on the other hand, struggled to exceed 50mph (80kph). Despite this marked difference, both engines were rated at 3.31 horsepower. At the time, quoted power figures were not a measure of actual output, merely a function of piston displacement and thus quite meaningless as a reflection of performance. Modern power figures, of course, describe actual output. Strangely, Harley chose to promote the flathead at the expense of the more advanced engine, probably because side-valves would soon comprise the vast bulk of the Milwaukee range.

Mechanically, the engine featured a lightweight aluminium alloy piston

■ ABOVE *The ohv "Peashooter" engine. The push-rods, rocker arms and exposed valves are clearly visible.*

■ LEFT *Dual "bullet" headlights first appeared on this 1929 500cc single, derived from the Models A and B. Note the front brake – another novelty introduced the previous year.*

■ LEFT *Stripped-down racing version of the ohv "Peashooter". Note low, pulled-back handlebars and spartan saddle.*

(initially iron for the side-valve machines) running in a cast-iron cylinder. Typically for the time, the overhead's valve gear was exposed, although the 21.1 cu in (344cc) single was the first Milwaukee engine lubricated by a proper mechanical pump. Nonetheless, a hand pump was retained for supplementary oiling when the engine was under extreme loads. Transmission was by the now-familiar three-speed sliding gear, driven by a foot-operated single-plate dry clutch.

By the time of the new single's debut in 1926, electrical equipment had leaped forward in specification and dependability. Although full electrical equipment was optional (Models A and AA came as standard with just a magneto to generate sparks), it was also comprehensive. Generator models featured a coil and distributor (to power and time the ignition), battery, horn, two-bulb headlight and tail-light, all controlled from a switch on the steering head – everything you might expect to find on a modern motorcycle, except stop-light and indicators. Less can be said for the cycle parts. True, the single wore the new type of teardrop petrol (gas) tank, which wrapped over the top frame tube rather than hung from it, as before. At the front, Harley's familiar sprung forks gave some comfort and control, but the rear end was rigid and would remain so for more than 20 further years. The rear hub did contain a brake – a 5¾in (146mm) drum – but the front wheel contributed nothing to retardation. It would be another two years before Milwaukee installed their first front brake. During the early 1930s, "21"'s sales were hit, partly by the relative success of the Series C single, but mainly by the Depression. Domestic supplies were halted during 1931 when just three examples were exported. The ohv model never reappeared, although flathead sales rallied slightly before the model was axed at the end of 1934.

■ ABOVE RIGHT *Note the gear lever (left) and fillers for oil and fuel. The switch console is a later addition.*

■ RIGHT *Although only $40 cheaper, flatheads such as this Model 26-B solo comfortably outsold the more exotic ohv singles.*

MODEL C SINGLE, 1929–34

In 1929, the Model A and B singles got a bigger brother with the introduction of the Model C. Displacing 30.1cu in (493cc), the newcomer's top end was essentially half of the old 61-inch Model F/J twin, mated to the 21-inch single's bottom end. This was clearly a more sound solution than the trick many American racers had been pulling for years – they had simply removed one top end and connecting rod from the J, blanked off the hole and let rip on the track. Road riders demanded something slightly more elegant.

Unlike the "21" however, this time no overhead-valve variant was offered; the model was resolutely side-valve, although the greater pulling power of the 30-inch motor meant that, for the modest uses for which most singles were destined, no overhead valves were required. Power was sufficient for a top speed approaching 60mph (96kph).

Compared to the smaller single, the "30" was both bored and stroked with even more undersquare dimensions of 3¹⁄₁₆ x 4in (78.6 x 101.6mm). Since it was also slower revving than the "21", a 42 per cent increase in capacity realised only a 25 per cent increase in power, from eight to ten horsepower. Both machines shared a similar three-speed transmission. An overhead-valve competition derivative, the Model CA (later CAC) was produced in very limited numbers. By the time of the Model C's debut in 1929, Harleys had begun to develop front brakes (they also

SPECIFICATIONS

Engine	side-valve single
Capacity	30.1cu in (493cc)
Transmission	3-speed
Power	10bhp
Wheelbase	57½in (1,460mm)
Top speed	around 56mph (90kph)

■ ABOVE *This Series C 500cc 3-speed single shows the low-line frame introduced in 1930.*

■ LEFT *A 1929 500cc single. At the time, the vibrant paint job was optional only on twins.*

■ ABOVE *This mammoth modern ElectraGlide might look a far cry from the early singles, but they are very much its ancestors.*

featured on the 45-inch twin that appeared in the same year). Like the rear brake, this was a simple, single-leading shoe drum, but activated by a lever on the right handlebar, as is the practice today.

Early examples shared the same frame and running gear as contemporary 21-inch singles, but during the second year of production the larger engine was installed in a chassis "borrowed" from the twin. This turned the robust little single into a "full-size" motorcycle – ironically with a lower seat height but increased ground clearance.

More ironically still, in 1933 it was joined by the Model CB, essentially a 30-inch engine in 21-inch running gear – a choice perhaps prompted by excess stock of the latter.

Worthy as the Model C was, the majority of American motorcycle buyers still hankered after twin-cylinder pulling power even during the depths of the Depression.

A measure of the singles' problem at home was that, during 1929, sales of the 21- and 30-inch singles combined were little more than half of those of the Series D twin – 3,789 units compared to 6,856.

Nonetheless, though comparatively unheralded in their own country, the sturdy little singles proved popular overseas as Harley-Davidson continued to develop its international markets, where the sheer weight and size of the big twins often posed problems to potential buyers. Not surprisingly, the larger single had soon became the dominant seller.

Initially priced at just $20 more than the $235 price-tag of the "21", the Model C comfortably outsold the smaller machine from 1930 onwards. More than 5,000 units of the popular Series C were produced in total over the life span of the model, which was to be six years in all.

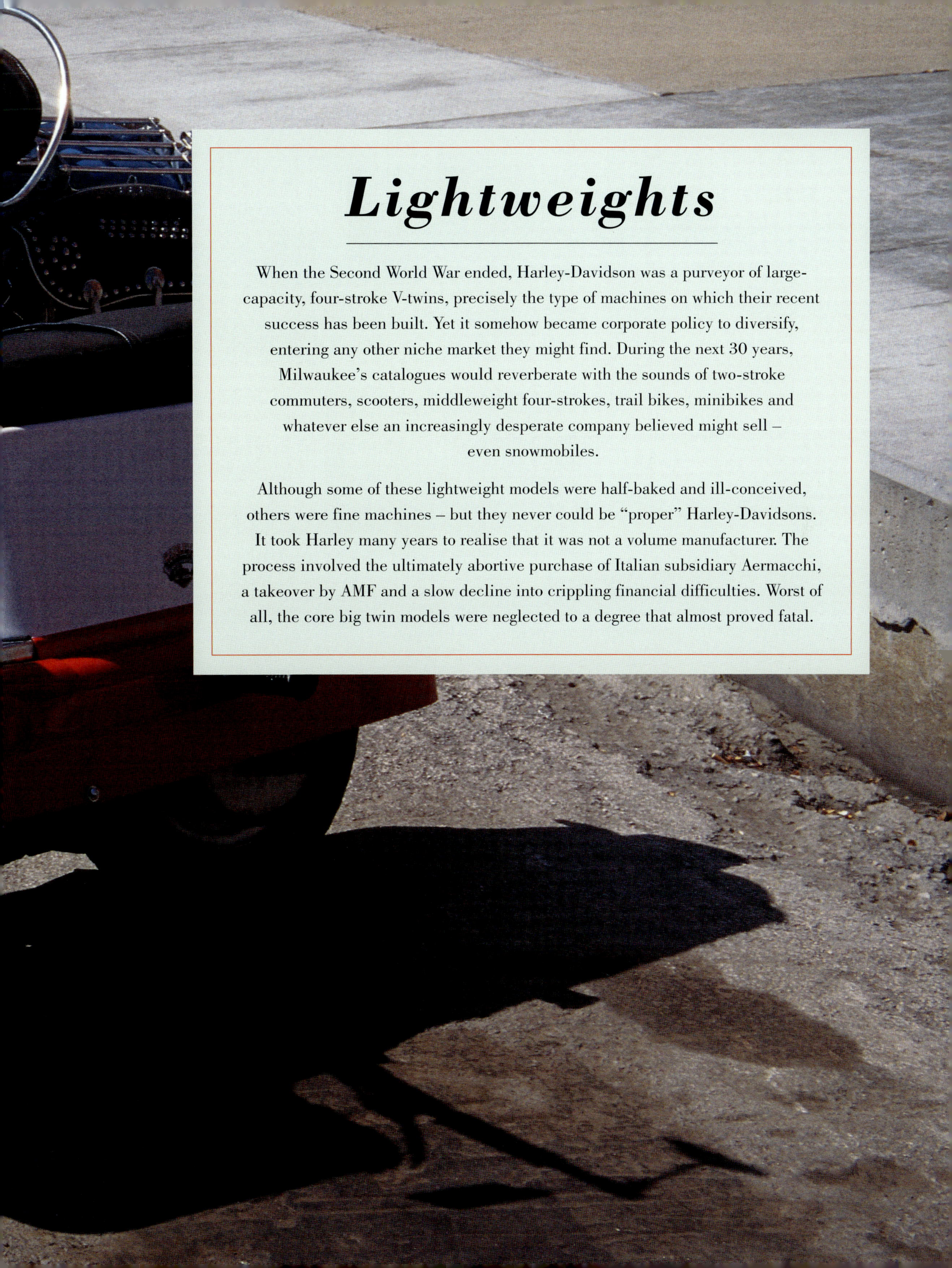

Lightweights

When the Second World War ended, Harley-Davidson was a purveyor of large-capacity, four-stroke V-twins, precisely the type of machines on which their recent success has been built. Yet it somehow became corporate policy to diversify, entering any other niche market they might find. During the next 30 years, Milwaukee's catalogues would reverberate with the sounds of two-stroke commuters, scooters, middleweight four-strokes, trail bikes, minibikes and whatever else an increasingly desperate company believed might sell – even snowmobiles.

Although some of these lightweight models were half-baked and ill-conceived, others were fine machines – but they never could be "proper" Harley-Davidsons. It took Harley many years to realise that it was not a volume manufacturer. The process involved the ultimately abortive purchase of Italian subsidiary Aermacchi, a takeover by AMF and a slow decline into crippling financial difficulties. Worst of all, the core big twin models were neglected to a degree that almost proved fatal.

STATESIDE STROKERS

■ LEFT AND BELOW LEFT *Two variants of the Milwaukee two-stroke derived from the German DKW. Note rigid rear end, "Tele-Glide" front forks and the fuel tank shape which would become the inspiration for the Sportsters.*

■ MODEL S-125, 1948–52 MODEL ST-165, 1953–9 MODEL B HUMMER, 1955–9

Harley-Davidson's first venture into the world of two-strokes owed much to the end of the Second World War. On the one hand, it was assumed that thousands of demobbed GIs would crave almost any motorcycle they could lay their hands on, and the 125cc single was considered the ideal low-cost candidate. Second, the design was basically that of the pre-war DKW RT125.

When partition placed the factory in the new East Germany, the design passed to the Allies as war reparations. British BSA's hugely successful Bantam was also a DKW copy, as was the very first Yamaha, the YA1 "Red Dragonfly".

Producing just three horsepower from its simple piston-ported, air-cooled engine, the S-125 must have been a profound disappointment to any American biker raised on big four-stroke power.

Juneau Avenue was evidently hopeful about selling these machines in huge numbers, producing more than 10,000 in the model's first year, but sales proved poor, settling to around 4,000 per annum even after the introduction of a "Tele-Glide" version with telescopic forks in 1951.

A bore increase in 1953, from 52 to 60mm, resulted in the slightly zippier 165cc Model ST. A restricted version, the STU, was also available.

Two years later, the Model B Hummer – using essentially the same 125cc engine and transmission as the first Model S – appeared in the Harley-Davidson catalogue.

From 1960 to 1961, an updated 165cc range continued as the 6bhp BT and BTU (restricted to 5bhp) Super Ten. Harley-Davidson's slogan for this model went: "keen wheeling for teen wheeling".

SPECIFICATIONS: S-125

Engine	2-stroke single-cylinder
Capacity	125cc
Transmission	3-speed
Power	3bhp
Wheelbase	50in (1,270mm)
Top speed	around 40mph (64kph)

■ ABOVE *The ST-165: the striking quartered tank emblem dates from 1957.*

■ LEFT *The first two-stroke was this Model S of 1948. Note the girder front forks.*

■ BELOW *The Pacer was the pure street version of the Model BT range of 165 and 175cc two-strokes.*

■ RANGER, PACER, SCAT, BOBCAT, 1962–6

This quartet was another attempt to broaden the Harley range and allow Milwaukee to compete as a mass-market player. In hindsight, the strategy was clearly misguided, but Milwaukee believed there was a niche market of buyers not quite ready for the new 250cc Sprint (nor for the big twins). The Ranger and its siblings were the result.

All four machines, designated Model BT, shared a two-stroke engine derived from the Super 10, but with increased stroke from 60 to 61mm for a capacity of 175cc on all but the 1962 Pacer and Ranger. As with the Topper, "full power" and 5bhp versions were built.

Models that year were the street-only BT Pacer, the dual-purpose BTH Scat and the BTF Ranger, a stripped-down, off-road variant without lights. The first examples had rigid rear ends, but models that had swinging-fork suspension appeared for 1963.

The Ranger was dropped for 1963 while the Pacer and Scat gave way to the BTH Bobcat in 1966.

Available in road and optional off-guises, this lasted for one year, proving to be the last of the American-built Harley lightweights.

SPECIFICATIONS: BOBCAT

Engine	2-stroke single-cylinder
Capacity	175cc
Transmission	3-speed
Power	8bhp
Wheelbase	52in (1,320mm)
Top speed	around 60mph (96kph)

■ TOPPER SCOOTER, 1960–5

The Model A Topper – which was Milwaukee's obvious attempt to cash in on the scooter boom which swept the Western world during the late 1950s – employed a 165cc two-stroke with identical bore and stroke to the old ST but with the cylinder laid down horizontally to reduce engine height.

Power was claimed to be 9bhp from the 1961-on high-compression engine (Model AH), with a "restricted" five-horsepower version (Model AU) sold in those American states which permitted the use of low output two-wheelers without a driver's licence.

Unlike earlier three-speed Harley strokers, this time the "Scootaway" transmission was automatic, using belt drive and variable flanged wheels to change ratios.

The system was unusual but by no means new – the Rudge Multi and American-built NeraCar had featured similar drives decades before – yet it did anticipate today's fully automatic commuter machines.

■ BOTTOM *A Topper in conventional livery. Although quite advanced, the $450 machine failed to cash in on the scooter boom.*

■ BELOW *A Topper Scooter, now used as Harley's corporate paddock transport.*

SPECIFICATIONS: TOPPER

Engine	2-stroke single-cylinder
Capacity	165cc
Transmission	variable belt
Power	5bhp or 9bhp
Wheelbase	51.5in (1,310mm)
Top speed	around 50mph (80kph)

Other Topper novelties included a rubber-mounted engine with reed-valve induction, a parking brake, under-seat stowage space and lawnmower-style hand-starting.

By all accounts, the boxy Topper was a quirky but competent device which might have fared better had it not arrived just as the scooter market went into decline.

Sales of the $430 machine went from almost 4,000 to just 500 during its six years on the books.

Ironically – given that Harley-Davidson by then had an Italian factory – being "Made in Milwaukee" was no substitute for the true Latin style of other more genuinely Italian scooters, such as those that were made by Vespa or Lambretta.

FORZA HARLEY

■ LEFT ***Stripped-down Sprints proved surprisingly adept at dirt-track racing.***

■ SPRINT, 1961–74

The Sprint family of four-stroke singles, unveiled in September 1960, was the first tangible result of Harley-Davidson's purchase of the Aermacchi concern in Varese, Italy. Compared to much contemporary Milwaukee hardware, this was a technically advanced machine derived from the existing 250cc Ala Verde model, with an in-unit overhead-valve engine and superb handling from its spine frame, telescopic forks and swinging-fork rear end. With its unmistakable horizontal cylinder, variants of the same engine went on to innumerable race wins, including the famous Isle of Man TT, and remain hugely popular (and competitive) in classic racing today.

American buyers – despite the invitation to "thrill to the dynamic, virile note of its Hi-Flo tuned exhaust" – never quite warmed to the Sprint's lack of cubes and relatively revvy nature, yet the bike was as capable a standard production machine as its siblings were racers. The stock street version, the Model C, claimed a potent (if slightly ambitious) 18bhp at 7,500rpm from its eager, free-breathing engine. This was joined by the Model H, an off-road variant, one year later, with high-compression pistons and an additional 1.5bhp. The "H" quickly became the more popular model and was used in a wide range of American competitions, from flat track to motocross as well as for purely recreational use.

The Sprint Model H later became known as the Scrambler, producing as much as 25bhp at a relatively giddy 8,700rpm.

In 1967, the original long-stroke configuration changed to short stroke – "The Sprint holds two land speed world records, so we improved it", went the ad. Two years later, the first 350 Sprints appeared, the ERS dirt racer and road-going 350cc SS. The SS was joined by the dual-purpose SX-350 in 1971 and given an electric starter two years later as the "Sprint" title was dropped from the range.

Pure road racing examples of the same 344cc single produced as much as 38bhp, good for 130mph (210kph) with

SPECIFICATIONS: SPRINT C (SS-350)

Engine	ohv horizontal single
Capacity	246cc (344cc)
Transmission	4-speed (5-speed)
Power	18bhp @ 7,500rpm (27bhp @ 7,000rpm)
Weight	unknown (355lb/161kg)
Wheelbase	52in/1,320mm (56in/1,420mm)
Top speed	around 75mph/120kph (85mph/136kph)

■ BELOW ***Note the carburettor's steep downdraught angle, which is a hallmark of Aermacchi design.***

■ BELOW ***This early Sprint enjoys pride of place in the Harley Museum.***

■ BELOW RIGHT AND LEFT *The M-50, one of Milwaukee's strange two-stroke mini-bike range. Left is a 1965 example. By 1966 (right) it looked rather more like a motorcycle. Such lightweights never truly caught on in the USA.*

racing streamlining. Road riders, with maybe 25bhp, had to be content with top speeds in the low nineties. Although a simple spine frame was always good enough for the racers, the final SS-350 inexplicably included a heavy and wholly unnecessary twin-downtube chassis.

With a career spanning 14 years, the Sprint can rightly be regarded as one of Harley's more successful forays away from its core big twin-activities.

The Sprint's arrival coincided with the appearance of advanced, lightweight machines from Japan and, to some extent, it profited from their success.

For the first time since the 1920s, motorcycling in the United States was developing a broad appeal, and the market was soaring.

In 1971 it would peak at 2.1 million new machines sold – a 40-fold increase in less than 20 years.

The Sprint's weakness was not the way it went (when the typically feeble Italian electrical system was not playing up), but in the way its price kept rising when Japanese machines seemed, year after year, to be offering much more for much less.

SPECIFICATIONS: M-50

Engine	2-stroke single-cylinder
Capacity	50cc
Transmission	3-speed
Wheelbase	44in (1,120mm)
Top speed	around 40mph (64kph)

■ BELOW *Trying hard to look like a "real" bike, this 1967 M-50 sports saddlebags and screen, despite a top speed of only around 40mph (64kph).*

■ M-50, M-65, 1965–71

In the mid 1960s Harley-Davidson's quest for wider markets led it into the 50cc domain, a move which was ultimately no more successful than its other oddballs of the time. Ironically those other V-twin warlords, the British Vincent company, had dabbled unsuccessfully with lightweights a decade earlier.

The range began with the M-50 in 1965 and a racier-looking Sport version 12 months later. Both were built in huge numbers – more than 25,000 in the first two years – causing massive oversupply and a sharp fall in price. 1967 brought an increase in capacity for the M-65 and Sport, and more realistic production figures.

For 1967, the original 50cc version developed much-needed extra power with the 65cc M-65, by which time some 4,000 unsold M-50s were flooding the market at knock-down prices.

Both models were available in standard and "Sport" guise, the latter with a racy fuel tank and seat.

A 65cc Leggero (which in Italian means "light") version was also built for the years 1970–1.

STRIVING FOR SALES

■ RAPIDO, TX, SX, STX, 1968–77

The Rapido family of machines was yet another attempt to find a profitable niche at the lightweight end of the market, this time with mainly off-road machines (although the first batch to be built were street bikes). Powered by a simple 123cc two-stroke single with four-speed transmission, the Rapido ultimately gave way to the five-speed, oil-injected TX, SS and SX models. Although often overlooked – not least by traditional big-twin dealers – the range established its pedigree in 1969 when three Rapidos completed an epic, 2,000-mile (3,2000km) ride across the Sahara, from Morocco to Nigeria. A smaller version of the TX, the 90cc Z-90, was produced.

SPECIFICATIONS: RAPIDO

Engine	2-stroke single-cylinder
Capacity	123cc
Transmission	4-speed
Wheelbase	48.9in (1,240mm)
Top speed	around 60mph (96kph)

■ SS AND SX SERIES, 1974–8

By the start of the 1970s, off-road machines were huge business in the American motorcycle scene. Inevitably, this market was hugely competitive, with prices pared to the bone – so much so that even the super-efficient Japanese factories would soon find themselves with massive amounts of unsold stock.

At the same time, environmental concerns were targeting the high hydrocarbon emissions of the two-stroke engine. It was into this unpromising scene that the off-road SX range was launched for 1974. The SX was joined by the street-only SS-250 in 1975 plus its larger dirt sibling, the SX-250, with the road-going SS-175 introduced for 1976. It was the off-roaders, however, that dominated production and sales. More than 25,000 machines were built in 1975, of which all but 3,000 were SX models. In the face of declining demand and over-supply, production slumped to 12,000 for 1976, then 1,400 in 1977 before disappearing almost completely as Harley-Davidson disentangled itself from its Italian partner in 1978.

These were actually quite competent motorcycles despite being very much copies of Yamaha's DT-series engines. The SX-250 in particular achieved quite striking competition success. More successful still was the MX250, derived from what was substantially the same engine. Both failed to survive the closure of Harley-Davidson's Italian operation in 1978.

■ TOP *Models such as this 1970 Rapido attempted to cash in on the Stateside boom in lightweight off-road machines.*

■ LEFT *An SX-250, one of the Italian two-stroke singles which tried to cash in on the trail-bike boom.*

SPECIFICATIONS: SX-175 (SX-250)

Engine	2-stroke single-cylinder
Capacity	174cc (243cc)
Transmission	5-speed
Wheelbase	56in (1,420mm)
Top speed	around 70mph/112kph (80mph/128kph)

■ RIGHT *Outlandishly racy, maybe, but such dual-purpose lightweights were too far from Harley's heritage to succeed.*

SPECIFICATIONS: BAJA SR-100	
Engine	2-stroke single-cylinder
Capacity	98cc
Transmission	5-speed
Wheelbase	52in (1,320mm)
Top speed	around 60mph (96kph)

■ BAJA, SR-100, 1970–4

Named after the notorious desert race down Mexico's Baja peninsula, this 98cc off-roader used a high-performance engine derived from the Rapido's (with the bore reduced from 56 to 50mm) but now with five-speed transmission. The little machine was surprisingly potent and almost 7,500 were built during its five year span. It was ultimately unable to overcome both environmental concerns and the increasingly sophisticated Japanese competition, despite the introduction of an improved, oil-injected SR-100 version for 1973.

■ MINIBIKES: SHORTSTER, X-90, Z-90, 1972–5

Anything further removed from big-inch cruisers would be hard to imagine, but that's exactly what Harley unveiled with the MC-65 Shortster of 1972. An obvious word play on "Sportster", the minibike used the M-65 engine and tiny 10in (254mm) wheels. Only 800 Shortsters were made before it grew to 90cc and became the X-90, which was built from 1973 to 1975. The Z-90 used the same engine, but in a quasi off-road chassis with larger wheels. "The Great American Freedom Machine" was how Harley billed the Italian-built two-strokes, intended mainly for hitching on the back of a camper van rather than as serious commuter machines. Almost 17,000 of these minibikes were made, plus a similar number of Z-90s.

SPECIFICATIONS: X-90	
Engine	2-stroke single-cylinder
Capacity	90cc
Transmission	4-speed
Wheelbase	40.75in (1,035mm)
Top speed	around 55mph (88kph)

■ LEFT *The X-90. Dismissed as "a menace" at the time, the minibike range is now considered cute and even collectable.*

■ SNOWMOBILE, 1970–5

Like the Topper Scooter, Harley's Snowmobile was a tardy response to a passing craze. The fad initiated by the Canadian Bombardier company in the mid-1960s produced many similar machines, most with the same mechanical layout. Milwaukee's version, released in 1970, was steered by paired skis linked to motorcycle-type handlebars at the front and driven by a broad belt at the rear. It was powered by a twin-cylinder two-stroke engine and the all-chain drive featured automatic transmission. There were two capacities (398 or 433cc) and electric or manual start. The Snowmobile was dropped from 1975, the victim of three consecutive mild winters.

■ RIGHT *Harley's snowmobile sold poorly. Maybe if they'd called it a SnowGlide...*

The First Twins

From a modern perspective, the expressions "Harley-Davidson" and "V-twin" are practically synonymous, yet it was not always so. Expanding the Harley range from singles to twins was a logical progression as Harley attempted to broaden its share in the rapidly expanding American market. The first American V-twin was the 695cc Curtiss of 1903 and Harley's first prototype was built three years later, making its first public appearance at the Chicago motorcycle show in 1907.

Exactly two years later, the Model 5-D twin was offered for sale, with the 45-degree configuration that is now a Harley hallmark. In almost every other respect, however, the engine was entirely different. As with the contemporary singles on which it was based, the F-head valve layout was inlet-over-exhaust, with the inlets of the "automatic" type, in which the valve was simply "sucked" open by the falling piston rather than being moved mechanically by a cam. After almost two decades of painstaking evolution, the F-head layout culminated in the legendary JH and JDH twin-cam models, the "superbike" race replica machines of their day.

As the 1920s drew to a close, side-valve engines became the Milwaukee norm, heralding an era dominated by flatheads such as the enduring "45" and the mammoth 80-inch VL – machines that put the muscle into Milwaukee.

EARLY TWINS

■ LEFT *A 1913 61-inch single speed twin. Although this example has no lights, an acetylene kit was supplied as an optional extra.*

With the single having amply demonstrated its ruggedness, the twin that evolved from it ought to have been the same – only more so. Like the singles, the twin was single-speed with belt final drive, one-piece heads and barrels with horizontal "beehive" finning. Capacity was 53.7cu in (880cc), although several development engines of varying capacity had been built and even raced during the previous two years.

Yet the Model D proved remarkably troublesome, with a mere 29 built in 1909 and just one in 1910. Harley-Davidson appears to have blamed its shortcomings on its automatic inlet valves, although other sources suggest slippage of the belt drive was at fault. Either way, when the re-engineered twin returned in 1911, it had both mechanical inlet valves and a simple but sturdy belt tensioning device which could be operated on the move by the rider's left hand.

Although still designated the Model D, other changes included a slightly reduced capacity of 49.5cu in (811cc), from a bore and stroke of 76.2 and 88.9mm respectively, the same as the 1904 single. Beehive finning had also given way to vertical cylinder-head finning. At $250, the asking price was the same as the twin of 1908.

SPECIFICATIONS: 1911 MODEL D

Engine	F-head V-twin
Capacity	49.48cu in (811cc)
Transmission	single speed, leather belt drive with freewheel "clutch"
Power	around 7bhp
Wheelbase	56½in (1,435mm)
Top speed	around 60mph (96kph)

■ ABOVE RIGHT AND BELOW *Two views of another 1913 twin. Note the long push-rods to the inlet valves, far more dependable than the earlier "automatic" mechanism. The colour is "Renault Gray".*

By all accounts, the revised twin proved far more dependable than its troublesome predecessor. Although little faster on the flat than the 30-inch single, it climbed hills far better – not least because the belt tensioner allowed the rider to maintain drive. Even so, a welter of improvements followed year on year. 1912 brought a new frame and a free-wheel clutch assembly in the rear wheel that freed the rider from the need to kill (and re-start) the engine if wishing to halt the machine. The same year saw the introduction of the first "one-litre" Harley, the 61-inch X8E, which also featured chain final drive. Although the two capacities were briefly produced in tandem, production of the smaller twin was dropped for 1913. The same year marked the debut of the

Model G "Forecar", a 61-inch twin with front-mounted luggage box – a sort of back-to-front precursor of the Servi-Car.

By this time, the engine was almost unrecognizable in its internal details from the original twin. Relatively exotic alloy steels were employed in high-stress areas of the engine, such as chrome vanadium steel for the "I" beam connecting rods, while roller and ball crankshaft bearings were widely used. A separate three-quart (2.8 litre) tank held oil for the total-loss lubrication system (used oil was either burnt by the engine or drained by hand from the crankcases). Like most contemporary engines, there was no oil pump: good old gravity and flailing engine parts moved the oil around the engine's internals and all the major bearings were of "self-lubricating" phosphor bronze. An auxiliary hand-operated oil pump had become standard in 1912, crudely metering about 25 "drops" of oil per minute.

Until this time, all Harleys had been single-speed, but in 1914 the Model 10F and Forecar debuted the two-speed rear hub. This astonishingly intricate device comprised no fewer than five bevel gears, yet was replaced by a true three-speed gearbox after only one year.

A measure of the twins' success is that, by 1915 the Harley-Davidson range comprised just two single-cylinder roadsters but six twins, including the three-speed Model K "Stripped Stock" – a race replica for its time. Among six "Speciality" twins were the even hotter "Fast Motor" K12 and out-and-out racers such as the KRH. This elaboration continued throughout the 61-inch F-head's astonishingly long career.

So comprehensive was its evolution that, by the time it was discontinued in 1929, almost no part from the original twin would fit.

■ ABOVE *By the time this twin was built in 1917, three-speed transmission was available for an extra $25.*

■ ABOVE RIGHT *The cam drive is clear in this sectioned F-head twin.*

■ LEFT *An exquisite 1916 board-racing twin. Note the Bosch magneto and single carburettor.*

■ BELOW *The timing side of a 1917 twin. Note valve-gear cutaways in tank.*

MODEL W SPORT TWIN, 1919–22

■ LEFT *The very Model W machine that set the Three Flag record, riding from Canada to Mexico in less than 75 hours.*

One of Harley-Davidson's most radical machines appeared as early as 1919. Developed during the war years and first shown to the public in 1918, the Model W "Sport Twin" was quite unlike the general expectation of what a Milwaukee twin should be. Its cylinders, rather than being tucked close together in a 45 degree V, were set 180 degrees apart. This was Harley's Boxer twin – but unlike BMW's more modern Boxers, this carried its cylinders fore-and-aft like contemporary British Douglas machines.

In theory, this somewhat unwieldy layout should have made the bike very long, but in practice the new model's wheelbase was actually three inches shorter than that of the existing V-twin – just 53½in (1,360mm). It was also low overall and carried its heaviest components in particular low to the ground – a considerable bonus on the rough roads of the time. It also weighed fully 100lbs (45kg) less than its sibling V-twins. Aesthetically, too, the "Brewster Green" Sport looked low and lean, with an elegance of line rarely achieved by previous V-twins. The engine's horizontally-opposed cylinders bestowed perfect primary balance, making it far smoother than the other big Vs in the Harley range. In fact, this was a most civilized mount all round.

As well as the standard equipment of magneto ignition and gas lights (fed by acetylene gas produced "on the move" by dissolving calcium carbide in water), optional equipment included coil ignition and true electric lighting. Engine lubrication was taken care of by an automatic pump, freeing the rider from the obligation of injecting just the right amount of oil at just the right time. The three-speed transmission was driven by a multi-plate clutch (albeit hand-operated) running in engine oil, just like a modern motorcycle.

The Sport's drive chain, enclosed in a steel case and lubricated by oil mist from the crankcase breather, was as close to zero-maintenance as chain transmission could get at the time. All in all, the Model W was a neat, light, economical and innovative piece of kit which Milwaukee clearly hoped would find a ready market, as riders were less disposed to the rougher pleasures of previous big twins.

SPECIFICATIONS

Engine	horizontally-opposed side-valve twin
Capacity	35.6 cu in (584cc)
Transmission	3-speed
Wheelbase	53½in (1,360mm)
Top speed	around 50mph (80kph)

■ LEFT AND ABOVE *It may look ratty, but it still works. The horizontal cylinders and low overall lines of this original Sport Twin are clear.*

Unfortunately the Sport had one major shortcoming – cubic inches, or the lack of them. It was way down on power compared to the existing 61-inch Harley V-twin and similar offerings from Indian. with a displacement of just 35.6cu in (584cc). To compensate, at least in part, it had to be revved hard – indeed it was reputed (very dubiously) to be the highest-revving internal combustion of its time. Yet even when thrashed, power was poor, with a top speed of little more than 50mph (80kph). Then, as now, America's motorcyclists demanded less revs and far more guts. Although its agility made it modestly popular for a while on Europe's more tortuous roads (almost one third of exports to Britain in 1919 were Sport Twins), the Model W was never a success at home. Production ceased in 1922, after just four years on the Milwaukee line.

■ ABOVE *Little can the builders of machines like the Sport Twin have realized the cultural tide they were unleashing.*

Model JD & FD Big Twins, 1921–9

Milwaukee's first 74-inch model, the so-called "Superpowered Twin" hit America's streets for the 1921 model year. Producing some 18 horsepower, the big engine was intended to compete with Indian's big twins and four cylinder models from Henderson and others. The "74" followed the practice of the "61" from which it evolved, employing inlet-over-exhaust valves (the F-head layout) driven by a single camshaft in a timing cover on the right side of the engine.

However, many major components – crankcases, cylinders and heads – were all new, and both bore and stroke were increased. The transmission was three-speed, the gears and shafts being located in a separate aluminium housing which was connected by enclosed chain to the left end of the crankshaft.

An "automatic" oil pump delivered lubrication for the engine's mixture of plain phosphor bronze, roller and ball bearings. As with almost every other motorcycle of the time, used oil was burned or dripped on to the ground. The multi-plate clutch, on the other hand, ran dry.

■ ABOVE *Sidecars, such as this mated to a Model J, were huge business.*

■ BELOW *An immaculately restored 1928 Model JD, one of the first to feature a front brake.*

Although often referred to generically as the JD, up to 1925 the 74-inch twin might more helpfully be called the Model D, with the addition of essentially the same prefixes as contemporary 61-inch twins. "JD" indicated a complete electrically equipped version, while the magneto model was designated "FD". Where fitted, electrical equipment comprised a six-volt generator, battery, contact breaker points and coil, headlight, tail light and oil

SPECIFICATIONS
74-INCH SUPERPOWERED TWIN

Engine	F-head V-twin
Capacity	74.2cu in (1,216cc)
Transmission	3-speed
Power	18bhp
Wheelbase	59½in (1,510mm)
Top speed	around 75mph (120kph)

■ RIGHT AND BELOW *This 1925 61-inch twin retains the original olive green colours with maroon and gold pin-striping, unlike the eye-catching example below.*

warning indicator light. An additional "S" in the model description indicated a sidecar model, with lower gearing and a 0.12in- (3mm-) thick steel spacer between cylinder and crankcase mouth to reduce the compression ratio. Other subsequent suffixes included such variables as piston material – A for aluminium, B for iron. The lighter weight and improved heat dissipation of the aluminium alloy pistons were particularly beneficial after their introduction in 1924.

A tubular steel, single-loop frame tied the whole thing together, the rider cushioned from the worst road shocks by a "Full-Floteing" Mesinger saddle. Front suspension comprised similar double-sprung girder forks to the smaller twin. Only a rear brake – a 7¼in (186mm) drum actuated by a long steel rod from a pedal on the right footboard – was fitted until 1928 when a front drum brake also became standard. For markets in which a second brake was mandated by law, an additional "stopper" – essentially a parking brake – could also be fitted. Other changes over the "74"'s life span included the use of "Alemite" surfaces for all chassis bearings in 1924. The rider would periodically inject these with grease from a purpose-made high-pressure grease gun, which did much to extend component life, especially in wet or dusty conditions. Less practical, but carrying echoes into the styling of Harleys today, 1926 found the big twin equipped with broad "balloon" tyres and a curvaceous "teardrop" fuel tank.

■ BELOW LEFT AND RIGHT *A lower frame carrying a teardrop-style tank first appeared in 1925, whilst front brakes finally arrived for the 1928 model year. The example below left clearly has neither.*

Over its eight-year career, the "74" proved itself a brisk performer which enhanced Milwaukee's reputation for building dependable motorcycles.

Some indication of its virtues – and not least of Harley's tradition of sticking with what worked – was that, at 87 x 101.6mm, the "74"'s cylinder dimensions remained almost unchanged up to the Shovelhead models of relatively recent times.

Clearly, the machine that would take its place in the future would have to be at least as special as the present one. Yet to begin with, at least, it would be anything but.

JH, JDH Two-Cam, 1928–9

■ BELOW *The difference between the Two Cam's timing cover and that of the standard twin is clear.*

■ BOTTOM *The 1928 JDH Two-Cam was only available for two years.*

Twin-cam and even eight-valve machines had formed the cutting edge of Harley-Davidson's official racing efforts since the First World War, yet the ordinary road-going motorcyclist could only dream of such performance. All that changed in 1928 when Harley offered a two-cam motorcycle to the general public at an affordable price. These special J-series machines were available for two years only, as the 61-inch JH and the awesome 74-inch JDH, which were priced at $360 and $370 respectively.

"The magic words 'two-cam' mean exceptional speed and power," extolled contemporary advertisements, with some justification. Not for the last time, Milwaukee was treading the fine line between effective salesmanship and encouraging public disquiet over bad boys on antisocial machines.

Both twin-cam engines featured inlet-over-exhaust valve operation driven by paired, gear-driven cams in a timing case on the right side of the engine. Instead of operating via Harley-Davidson's customary roller arms, the cam lobes acted directly on tappets, offering more accurate valve control, higher revs and improved combustion. The height of each cylinder's inlet valve necessitated flamboyant clearance cutaways in the narrow fuel tank, which gave the "JH" its characteristically racy appearance.

SPECIFICATIONS

Engine	2-cam, F-head V-twin
Capacity	60.33cu in (988cc) or 74.2 cu in (1,216cc)
Transmission	3-speed
Wheelbase	60in (1,525mm)
Top speed	around 85mph (137kph)

The two engines differed in both bore and stroke, as well as in the use of Dow metal pistons, but were built on essentially the same crankcases. These were connected by roller primary chain to a multi-plate dry clutch and three-speed gearbox, which in turn drove the rear wheel by chain.

As well as the choice of capacities, two specifications of the Two-Cam were offered, although numerous racing specials would be created in private hands. As well as the competitive potential of stripped-down Model Js, Juneau Avenue anticipated a demand for an exclusive road version – or "superbike" as it might be known today. Thus the Two-Cam was available with full electrical equipment, carburettor air cleaner, fully valanced mudguards and front and rear brakes.

Echoes of the machine's racing pedigree were retained, however, in the slimline "sport" chassis, single seat and racer-style two-gallon (7.5 litre) fuel tank.

Even as a roadster, the Two-Cam was billed as "the fastest model ever offered by Harley-Davidson" with the JDH specially recommended "for greatest speed and maximum performance."

With an 80-inch version available on special order in 1929, this olive green projectile was no less than the American equivalent of Brough Superior's sensational SS100 in Europe.

Yet even this degree of exclusivity was priced too high for an American market more interested in cars, and the Two-Cams passed into legend after spending a very short two years in the Harley-Davidson range.

■ BELOW *Reflected glory: an Evo-engined Low Rider basks in the setting sun.*

45-INCH TWIN, 1929–51

One of the most enduring motorcycles in Harley-Davidson's history was announced in October 1927, hitting the road just over 12 months later. The Model D, as it was first styled, was the first of a new generation of side-valve "flathead" V-twins – far cheaper to create than the relatively complex F-head engines. Not much more than a pair of 21-inch "Ricardo" singles on a common bottom-end, it featured three-speed transmission and a spindly frame almost identical to the little single's.

If the beginnings were lacklustre, improvements came fast. Within a year, the "45" benefited from a sturdy new frame with lower saddle but increased ground clearance. It was now available in four guises: D (low compression solo), DS (sidecar), DL (high compression Sport Solo) and DLD Special Sport Solo. Two years later, it emerged from a comprehensive redesign as the Model R. This included aluminium pistons in place of Dow metal (with magnesium offered as a special option from 1933), new crankcases with improved oiling and a sturdier frame.

■ LEFT *An early Model D "45". The unfinned timing cover is one obvious difference from the later Model W.*

SPECIFICATIONS: 1929 MODEL DL

Engine	side-valve V-twin
Capacity	45.3cu in (742cc)
Transmission	3-speed
Power	around 22bhp
Weight	395lbs (179kg)
Wheelbase	56½in (1,435mm)
Top speed	around 65mph (105kph)

In 1933, of course, the Depression was at its deepest. A sign of these cash-strapped times was that this much-improved machine now cost just $280 – $10 less than the Model D had at its introduction. After a further steady regime of continuous improvement, the "45" was transformed once again to become the Model W in 1937. Although the most obvious difference was the adoption of styling from the Knucklehead released the previous year, there were numerous engine

■ LEFT AND RIGHT *The inspiration for the "flathead" nickname is obvious (left). Note the streamlined instrument console, which remains a Milwaukee hallmark.*

improvements as well, with its troublesome crankcase oiling and breathing system getting the lion's share of attention.

The range now comprised not only standard (W), sidecar (WS), Sport (WL) and Special Sport (WLD) models, but also the WLDR Competition Sport Special, a mean-looking stripped-down racer – though by 1941, the WLDR machine was a "Special Sport" roadster, the racer being known by a simple "WR". Four-speed transmission, adopted from the bigger twins, appeared in 1938 and by 1940 the WLA Army version was on the books. By now, the WLD and WLDR versions carried light alloy cylinder heads with more fin area and a larger carburettor, improvements that would not reach the base models for another five years.

Indeed, the engine would receive almost no more significant changes during the WL's final decade – a far cry from the 1930s when anything from 15 to 30 modifications were made each year. Instead, Harley-Davidson directed its efforts into its overhead-valve models, confining the "45" mainly to cosmetic revisions, partly inspired by the Hydra-Glide. Civilian production of "45"s ceased after 1951, although some military versions were produced later, and the same side-valve engine would continue to power the Servi-Car into the 1970s. The WL is – and was for most of its life – a crude, heavy machine better suited to the American Prairies or war-torn battlefields than any road with bends. By the time it went out of production, it was a motorcycling dinosaur. Though it was slow, outdated and cumbersome, it was also strong as an ox and almost indestructible: this model had proved itself to be a tough old Hog that for more than two decades had dependably delivered the bacon for Harley-Davidson.

■ OPPOSITE BOTTOM LEFT AND RIGHT *Art-deco influences are clear in the styling of these two striking WL45s. The inspiration for modern Springers is clear in the girder forks, especially on the chrome-plated example on the right.*

■ LEFT *A 1942 WL45, one of the last pre-war civilian models. The "Boat-tail" rear fender appeared in 1939.*

74-INCH SIDE-VALVE TWIN, 1930–48
80-INCH SIDE-VALVE TWIN, 1935–41

Far from being the dependable machine the market required, the model which propelled Harley's big-inch fortunes into the troubled 1930s was even more bothersome than that very first V-twin of 20 years earlier. Launched just in time to see the New York stock exchange collapse in 1929, the Model V "Big Twin" began life as a fiasco.

With the original twin, valvegear was the problem. With this new 74-inch model it was almost the entire machine. As William H. Davidson recalled: "bad engine... bad clutch... flywheels too small... frames broke... mufflers became so clogged the engine lost power."

It's a mystery now – and probably was for Harley at the time – why the first of this line were so very poor. The cylinder heads, though now of side-valve layout, retained the proven "Ricardo" pattern of the earlier single.

At 87.3 x 101.6mm, the bore and stroke dimensions were unchanged from the Model D. As before, a single dependable Schebler carburettor metered fuel via a forked manifold. Testing showed that power was up 15 per cent on the old "74".

SPECIFICATIONS: 74-INCH (80-INCH) TWIN

Engine	side-valve V-twin
Capacity	74.2cu in/1,216cc (78.9cu in/1,293cc)
Transmission	3-speed (4-speed from 1937)
Wheelbase	60in (1,525mm)
Top speed	up to 90mph (145kph)

There were novelties, of course, but nothing suggesting the trouble to come. Primary drive was now based on duplex chain, far stronger than the single chain used previously. Revisions to the oil-circulation system promised the rider a less oil-soaked time, as did full enclosure of the valvegear, which was impracticable on the old ioe twin. Other improvements that ought to have been welcomed by serious users included interchangeable quick-release wheels (at a time when punctures were a

■ ABOVE *The mighty VL, the top of the Milwaukee range before the arrival of the Knucklehead.*

■ LEFT *A 1936 VLH 80-inch twin. The spring shield on the girder forks was new for that particular year.*

■ ABOVE LEFT ***Hand gear-change would remain a Milwaukee norm until the 1950s. The foot pedal operates this VL's "suicide" clutch.***

■ ABOVE RIGHT ***A drab army 74-inch twin. Note the metric engine capacity in the "1200" on the tank.***

daily hazard) and an improved electrical system with better weather protection. The frame, too, was new: lower, heavier and reputedly sturdier than before.

For a company trading on unsurpassable reliability, the "74"s problems were serious indeed. No matter how handsome the new machine was, dressed in olive green with red pin-striping, no-one would buy it if it didn't work. To its credit, Milwaukee dropped everything to fix all the faults and the Model V proved dependable for the rest of its days.

■ ABOVE AND BELOW ***With the change to four-speed transmissions in 1937, the Model V became the Model U, one year before this handsome 80-incher was built. Note the revised timing cover.***

Having benefited from the fixes applied to the 74-inch model, the 80-inch model released for 1935 proved almost completely problem-free. The bigger engine was substantially similar to the contemporary "74", the extra capacity resulting from an increase in stroke from 101.6 to 108mm.

For 1937, the V-series gave way to the U-series big twins, with four-speed transmission, improved engine oiling and both the running gear and styling from Knucklehead twins. Both were capable of up to 90mph (145kph), had vestigial brakes and no rear suspension. Production of the "80" effectively ceased after 1941.

NAME GAMES

Not for the first time, Harley-Davidson's model nomenclature looks confusing viewed from decades distant. Sometimes called the "VL", the 74-incher was available from the outset as a straight Model V, with "VL" representing the high compression version, "VS" the sidecar puller and "VC" signifying the use of nickel iron rather than light alloy pistons. This continued until 1934, when options included the VLD ("Special Sport solo" with TNT motor), VD (low compression, solo), VDS (low compression, sidecar gears) and VFDS (heavy duty commercial, TNT motor). In 1935, the 80-inch model appeared and was dubbed VLDD (Sport solo) or VDDS (sidecar), alongside existing 74-inch models. This all changed for the 1937 model year, with "U" replacing "V" (alphabetically backwards). From then on, all the big side-valve twins' model designations began "U-" (80-inch models were indicated by a subsequent "H"). Thus a simple "U" indicated the basic 74-inch model and the plain "UH" was the equivalent 80-inch model.

WLA & XA

■ LEFT *The redoubtable WLA. Note the large auxiliary air-cleaner to prevent the motor choking in dusty conditions.*

■ **WLA, 1940–5**

If the Willys Jeep was the archetypal American military four-wheeler during the Second World War then Harley-Davidson's rugged old 45-inch flathead twin was its two-wheeled equivalent. By the time the United States entered the war in December 1941, the "45" had proved itself during a dozen years of civilian development and was the obvious choice for an army workhorse. The first example, dubbed WLA (the A stood for "army") appeared in 1940 and was initially scarcely more than a drab green WL. By 1941, it had acquired blacked-out auxiliary lights, an oil-bath air-cleaner (intended for North African conditions) and a quieter fishtail exhaust. Depending on the precise military requirements, luggage racks were added, front and rear, plus a gun scabbard and under-sump bash plate.

That pivotal year also brought the first of around 18,000 WLC models built for the Canadian military, which differed principally in having a foot-operated gear change on the right, rather than hand-change on the left. Anti-hertz suppressors and more comprehensive blackout gear were added later, and by late 1943 – the year in which WLA/WLC production peaked, at over 27,000 – even the crankcases were painted olive drab. Each machine bore a plate warning the rider not to exceed 65mph (105kph), not that the WLA was capable of very much more. Of around

■ BELOW LEFT AND RIGHT *The key to the WLA's success was its low-tuned, dependable engine, which had already enjoyed over a dozen years of development since the original Model D of 1929. Later examples had slotted "black-out" lights.*

■ LEFT *Although American-liveried models are best known, over half of military WL production went to other countries' armies.*

SPECIFICATIONS: WLA

Engine	side-valve V-twin
Capacity	45.3cu in (742cc)
Transmission	4-speed
Power	around 22bhp
Weight	varied with specification
Wheelbase	59½in (1,510mm)
Top speed	limited to 65mph (105kph)

SPECIFICATIONS: XA

Engine	side-valve horizontally-opposed twin
Capacity	45.1cu in (739cc)
Transmission	4-speed
Power	around 25bhp
Wheelbase	59½in (1,510mm)
Top speed	around 65 mph (105kph)

88,000 WLs produced for war-time service, many went to Russia, of which later examples were specified WSR models. It is reputed that some 30,000 Red Army Harley-Davidsons entered Berlin as the war in Europe drew to a close. Milwaukee's contribution to the war effort was marked by no fewer than three Army/Navy "E" awards for excellence in military production – although this was to backfire commercially on the company when thousands of WLAs were sold as war surplus after 1945, damping-down the post-war recovery.

■ LEFT ***Most observers would fail to recognize this as Milwaukee iron: the horizontally-opposed XA twin.***

■ BELOW ***Note the shaft drive coupling and large air-cleaner on this flathead XA.***

■ BOTTOM LEFT ***Although most XAs were intended for North African use, this example is painted in non-desert livery.***

■ BOTTOM RIGHT ***Note the instruction plate: the military ensured that as little as possible was left to chance.***

■ XA, 1942–3

Although Milwaukee built some military versions of the 74-inch side-valve twin (UA) and even fewer ELC Knuckleheads for the Canadian forces, the factory's second-string army model was the curious XA. Powered by a horizontally-opposed 45.1cu in (739cc) twin with shaft final drive and plunger rear suspension, the XA was expressly designed for use in the North African desert. The transmission was four-speed, with foot change and twin carburettors feeding the two side-valve cylinder heads. This may seem reminiscent of contemporary BMWs: this was a direct copy of the German machine. Juneau Avenue did not copy the opposition's dependability, for it reputedly suffered serious bearing failures due to the Sahara's heat and sand. As a result, only around 1,000 XAs were built, all during the years 1942–3, though this may have been because the North African campaign was drawing to a close. There was also a rare XS variant with sidecar. A civilian prototype derivative of the XA was tested during 1946 but failed to reach production.

SERVI-CAR, 1932–74

Although we think of them now as kings of style even when carrying the Highway Patrol along California's freeways, in their earlier years Harley-Davidsons were no strangers to humble workaday vehicles. As early as 1913, the range included a "Forecar" delivery van, the Model 9-G, essentially a 61-inch F-head twin with front-mounted luggage box. Sidecars and sidecar accessories had been an integral part of the Milwaukee range since 1916, with a huge sidecar production facility in operation at Juneau Avenue since 1926.

With the Wall Street Crash and its aftermath placing a particular premium on cheap, dependable commercial transport, it was perhaps no surprise that 1932 marked the debut of one of the strangest – and most enduring – Harleys ever produced. The Model G Servi-Car was a more-or-less conventional V-twin from the saddle forward, but the rear looked for all the world like an ice-cream van. Although it resembled a car rear axle crudely grafted on to a conventional bike (and topped off with a metal and fibreglass boot (trunk)), the Servi-Car was a practical and cheap working vehicle which found a steady market in Depression-torn America.

Some suggested that it was inspired by Far East rickshaw-style machines; however, the Servi-Car was initially

■ LEFT *Servi-Cars proved adept at many tasks, although cooling ice cream in an inferno probably wasn't one.*

■ ABOVE LEFT AND LEFT *A Servi-Car kitted out for police duty, as so many examples were. Note the additional lights and large siren on the front mudguard.*

SPECIFICATIONS

Engine	side-valve V-twin
Capacity	45.3cu in (742cc)
Transmission	three forward speeds, one reverse
Power	around 22hp
Wheelbase	61in (1,550mm)
Width	48in (1,220mm)
Top speed	around 60mph (96kph)

■ RIGHT *Proving that any Harley can be customized, although tassels were never a Servi-Car factory option.*

intended for the recovery of broken-down cars – hence the tow-bar and huge 60 amp/hour battery fitted as standard. Perhaps surprisingly, given the fraught circumstances of the time, it combined both sound design and solid engineering – so tough and enduring in fact that it remained in production from 1932 until 1974. From the outset, it employed a purpose-built frame with chain drive from the gearbox turning a car-type rear axle complete with differential. It enjoyed conventional drum brakes in each wheel, plus a parking brake mounted inside the rear axle housing. Power came from the same 45.3cu in (742cc) flathead V-twin fitted to the Model R. It may have been sluggish but it was undeniably dependable.

The first examples had the same three-speed gearbox as the roadster solo but within two years a reverse gear (not to mention contemporary art-deco styling motifs) had been added. By this time, the three-wheeler range was popular with police, garages, motoring organizations and small businesses alike and comprised no fewer than five models. In fact it was almost everything such enterprises needed: practical, reliable and cheap.

Above all, it was easy to drive, so there was usually need for only a minimum of operator training. One clever and user-friendly touch was the adoption of the same 42in (1,067mm) wheel track as the typical car – inexperienced Servi-Car drivers would not need to forge their own ruts in mud and snow. At its introduction, it was priced at just $450; by 1969 this had risen to $2,065.

With such a lengthy life-span, inevitably there were other changes too numerous to list. A radical styling change was introduced in 1937, echoing the new 61-inch Knucklehead (indeed the factory briefly dabbled with a prototype shaft-driven Knucklehead Servi-Car). This included a white-faced speedometer calibrated to 100mph (161kph), which would have been terrifying were it not at least 35mph (56kph) over the machine's capabilities.

At the same time, the revised flathead twin from the Model W provided the power – and would continue to do so for the rest of the Servi-Car's days.

Electric start was finally added in 1964 and rear disc brakes toward the end of 1973, at which time annual sales still exceeded 400. Volume production of Servi-Cars ceased after 1973, although some were made to order the following year.

The Model G's most obvious drawback – the absence of heater and roof – had finally brought about its demise, although it could still be seen in service with United States' police forces well into the 1990s.

■ RIGHT *This is a more original example, and here it is painted in colours of the fire department.*

MODEL K, 1952–6

If a single model demonstrated Milwaukee's problems during the post-war years, it was surely the Model K, unveiled in November 1951. Virtually a technological throwback, the "K" was born into an age when competition from Europe was intensifying almost monthly. Opposition machines offered high-performance overhead-valve engines with 100mph- (161kph) plus performance and the finest chassis ever built. In response, Harley-Davidson offered as its premier model an antiquated, long-stroke, side-valve twin as its premier sports model, which struggled to reach 80mph (129kph).

Advertised as "America's Most Sensational Motorcycle", the "K" was "designed to outperform, outride, outlook, outvalue ... any motorcycle in its class." Of course, this was only true if a class existed for absurdly slow and out-dated machines – which it might if Milwaukee's plea for a 40 per cent tariff on imported motorcycles had succeeded in May 1951. Harley literature claimed 30 horsepower for the Model K, only a little less than the contemporary 650cc Triumph Thunderbird. Whether true or not, the V-twin was no match for the 103mph (166kph) Britisher. Yet remarkably, Joe Leonard became first American national champion in 1954, on a machine substantially derived from the K. Its other saving grace was that it was the only large-capacity motorcycle Hollywood stars could be insured to ride – in other words, the K was so slow, it was considered safe.

SPECIFICATIONS

Engine	side-valve V-twin
Capacity	45.3cu in (742cc)
Transmission	4-speed
Peak power	30bhp
Wheelbase	60in (1,525mm)
Top speed	around 80mph (130kph)

True, the K was the first Harley-Davidson twin to feature suspension at both ends: "easy riding" double-action telescopic forks up front with a swinging-fork rear end (oddly, a sprung seat was retained.) By the standards of Triumph, BSA and Norton in particular, the handling was ponderous and mushy, although the eight-inch (200mm) brakes weren't bad for the time. It offered a hand-operated clutch and in a demonstration of supreme optimism, its speedometer was graduated to 120mph (193kph).

Nor was the K dependable, at least initially, as it was beset by a variety of performance and reliability problems. Perhaps the worst was its habit of breaking its "large, rugged" transmission gears, until a switch to forged parts after 1954. In many other respects, the bike was sturdy and sensibly conceived, such as in the use of taper-roller bearings for the swing-arm pivots. Bore and stroke were identical to the WL's: 70 x 97mm. The four-cam, air-cooled engine enjoyed generous finning to its aluminium heads and iron

■ TOP ***Aided by a 30.5cu in (500cc) limit for ohv engines, the side-valve 45.3cu in (742cc) Model K fared better on the track than on the street.***

■ ABOVE AND LEFT ***The best of the breed: a KHK in strident yellow.***

barrels, and it featured in-unit construction of engine and gearbox, with triplex chain drive, long before this became widespread among competitors.

Some years after the age of the K, Harley revealed what many had suspected – that it was only a stop-gap model to see the company through until something better could be developed. Although history records that the Model K was superseded by the Sportster, something more radical was envisaged originally. The familiar 45-degree V layout was dropped in favour of a wider 60-degree engine to be known as the KL, with "high" cams, twin carburettors and side-by-side rather than forked connecting rods. This would have increased secondary vibration, although the wider V angle would have gone some way to reducing primary imbalance.

Evidently, the KL project ran into patent conflicts with Vincent and ran out of development time, although it is possible that the progress of European machines convinced Harley that something even more potent was required. By way of a stop-gap to the stop-gap, a drastic 19mm increase in stroke raised the Model K's capacity to 55cu in (883cc) for 1954, and power to a claimed 38bhp, in an attempt to stay at least within sight of the Brits. The cover of *The Enthusiast* showed one Elvis Aaron Presley on board just such a machine in 1956, by which time work on the model's successor was already well in hand. As well as the basic KH, a tuned Super Sport Solo KHK model with high-lift camshafts, polished ports, leaner styling and lower handlebars arrived in 1955. Though they were ostensibly intended for racing, most found their way on to America's streets where they proved far more acceptable to American sports riders – their top speed exceeded 90mph (145kph). After 1956, the old flathead expired and was replaced by the first of the overhead-valve Sportsters. As the KR and KRTT, it soldiered on for more than a decade as Milwaukee's principal racing iron.

■ TOP ***Pictured here is a handsome example of a 1956 Model K.***

■ LEFT ***The K probably looked cooler than it went, especially here at Daytona Beach, Florida.***

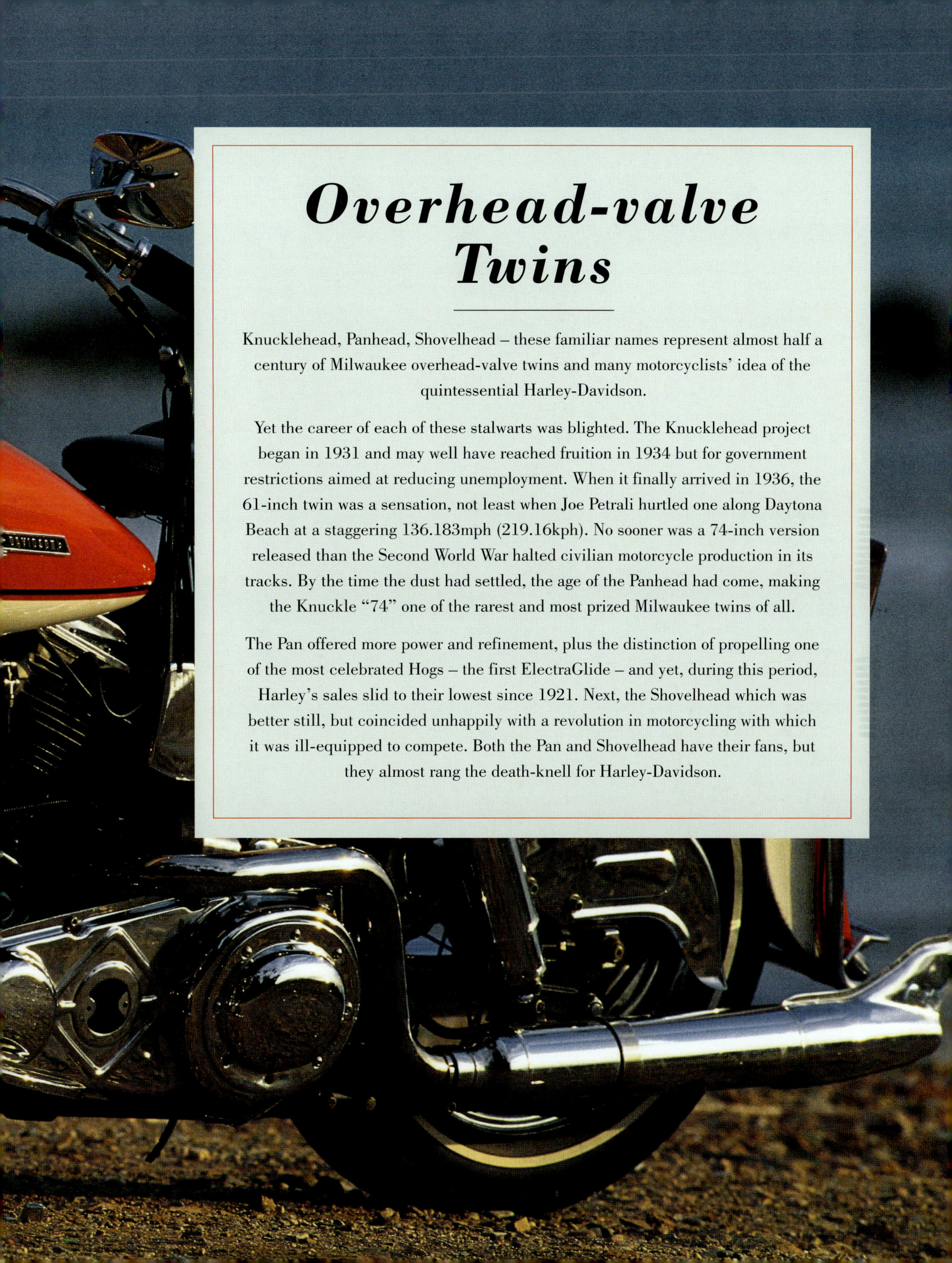

Overhead-valve Twins

Knucklehead, Panhead, Shovelhead – these familiar names represent almost half a century of Milwaukee overhead-valve twins and many motorcyclists' idea of the quintessential Harley-Davidson.

Yet the career of each of these stalwarts was blighted. The Knucklehead project began in 1931 and may well have reached fruition in 1934 but for government restrictions aimed at reducing unemployment. When it finally arrived in 1936, the 61-inch twin was a sensation, not least when Joe Petrali hurtled one along Daytona Beach at a staggering 136.183mph (219.16kph). No sooner was a 74-inch version released than the Second World War halted civilian motorcycle production in its tracks. By the time the dust had settled, the age of the Panhead had come, making the Knuckle "74" one of the rarest and most prized Milwaukee twins of all.

The Pan offered more power and refinement, plus the distinction of propelling one of the most celebrated Hogs – the first ElectraGlide – and yet, during this period, Harley's sales slid to their lowest since 1921. Next, the Shovelhead which was better still, but coincided unhappily with a revolution in motorcycling with which it was ill-equipped to compete. Both the Pan and Shovelhead have their fans, but they almost rang the death-knell for Harley-Davidson.

KNUCKLEHEAD, 1936–47

It's difficult to appreciate the impact Harley-Davidson's first overhead-valve roadster twin must have had on a motorcycling public that was emerging groggily from six long years of Depression. In fact, no Milwaukee model before or since was ever quite so comprehensively new. Even the latest Twin Cam, remember, is installed in largely familiar running gear.

Not so with the legendary Knuckle. Not only was the engine a major departure, but it sat in an equally new twin-cradle frame, with just the mudguards and generator remaining from the flathead VL. Its striking styling owed much to the art-deco innovations of the Depression years, capped by a teardrop-style tank, complete with an audacious white-faced Stewart-Warner speedometer calibrated to 120mph (193kph). Fanciful, perhaps, but factory

■ LEFT *The overhead-valve Knuckle was the biggest development in years.*

■ ABOVE *Milwaukee makes metal come alive.*

■ BELOW *This 1946 FL Knucklehead looks better now than it did when new.*

SPECIFICATIONS

Engine	ohv V-twin
Capacity	60.32 or 73.66cu in (989 or 1,207cc)
Transmission	4-speed, hand change
Power	40 or 45bhp
Weight	565lbs (256kg)
Wheelbase	59½in (1,510mm)
Top speed	up to 90mph (145kph)

■ LEFT AND BELOW ***A finned timing cover (left) identifies this as a post-1941 Knucklehead. Compare this with the "smooth case" example below. A host of other changes also came in for 1942.***

testers had reported 100mph (161kph) during development. Little wonder that would-be owners queued in droves when the first examples were shipped to dealers in January 1936, despite the $380 Knuckle costing $40 more than a contemporary 80-inch twin.

Designed by William S. Harley and Lothar A. Doerner (the latter tragically killed while testing a 1937 model), the 60.32cu in (989cc) twin underwent no fewer than 70,000 hours of testing, according to contemporary claims. As with previous mainstream models, the Knuckle was initially available in three guises: E (standard, discontinued after 1937 but restored during the Second World War), ES (sidecar) and EL (high-compression sport). All proved free-revving and eager, while the EL in particular – with 40 horsepower at 4,800rpm – offered a huge performance increase over the laggard side-valvers. Even the mighty 80-inch VL couldn't come close to an ohv twin.

Yet despite the time-consuming route to production – and not for the first time – there were initial problems.

Many changes were implemented during the first year of production, including frame reinforcing and revisions to the kick-start gears. The rocker assemblies became enclosed for 1938, by which time the patented tank-mounted instruments also included warning lights for low oil pressure and generator output.

But the 61's worst fault concerned its dry-sump lubrication. Some parts got too little oil while others – including the road underneath – got too much. A partial fix was introduced in 1937 but the glitch was not completely solved until the arrival of the centrifugally-controlled oil pump bypass of the 74-inch (Model F) Knuckle of 1941. The crankshaft main bearings had been up-rated in 1940, perhaps in anticipation of the extra loads on the bigger engine. The arrival of the more potent "74" also brought larger 8½in (216mm) diameter flywheels, revised crankcases, an up-rated seven-plate clutch and a carburettor choke increased to 1⅛in (28.6mm). By now, the two ohv models combined were comfortably out-selling Milwaukee's established range of side-valve twins. Given further development, the Knuckle could surely have become better still, but with the outbreak of war in December 1941, production concentrated almost exclusively on military side-valve twins and development of the ohv models all but ceased.

Milwaukee lore has it that the very best of the big Knuckles were those built in that final pre-war year, but hostilities meant that relatively few Model Fs reached the road until 1947, when the line's reign was almost over.

Not surprisingly, that first overhead-valve "74" remains one of the most prized Harley roadsters of all.

By 1948, however, a new pretender was on the scene: the age of the Panhead had arrived. At last it was goodbye, finally, to oil leaks from the rocker box, which was a problem that had never been completely solved on the Knucklehead.

HYDRAGLIDE, 1949–57

■ BELOW RIGHT *Although the Panhead shared its bottom-end with the Knuckle, the heads, valve-gear and oil feeds were new.*

■ BOTTOM *The HydraGlide name came from the bike's new telescopic front forks, then becoming widespread on motorcycles worldwide.*

For the 1948 model year, Harley-Davidson had unveiled its new Panhead engine, mating it to a revised "Wishbone" frame with characteristic "dog-leg" front downtubes. Within a year, it had been eclipsed by the first of Milwaukee's "Glide" models.

Although retaining a rigid rear end, the HydraGlide broke with the company's usual reliance on leading-link sprung forks. Instead, here was a Hog with a modern oil-damped telescopic front-end. As if to compensate for this fit of novelty, the Hydra persevered with a uniquely American hand-change gearbox until 1952 and even later as an option for true die-hards.

For the present, however, it was as close to modern as heavyweight Harleys would get. Billed with characteristic restraint as "the nearest thing to flying and as modern as a spaceship," the first HydraGlide was, in truth, only a relatively slight departure from the model that went before.

SPECIFICATIONS

Engine	ohv V-twin
Capacity	60.32 or 73.66cu in (989 or 1,207cc)
Transmission	4-speed, hand change
Power	around 50/55bhp
Weight	560lbs (254kg)
Wheelbase	59½in (1,510mm)
Top speed	around 95mph (152kph)

As was company tradition, a host of detail changes would follow year-on-year. Many of these would be cosmetic (the speedometer alone received an astonishing degree of attention), but most concerned the internal workings of the engine and chassis, making the final HydraGlide of 1957 very different from the first. It should be remembered, however, that in the American automotive industry in general, the 1950s and 1960s were characterized much more by developments in styling than in functional engineering.

In essence, the Panhead engine comprised new cylinders and heads grafted on to the Knucklehead bottom end. The heads were now aluminium with hydraulic valve lifters (tappets), and internal oilways had replaced the Knuckle's external lines.

Like the Knucklehead it replaced, this new Panhead was produced in both 61- and 74-inch (989 and 1,207cc) versions, designated models E and F respectively. Six versions comprised the initial range: Model F Sport Solo, FL Special Sport Solo and FS Sidecar twin, with the designations repeated for the 61-inch motor. All featured four-speed transmission, while sidecar models had lower gearing and reduced compression ratios. At their launch, all sprung-fork Model Es cost $635, with the larger engine adding a mere $15 to the price. Within a year, the introduction of the HydraGlide had upped those figures by precisely $100. Just to be on the safe side, sprung-fork models – designated ELP and FLP – remained in the range for one transitional year.

Of literally hundreds of detail changes, the first major improvement came in 1950 when revised cylinder

■ BELOW *Add electric start and rear shock absorbers and you'd have an ElectraGlide. The real thing was to take another 17 years.*

■ BELOW *White tassels probably weren't around when the HydraGlide was king of the road, but whitewall tyres certainly were.*

heads with larger ports added a claimed ten per cent more power. The 61-inch Model E was dropped for 1953, by which time annual sales of the smaller Panhead had slumped to below 1,000. The same year – the company's fiftieth anniversary – brought about Harley-Davidson's familiar "mid-series" bottom-end redesign. This included major changes to both crankcase halves as well as the relocation of the hydraulic lifters from top to bottom of the pushrods. A new "straight-leg" frame was brought in for 1954, followed by the FLH Super Sport model (the "H" stood for "hot") 12 months later, with gas-flowed heads and 8:1 compression ratios.

Even the FLH was no tyre-shredder, though, retaining the low-revving, high-torque virtues of every Milwaukee V-twin. These were very much machines in the American tradition, having ponderous steering, limited ground clearance, marginal brakes and hand gear change.

In terms of styling, the HydraGlide was pure 1950s – or perhaps pure 1990s, since so many modern Harley models echo its visual themes. Central to this was its low-slung profile with "Air-Flow" front and rear fenders (mudguards).

A chrome-plated tubular steel front "safety guard" was offered as an option from 1950, with "HydraGlide" emblems available one year later – both mimicking those gracing the very latest FLs.

It had some early "innovations" – like black silencers and fork sliders – that did not last, but overall the Hydra-Glide made an impact that is still very much with us today.

■ LEFT *Yes, this 1953 HydraGlide could almost be a year 2000 Softail, That's precisely the point of Retro-Tech.*

FL DuoGlide, 1958–64

■ BELOW *It was still a Panhead, but with the arrival of the DuoGlide the FL had springing at both ends.*

By 1958, Harley-Davidson was already in grave difficulties as annual sales hovered around a paltry 12,000 under intense competition from European machines. To make matters worse, the start of the Japanese invasion was just one year away – though no-one knew it at the time – with the arrival of Honda into the American market.

One way in which the company responded was through increased diversification of its range – first the Model K, and then the Sportsters took different directions from the heavyweight twins. But by the late 1950s, the latter – the FL models – were woefully outdated and badly in need of a major overhaul. Instead, they got little more than a facelift.

After the HydraGlide, the DuoGlide was the logical next step. As well as real, oil-damped telescopic front suspension, the Duo floated on a swinging-arm rear end, hence the name. This was a major improvement on the face of it, even though the Model K had beaten it comfortably for the distinction of being the first Harley-Davidson twin with rear suspension. By the time it appeared in 1958, however, pretty much everything it offered had already been done – and done better – by every other major motorcycle manufacturer, with the exception of the Duo's hydraulic rear brake. Unfortunately this was little more than a gimmicky novelty, since both hubs contain tiny, ineffective single-leading shoe drums.

With major engine revisions having been implemented in 1953 and in 1956, the DuoGlide's engine might as well have been called the "Panhead Mark II". It also benefited from more generous finning than previous Pans for 1958, as well as an up-rated generator. With the 61-inch Pan long departed, all DuoGlides enjoyed 74-inch (1,207cc) power. The range offered a choice of hand or foot gear-change and Sport or Super Sport ("H") tune, making four models in all. In 1958, the hotter specification added $65 to the standard $1,255 purchase price.

Central to the machine's layout was a new "Step-down" frame with larger diameter backbone and attachment

SPECIFICATIONS	
Engine	ohv V-twin
Capacity	74cu in (1,207cc)
Transmission	4-speed
Power	55bhp
Weight	575lb (261kg)
Wheelbase	60in (1,525mm)
Top speed	around 95mph (152kph)

■ ABOVE *The distinctive speedometer is original; the handbag is not.*

■ LEFT *The chrome crash bars, fender rails and panniers were available as part of 16 Harley-Davidson option groups.*

■ RIGHT *As soon as Milwaukee installed rear suspension, some riders wanted to take it off. This hardtailed 1958 DuoGlide is similar to Hopper's* Easy Rider *mount.*

■ BELOW *An original 1961 example shows how Harley intended it to look.*

points for the twin rear shock absorbers. These incorporated oil-damping (typical of the time, for rebound only) and their springs were enclosed in gleaming chrome-plated shrouds. The new frame necessitated many other modifications – to the oil tank, toolbox and fork yokes – although the first Duos looked rather like soft-tailed HydraGlides.

If the Duo's looks weren't enough for aspiring owners, 1958 also introduced a huge expansion in the number of factory "option packs" including no fewer than nine for the new DuoGlide. These comprised accessories groups for "Chrome Finish", "Road Cruiser" and "King of the Highway", with a bewildering array of lights, luggage items and other paraphernalia. The "King of the Highway" package included front and rear nudge bars, twin rear lights and a dual exhaust system.

Unfortunately it didn't sell very well, being particularly unsuited to most export markets, although it accounted for around 40 per cent of Milwaukee's sales at home. The Duo didn't much like corners, and was woefully under-braked. Even the "H"-designated Super Sports models, with optional high-lift camshaft and higher compression pistons, weren't rapid. Vibration was intense at high engine speeds, leaving much of their potential power unused most of the time, except by the most determined riders – who would probably seek the high-rev thrills of a Triumph Thunderbird anyway.

Then, as now, the DuoGlide was about a different sort of motorcycling, with its big, slow-revving engine and charismatic looks. It was indisputably a Harley, with all the attributes and vices of the breed. And it was also indisputably beautiful.

FL ELECTRA-GLIDE, 1965

■ ABOVE *The first of the breed, the 1965 ElectraGlide. The large battery box distinguishes it from earlier DuoGlide.*

Of all Harley-Davidson models, surely the enduring FL ElectraGlide is the one that best epitomizes the breed. The "FL" designation actually arrived with the first 74-inch Knucklehead of 1942 and has since been ever-present in the Milwaukee range. The model that has carried those laurels with the greatest distinction has been the thundering ElectraGlide – the quintessential model since its 1965 debut.

Yet for all its lusty pedigree, that first ElectraGlide was little more than a DuoGlide with the addition of 12-volt electrics and an electric starter which – initially, at least – did not prove altogether very dependable.

Just as there was a 12-month hiatus between the introduction of the Panhead and the HydraGlide, Harley-Davidson waited until 1966 before giving the Glide something new. From its second year of production, it was powered by the new Shovelhead mill with its (relatively) more efficient "Power-Pac" heads. Initial examples used the alloy-headed Panhead engine which had first appeared in 1948 and gone on to propel the first Glide (the HydraGlide of 1949) and the DuoGlide of a decade later. The Hydra- had been the first big twin with telescopic forks while the Duo- added swinging arm rear suspension.

The starter motor itself lived behind the rear cylinder and engaged on the rear of the primary drive. The DuoGlide frame had to be opened up slightly to accommodate it, yet still there was no room for the earlier model's tool kit. Surprisingly for a unit "borrowed" from an outboard motor, the first starters were

SPECIFICATIONS: 1965–1970	
Engine	ohv V-twin
Capacity	73.66cu in (1,207cc)
Transmission	4-speed
Power	around 55bhp
Weight	595lbs (270kg)
Wheelbase	60in (1,525mm)
Top speed	95mph (152kph)

■ ABOVE LEFT *It would do considerably more than 12mph (20kph), but in Harley-land style counted as much as numeracy.*

■ LEFT *For little more than $1,500, this Milwaukee dream could be yours – in 1965.*

■ RIGHT *As leaps forward go, the ElectraGlide was conservative: both hand-change and foot-change versions were available until 1972.*

■ BELOW *The last of the Panheads: in 1970 the Shovelhead took its place.*

troublesome when damp and the kick start was prudently retained. Harley later adopted Homelite starters, which proved much more reliable.

Like all Harley big twins, the ohv engine ran forked con-rods to eliminate rocking couple (so the rear cylinder was precisely, rather than roughly, masked by the front). Primary drive was by chain to a four-speed box (with a sidecar option, up to 1980, of three forward and one reverse). Capacity was 74cu in (1,207cc): the current 81.74cu in (1,340cc) dimensions didn't arrive until 1970 with the new generation of "alternator" Shovelheads. The rest was almost unchanged from the DuoGlide, complete with five-inch (127mm) whitewall tyres and running boards, although for the first time a five-gallon (19-litre) "Turnpike" tank was fitted. Of the four-model range, two versions retained hand gear change, which would remain an option until 1972.

In short, this was never a state-of-the-art machine. Indeed the "King of the Road" touring pack offered in 1966 required the rear shock absorbers to be relocated forwards, to the detriment of the Glide's handling, which had already proved to be rather pedestrian.

For all that, it's a strikingly handsome machine – one which looks far better than it performs. Like most Harleys, the rear brake is good but, prior to the arrival of a front disc in 1971, no prudent rider would choose to stop a Glide in a hurry.

This is a device for getting into top gear and staying there as you cruise serenely to the next horizon.

FX SuperGlide, 1971–84

In the late 1960s, customizing was king. In California in particular, Harley-Davidson owners were tearing their machines to pieces, discarding one piece and adding another to produce unique examples of what were to become known as "blend" bikes. Nowhere was this more publicly demonstrated than in the film *Easy Rider*, with Peter Fonda cruising to New Orleans on the outrageous "Captain America" alongside Dennis Hopper's hardtailed DuoGlide.

Milwaukee's response was as startling as it was controversial. When the SuperGlide was unveiled for the 1971 model year, it was the first example of a genre quickly dubbed "factory custom". The influential *Cycle* magazine's misgivings were typical.

"Is the American motorcyclist ready to ride around on someone else's expression of personal, radical tastes?" it asked, before testing the newcomer and answering its own question enthusiastically in the affirmative. Such was the SuperGlide's impact that almost every major motorcycle manufacturer has since produced its own interpretation of the "factory" custom – invariably to less effect than Harley's original. From a modern perspective, taking into account models such as the Springer Softail, the FX wasn't actually all that radical. Styled and conceived by Willie G. Davidson, it was essentially a combination of heavyweight FLH frame, 74-inch Shovelhead engine (which still carried "FLH" on the timing cover) and running gear, with the front end from the existing XLH Sportster. The rear end's styling was dominated by a fibreglass boat-tail stepped seat and integral rear mudguard which had debuted as an option on the Sportsters the previous year. Although widely viewed as a defining element of the model, this lasted for only one year and was quickly replaced by a more conventional rear mudguard.

■ LEFT *By the 1970s, customs were all the rage. Willie G.'s official version was less flamboyant than this "Captain America", but its impact was more enduring.*

■ BELOW LEFT *Part Sportster, part FL, the SuperGlide was an instant hit, with 4,700 built in the first year.*

Compared to the FLH, the SuperGlide also had pegs in place of footboards, with foot controls revised to suit. Both exhausts were low-level feeding paired silencers on the right hand side. Wheels were 19in (483mm) front, 16in (406mm) rear, both equipped with fairly feeble drum brakes. The 3½ gallon (13 litre) fuel tank included a built-in speedometer. Functionally, it was a far from perfect machine, although it went and handled far better than the FLH

■ BELOW *In 1974 the SuperGlide gave rise to the FXE. Twin discs first appeared for 1979.*

■ BOTTOM *Although the SuperGlide's most eye-catching feature, the "boat-tail" rear end was an option rather than standard equipment.*

■ BELOW *A later, disc-braked FX. Note the "AMF" logo on its tank.*

SPECIFICATIONS: 1971–80	
Engine	ohv V-twin
Capacity	73.66cu.in (1,207cc)
Transmission	4-speed
Power	around 60bhp @ 5400rpm
Weight	590lbs (267kg)
Wheelbase	61in (1,550mm)
Top speed	105mph (169kph)

from which it was derived, not least because it was more than 66lbs (30kg) lighter. The hybrid instantly struck a chord and sold well – 4,700 units in its first year, almost as many as the established FLH ElectraGlide. After two years, it acquired hydraulic disc brakes at both ends and improved suspension with stiffer springs. A year later, an electric start option, the FXE, was added. Japanese Showa forks were added in 1977, electronic ignition in 1978 and twin front discs in 1979, before it developed 80-inch Shovelhead power for 1981. For the final year of production in 1984, five-speed transmission was added; the FXR and FXRS Super Glide II models were also on the Milwaukee stocks, comfortably out-selling the old stager. Although almost two decades would pass from the SuperGlide's launch to the turnaround in the company's economic fortunes, it's impossible to overstate the effect the model has had on Harley-Davidson's affairs. The FX invented the concept of the factory custom and led to landmark models such as the FXEF Fat Bob in 1979 and Sturgis 12 months later.

Police Bikes

■ LEFT *"You mean they actually pay you to ride one of those?" A police hogger at Daytona.*

■ CENTRE AND BELOW LEFT *Police bikes may be utilitarian, but that's no reason why they shouldn't look good, too. Rarely has so much chrome plate been put to law enforcement use as on these Shovelheads.*

The first police Harley was bought by the city of Detroit in 1908. Specially equipped machines took a little longer, but by 1924 more than 1,400 police forces across America had at least one Harley-Davidson in their ranks. Two years later, an office was established at Juneau Avenue to handle fleet sales to police forces, and it was from this that the first factory police option packs began to emerge. Previously, most modifications had been undertaken by the customers themselves. Incidentally, the first order from CHiPs – the California Highway Patrol – was for the 74-inch Model JD in 1929. Twelve months later, bikes could be equipped with that most vital piece of law-enforcement equipment: the Police Special speedometer. By 1935, two police option packs were available for inclusion on any of the big-twin models.

During the 1950s, the HydraGlide and then the DuoGlide – fitted with one of three option groups – became the "standard" police two-wheeler (for a time the Servi-Car had up to four distinct option packs). The arrival of the Shovelhead in 1966 continued the theme, until the first specific Police model hit the stocks for 1974. The FL-Police was essentially a 74-inch ElectraGlide with basic police equipment included as standard. Almost 800 were sold that year.

From 1979, the 80-inch Shovelhead FLH-80 began to displace the old FLH-1200 as the standard police model and, by 1982, Harley's law-keeper was known simply as the FLHP, available variously with chain, enclosed chain or belt final drive.

Today's police range comprises the FXRP CHiP and FLHT-Police, which are based on the Evo-engined Low Rider and ElectraGlide respectively, and each has special equipment, including an up-rated electronics system, coloured pursuit lights, radio carrier and siren switches (the siren is optional, though).

An indication of the importance of the police market can be gleaned from the sales figures for 1991, when more than 1,500 police machines were sold.

■ BELOW *There are limits. Unless their riders are off-duty, these Harleys are definitely not police machines.*

FXS Low Rider, 1977–85

■ BELOW *The Low Rider was built by Milwaukee, but born in the biker heaven of the United States.*

These days, the Low Rider range is as essentially Harley-Davidson as the Sportsters and heavyweight Glides, yet it wasn't until 1977 that Willie G. brought us the first Low Rider model. The FXS Low Rider was, in essence, another reworking of the seminal Super Glide theme, which in turn was to spawn yet another dynasty of Milwaukee hardware.

Described as "one mean machine" in Harley-Davidson's own publicity, the FXS was a new type of custom cruising model, intended to be as content cruising wide-open prairies as downtown avenues. It was finished in menacing gunmetal grey with flat, drag-style handlebars on pulled-back risers, resonating echoes of the choppers that countless enthusiasts had created in the past. The laid-back name came from a seat height of just 27in (686mm), a characteristic which would appear again in the Huggers of the future.

Although the 80-inch Shovelhead first appeared on the FLH ElectraGlide in the Low Rider's debut year, the FXS was initially powered by the established 74-inch Shovel. The engine came finished in crinkle black paint with highly polished outer covers. Both exhaust pipes curved back along the right side below a new "1200" air-cleaner cover, before thumping the atmosphere through a single chromed muffler. The revised frame was heavily raked and fitted with highway pegs, allowing the rider to stretch out, like the latter-day *Easy Rider* the styling sought to emulate.

Chassis components included Japanese Showa telescopic forks, chromed twin rear shock absorbers and dual front disc brakes. Sadly, the stoppers were still disconcertingly feeble in their effect, although the rear was relatively fierce with massive leverage available at the pedal. The puny forks, too, were prone to flex while the short-travel rear suspension units were at the same time

SPECIFICATIONS

Engine	ohv V-twin
Capacity	73.7cu in (1,207cc)
Transmission	4-speed
Power	60bhp
Weight	550lb (249kg)
Wheelbase	63in (1,600mm)
Top speed	98mph (158kph)

■ LEFT *The FXS-1200 Low Rider was described as "one mean machine" when it first came on to the scene.*

■ BELOW *This 1985 FXRS Custom picks up the tradition of V-Twin power that was started by the Knucklehead, Panhead and Shovelhead.*

both harsh and under-damped. It would be a while before any heavyweight Harley aspired to even the sketchiest handling prowess.

Quicksilver handling, though, wasn't what the FXS was all about. The model was an instant success, hitting the public's wish-list almost as soon as it was unveiled. It was comfortably out-selling the SuperGlide by its second year, with almost 10,000 examples built. Clearly, the Low Rider concept was here to stay and the breed has benefited from a steady stream of improvements in every succeeding year. Along the way, they've spawned eye-catching sister models, such as the 80-inch FXB Sturgis of 1980 – the year after the FXS itself was first offered with the larger Shovelhead mill.

The biggest novelty came in 1983 with the much revised FXSB Low Rider. The "B" represented the adoption of the Aramid-fibre toothed belts first seen on the Sturgis for both primary and secondary drive.

A small number of late-1984 examples may have received the new 80-inch Evolution motor, but it wasn't until the FXRS "Custom Sport" Low Rider of 1985 that this much-improved engine became widespread. By the time five-speed transmission was grafted on to the same model 12 months later, the modern Low Rider series had arrived.

■ ABOVE AND LEFT *The FXS caught on almost instantly, becoming Milwaukee's best-selling model by 1978.*

■ BELOW *Although built in 1992, this Low Rider Sport displays features similar to the original FXS.*

FLT TourGlide, 1980

■ BELOW *Early TourGlides are easily distinguished by their huge twin headlamp fairing.*

Like most things Harley-Davidson, the TourGlide didn't suddenly appear out of the Milwaukee ether, it just sort of evolved. One fundamental element, the 80-inch Shovelhead engine – a long-stroke derivative of the old "74" – first appeared on the 1978 FLH Electra-Glide. Another arrived one year later with the FLH Classic, offered as standard with special paint and wheels as well as a complete set of "Tour Pak" touring extras. The Tour Pak was ultimately to become the heavyweight long-haul norm, comprising saddlebags, luggage rack, "batwing" fairing and chromed crash bars.

In 1980, Harley bundled the two together, adding a few other choice ingredients for good measure, and the FLT TourGlide was born. The most obvious change was the replacement of the ElectraGlide's handlebar-mounted fairing with a bigger, more protective frame-mounted fairing, now equipped with twin headlights. There was an improved new frame with "sport bike"

SPECIFICATIONS	
Engine	ohv V-twin
Capacity	81.6cu in (1,338cc)
Transmission	5-speed
Power	65bhp
Weight	765lb (347kg)
Wheelbase	62½in (1,590mm)
Top speed	100mph (161kph)

■ LEFT *Additional long-distance kit allowed heavyweights such as this late-1970s ElectraGlide to evolve into the TourGlide series.*

■ RIGHT *In 1981 the FLTC Classic arrived, to be followed by further Tour-Glide variations.*

geometry and a box-section backbone. Fabricated from both tubes and forgings, the frame was further modified at the rear to increase suspension travel. At the front, it now extended forward of the head-stock for more secure fairing mounting.

Less obvious – unless you were riding one – were a host of engine improvements also bestowed on the FLT. Rather than existing separately, the engine and transmission were now bolted rigidly together, gaining the benefits of unit construction without the drawbacks. The transmission itself was now five-speed for the first time on any big twin Harley-Davidson roadster, permitting even more long-legged gearing than before. A new Motorola electronic ignition virtually guaranteed dependable running at all engine speeds (or perhaps not: within a year it gave way to the superior V-Fire II system).

Final drive was still by roller chain but now fully-enclosed in its own oil-bath, a useful asset on any long-distance machines. Chain was superseded by a toothed belt drive on the FLTC Classic of 1984, which became standard across the FL range the following year.

Despite some initial scepticism, the Aramid fibre belts – made from a similar material to that used in bullet-proof vests – had worked well on the lighter V-twins, lasting four times as long as a chain, at similar cost but without the mess. By 1993, they would be a welcome feature on every Harley-Davidson model.

If that particular virtue was still in the future, an equally compelling one first appeared on the inaugural TourGlide. In contrast to previous rigidly-mounted engines, for the first time the FLT engine was installed using a clever three-point rubber-mounting system designed to isolate the rider from the worst of the big V-twin's vibration. In essence it couldn't be simpler, but the effect transformed the machine, making it smoother and more usable than any previous big twin.

Anyone with $6,013 to spare in 1980 could buy what was undoubtedly the smoothest, most comfortable and lavishly-equipped motorcycle Milwaukee had ever produced, a machine tailor-made for demolishing large distances.

The TourGlide might not be everyone's idea of motorcycling but it launched a generation of Milwaukee luxury tourers to which rival manufacturers have yet again paid the ultimate compliment: most of them have since tried to copy it.

■ LEFT *All Tour-Glides enjoyed five-speed transmission and rubber engine mounts. The Evo powerplant brought further refinement from 1984.*

Sportster
883

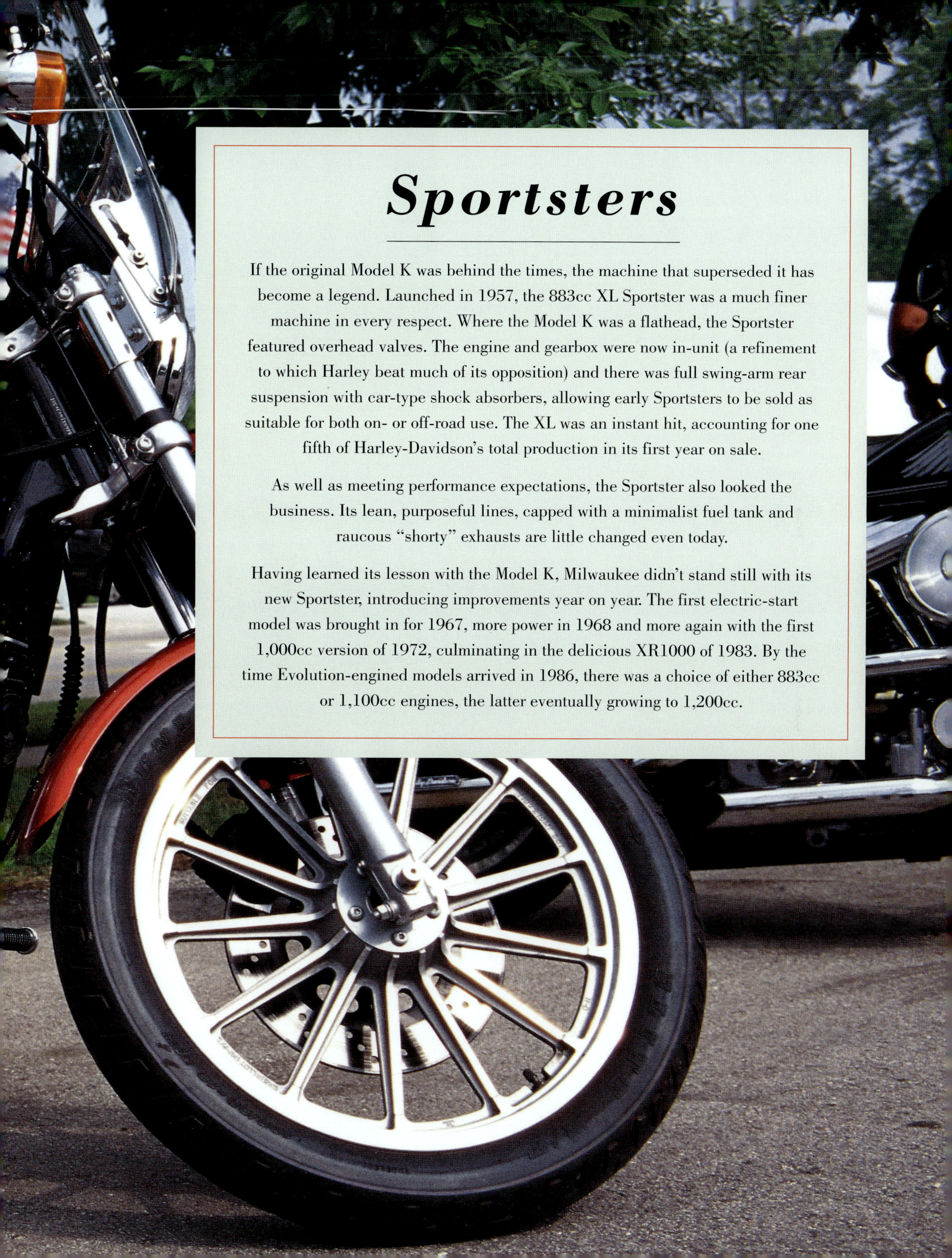

Sportsters

If the original Model K was behind the times, the machine that superseded it has become a legend. Launched in 1957, the 883cc XL Sportster was a much finer machine in every respect. Where the Model K was a flathead, the Sportster featured overhead valves. The engine and gearbox were now in-unit (a refinement to which Harley beat much of its opposition) and there was full swing-arm rear suspension with car-type shock absorbers, allowing early Sportsters to be sold as suitable for both on- or off-road use. The XL was an instant hit, accounting for one fifth of Harley-Davidson's total production in its first year on sale.

As well as meeting performance expectations, the Sportster also looked the business. Its lean, purposeful lines, capped with a minimalist fuel tank and raucous "shorty" exhausts are little changed even today.

Having learned its lesson with the Model K, Milwaukee didn't stand still with its new Sportster, introducing improvements year on year. The first electric-start model was brought in for 1967, more power in 1968 and more again with the first 1,000cc version of 1972, culminating in the delicious XR1000 of 1983. By the time Evolution-engined models arrived in 1986, there was a choice of either 883cc or 1,100cc engines, the latter eventually growing to 1,200cc.

THE FIRST OF THE BREED

■ RIGHT *In 1957 the first of the Sportsters proved to be a giant leap forward from the primitive side-valve Model K.*

After the debacle of the side-valve Model K, the Sportster series roared across America like a refreshing gale. At its heart was an overhead-valve engine displacing the same 883cc as the XLs of today. In those days, however, both the cylinder barrels and heads were of heavy cast iron, the latter with a hemispherical combustion chamber.

Each valve had its own gear-driven camshaft, operating the valve via "High Speed Racing" roller tappets and solid push-rods. A single Linkert carburettor fed mixture into the cylinder, where shallow domed pistons offered a compression ratio of 7.5:1. In 1957, peak power was around 40bhp but this rose considerably with the ported, high-compression "H" and "CH" versions, reputedly reaching 58bhp at 6,800rpm by the mid-1960s. By then, a good one could exceed 110mph (177kph).

Cosmetically, even fully-equipped versions of the XL were as lean as motorcycles can be – an attribute most retain to this day. Not so much as a pillion seat was permitted to mar their purposeful lines. The chassis was adequate if altogether less persuasive. A combination tubular steel and cast iron frame married "easy riding" telescopic forks and twin rear shock absorbers, with the swing arm pivoting on taper roller bearings. Each 18in (457mm) wheel held an underwhelming eight-inch (200mm) drum with shoes one inch (25mm) wide.

In truth, the handling wasn't great, although (for a Harley) the Sportster was light and low enough for a good rider to manhandle it into shape. An improved front fork helped matters from 1968 but the XL only really began to behave with the appearance of a lighter and stiffer frame, universally praised in press road tests, in 1982. By this time, the old one was very much feeling its age. Those first Sportsters were comparable with almost anything on the road and, at $1,103 apiece, sold like "Competition Hot-cakes". By the late 1960s, this was comfortably Harley's best-selling range.

SPECIFICATIONS: XL SPORTSTER 1957

Engine	ohv V-twin
Capacity	883cc
Transmission	4-speed
Power	40bhp
Weight	438lbs (199kg)
Wheelbase	58.5in (1,485mm)
Top speed	95mph (152kph)

■ ABOVE RIGHT *The mercurial "H" stood for high-compression and was intended to signify that this machine was hot.*

■ BELOW *By 1970, the Honda CB750 had arrived, yet the XL had feeble brakes and relatively lacklustre performance.*

■ BELOW *Fiddly detailing is rare on the XL range, which favours fuss-free lines.*

■ LEFT *The XLCH, which is commonly dubbed "Competition Hot". Sportsters remain the only Harleys to use unit construction engines.*

■ **SPORTSTER EVOLUTION**

Since its introduction in 1957, the XL Sportster has been the bread and butter of the Harley-Davidson range. Within a year, the stock Sporty had been joined by the high-compression XLH Sportster Sport, the legendary XLCH "Competition Hot" (as it is commonly called, although it actually meant "Competition High-compression") and the stripped-down XLC Sportster Racing. Perhaps surprisingly, the latter, intended for off-road use, lasted for only one year.

Originally marked for a life on dirt, the XLCH featured the 1.8 gallon (8.2 litre) "peanut" tank (standard was 3.5 gallon /16 litres), big valves, magneto ignition – and neither lights, speedometer nor battery. It was superseded by a fully road-equipped XLCH one year later. Detail changes included a switch to 12-volt electronics in 1965, two years before the first Sportster electric start – or "Push the button... ZAP... and away you go" as Milwaukee promoted it.

For 1971, the previous dry clutch gave way to a wet one. The first 1,000cc examples were the XLH/XLCH Super H and Super CH of 1972, the extra displacement coming from a 4.5mm increase in bore size to offer around 60bhp. (The captivating XLCR and XR1000 are dealt with in detail later.) Another spin-off from the Sportster line was a series of hybrid models, hoping to hit any untapped market niche. The XLT Touring came out in 1977, equipped with saddlebags, high bars and a thicker seat. More than 1,000 were built in the first year, a mere six in the second, giving way two years later to the XLS Roadster, with extended forks, highway pegs and a 16in (406mm) rear wheel. That year might be remembered as the last year of the legendary XLCH. A lasting hybrid was the optional Hugger package of 1980, offering shorter shocks and a thinner seat – this was a precursor of the true Hugger models of today. The equally far-reaching XLX61 came out in 1983, a stripped-down, budget-priced version of the XLH1000 aimed at cash-strapped riders. It has been Milwaukee policy ever since to produce a cut-price "entry-level" model. When the 883 and 1,100cc Evolution models arrived for 1986, it was to be the beginning of a new chapter in the Sportster story.

■ LEFT *The very first of the Sportsters, from 1957. The Model S-inspired fuel tank came later.*

XLCR Cafe Racer, 1977–8

If black truly is beautiful, then the XLCR was sublime. So dark, it practically drank in the light, the Café Racer was another of Willie G. Davidson's variations on an old theme, in this case re-working the basic 1,000cc Sportster which had first appeared in 1972. When it arrived for the 1977 model year, the XLCR looked revolutionary – the most unashamedly different Harley-Davidson yet.

At its heart was the then biggest XL engine grafted into a redesigned frame, with extended rear frame rails allowing more vertical shock absorbers than before. Most striking of all was the "Black-on-Black" paint job. This included gloss black bodywork, crinkle-black engine finish and a black Siamesed exhaust which snaked together below the air-filter housing – which, naturally, was black.

The 3.8 gallon (14.5 litre) fuel tank – black, of course – was unique to the XLCR, as were a fibreglass "bikini" fairing and single seat. The latter ended with a racing-style "bum stop" – although a dual seat option was available for 1978, the model's second and final year of manufacture. Cast aluminium Morris wheels, as well as rear-set "race replica" footrests and controls, were also provided as standard.

The move to more vertical shock absorbers was a not particularly successful attempt to improve the Sportster's habitually sloppy handling.

At the same time, twin hydraulic front discs were fitted in much-needed pursuit of improved braking. They proved moderately powerful, if rather lacking in feel.

■ ABOVE *The stylish XLCR, with its "race replica" footrests, did not produce the kind of sales that Harley had hoped for.*

SPECIFICATIONS

Engine	ohv V-twin
Capacity	992cc
Transmission	4-speed
Power	around 60bhp
Weight	540lbs (245kg)
Wheelbase	58.5in (1,485mm)
Top speed	110mph (177kph)

■ BELOW *In truth the XLCR looked better than it went.*

■ BELOW *In 1977, riders were required to enjoy the machine alone. A dual seat became an optional extra for 1978.*

■ BELOW *The problem wasn't so much the name on the tank as the AMF logo on the side panel. Just nine were made for the 1978–9 model year.*

25mph (40kph) slower than rival sports machines, with equally inferior handling and braking. Worse still, the XLCR bore all the worst hallmarks of the AMF years. Contemporary road tests might praise the marque's "indefinable magic" but they would equally slate the Café Racer (and its siblings) for being "appallingly built and hideously unreliable," to which was usually added "prohibitively expensive".

By the end of the model's brief reign, Harley-Davidson's share of the American motorcycle market had slumped to a paltry four per cent, yet it would be several years before the reborn company would seriously set about tackling its manufacturing shortcomings. This wasn't specifically the fault of the XLCR, of which just 3,124 examples were built, but this model did illustrate Harley-Davidson's problem – that beauty had to be much more than skin-deep.

Visually, this "top Sportster" was superb. True, it wasn't to everyone's taste, but most bikers would cast admiring glances at this stylish symphony in black. For all its eye-grabbing credentials, however, the XLCR was far from a runaway success.

On the one hand, most Harley die-hards found it visually too radical. On the other hand, more neutral buyers found sport-bike image and performance far more effectively packaged in Japanese and Italian machines. For all that, the XLCR is a desirable classic now, though at the time it was neither a vintage Harley-Davidson model nor a competent sports machine.

With around 60bhp and a top speed close to around 110mph (177kph), the XLCR was certainly no slug, but the bald truth was that it went at least

XR1000 Sportster, 1983–4

Unveiled at Daytona in March 1983, the XR1000 was the closest Harley-Davidson fans would ever get to a road-going XR racer. Even this far on, it's still many people's idea of the ultimate Harley Sportster. This should have come as no surprise because the big XR roadster was designed (and the prototype built) in the official factory race shop under the direction of Dick O'Brien. The 1000 could scarcely have enjoyed a better pedigree – O'Brien had managed Harley-Davidson's racing efforts since 1957 and overseen every moment of the XR750's career. Fittingly, O'Brien retired in the same year as the XR1000 roadster was released, making it an appropriately snarling swansong.

The $6,995 1000 wasn't quite a big-bore factory racer with lights but it was pretty special all the same. The engine employed a normal Sportster bottom end capped by special cylinder barrels, heads, fuel and exhaust systems. The aluminium heads were based on those of the racing XR, each reputedly shipped to Los Angeles to be ported and polished by legendary tuner, Jerry Branch (although it's likely that Branch simply oversaw the work, since a total of 1,777 XR1000s were built).

Induction was in the capable hands of twin 1½in (36mm) Dell'Orto carburettors with accelerator pumps, each breathing through huge, free-flowing K&N air filters stacked, flat-track style, on the engine's right side. Although stock Sportster camshafts were employed, valve-lash was adjusted by

■ ABOVE *Not quite a racing XR750 for the road, but visually the XR1000 came pretty close.*

SPECIFICATIONS:	
Engine	ohv V-twin
Capacity	998cc
Transmission	4-speed
Power	70bhp
Weight	487lbs (221kg)
Wheelbase	59.3in (1,505mm)
Top speed	115mph (185kph)

■ RIGHT *Possibly the most prized of all AMF-era models, the XR1000 was race boss Dick O'Brien's major contribution to Harley roadsters.*

■ RIGHT *This example has been customized to superb effect with a flat-track style rear mudguard and seat.*

■ BELOW *Strangely, Milwaukee didn't offer the XR in their classic orange and black racing livery until 1984. In comparison this relatively standard machine looks mundane.*

racer-style eccentric rocker shafts. The push-rods, too, were special lightweight alloy components. Lumpy pistons gave a 9:1 compression ratio. Paired high-level black megaphone exhausts growled back along the machine's left side.

This bespoke engine was red-lined at 6,200rpm but there was no earthly need to spin it that high, since the spread of power was immense.

Peak power – a claimed 70bhp – arrived at 5,600rpm but the engine pulled strongly from as few as 2,000rpm. Maximum torque was 48lb/ft (65Nm) at just 4,400rpm. The speedometer was calibrated only to 110mph (177kph), a figure a good XR could reach comfortably.

With optional performance kits offering more than 90bhp, the sky was almost the limit.

In truth, the XR's chassis was far less impressive than its engine. The frame and running gear were based on the XLX61, which was also new for 1983, with a nine-spoke, cast 19in (483mm) front wheel and 16in (406mm) rear. Rear suspension was in the hands of twin shock absorbers of no great quality, adjustable only for spring pre-load. Travel was quite short and the action harsh, making the XR nervous when ridden hard on bumpy surfaces. The brakes, however – twin 11½in (292mm) front discs – were surely the best Harley-Davidson had put on any roadster model up to that time and improved even further for 1984.

During the model's second year, it was offered with optional black and orange "factory" racing paintwork as well as the original steel grey. This seemed to be a suitably fitting livery for such a great machine.

The XR1000's reign as the ultimate sporting Harley-Davidson ever to have been produced by Milwaukee came to an end when production of this model ceased in 1984.

■ BELOW RIGHT *That's better: the same colours flown by Jay Springsteen, Scott Parker and the rest of the champion racers.*

XLH883, 1986–PRESENT

■ LEFT *The 883 is just the coolest thing on the road.*

With a price tag of just under $4,000 when introduced as the XLX61 in 1983, the basic Sportster was precisely the type of entry-level machine so conspicuously absent from the Harley-Davidson stables in the past. This was a piece of genuine Milwaukee hardware at a price almost anyone could afford. In 1986, the deal was made even better with the appearance of Evolution engines across the Sportster range and the arrival of the XLH883. Then, just 12 months after that, would-be 883 owners got an even more irresistible package with the announcement of Harley's innovative buy-back scheme: "Trade in your XLH against an FX or FL within two years and we'll guarantee $3,995 on your old machine." How could anyone lose?

The smallest Sportster was the last model to benefit from the wave of refinements sweeping through the Milwaukee range. But in two short years from 1992, Harley-Davidson's bargain-basement superbike progressed from being the runt of the Harley-Davidson litter to become a thoroughly competent machine. There were dozens of detail changes over those two seasons, but two stand out. First came five-speed transmission for 1992, followed 12 months later by belt final drive.

SPECIFICATIONS	
Engine	ohv V-twin
Capacity	883cc
Transmission	5-speed
Power	52bhp
Weight	489lb (222kg)
Wheelbase	60.2in (1,530mm)
Top Speed	103mph (166kph)

The extra gear transformed the smallest Harley from a relatively buzzy, busy machine into a far more laid-back device, with the bonus of a better gear-shift. The tooth-belt drive made it smoother still, with the added benefits of low maintenance and cleanliness.

The first belts – pioneered by Harley-Davidson and the Gates company that manufactures them – aroused a degree of suspicion. However, thanks to space-age Aramid fibre reinforcement (similar to Kevlar – they last at least four times as long as a chain, cost about the same

■ BELOW LEFT *No frills, no tassels and bereft of baubles, the 883 is the most honest-to-goodness model in the Milwaukee range.*

■ BELOW RIGHT *The least expensive, lightest and easiest Harley to handle is popular with male and female riders alike.*

and are practically unknown to fail. This was to make the XLH slightly more of what it was always good at – being a lean, spare and handsome means of filling practically all the space between headstock and rear spindle. There are no tassels, no gratuitously shiny but ultimately useless bits – just plain, single-seated function.

Of course, like all Harleys, the function in question has relatively little to do with sheer speed, handling or stopping. The 883 is essentially a cut-down cruiser, its low-profile Hugger stablemates all the more so. It looks cool while allowing its rider to appreciate, with as little intervening sanitation as possible, the most intimate doings of the internal-combustion engine.

Peak power from the 883cc engine is around 52bhp at a distinctly unruffled 5,500rpm – 1,000rpm after the arrival of maximum torque of 52lb/ft (70.5Nm). Acceleration is brisk rather than vivid, although the ample torque means there's always power on hand.

This motorcycle might be smaller than any other that Harley has produced, but crank open the throttle at almost any revs and the Sportster lunges forward on the same irrepressible wave of power. Without the rubber-mounting available on some larger models, engine vibration can be intense at high revs. There is no question that the 883 series represents good quality and value.

As well as the basic 883, there's also the Hugger – a variant dating back to 1979 and so called because it squats even lower to the ground.

They hardly depreciate and, with a bit of care, they can all last practically forever. Best of all, however, more than 40 years after the introduction of the original XL, the 883s continue to embody the same frill-free virtues.

For a chunk of a legend, the 883 really is a steal.

■ ABOVE LEFT AND ABOVE ***Although this was the last model in the range to benefit from five-speed transmission and belt final drive, the Evolution-engined 883 has sold consistently well.***

■ LEFT ***A 1996 Hugger 883, even lower to the ground than the stock Sportster.***

XL1200S Sportster Sport, 1996–present

By the mid-1990s, the redoubtable Sportster family was approaching its fortieth birthday – and beginning to show it. True, Evolution V2 engine technology had reached the old XL steeds on the 883 and 1100 Sportsters for the 1987 model year. Twelve months later, Milwaukee unleashed the first of the family's 1,200cc models, the XLH. Essentially this was the old 1,100 engine with the bore increased from 85.1 to 88.8mm. The stroke remained unchanged at 96.8mm, the same as the 883. Other than a change to five-speed transmissions and belt drive across most of the Sportster family in 1991, the range remained largely unchanged until the appearance of the 1200S in 1996. Along the way, it had definitely lost some of the fire that had burned in the first of the breed all those years before.

Those first Sportster Sports were perhaps a case of "close, but no cigar." Initially, their chief distinction was the adoption of improved, fully-adjustable suspension components at both ends, mated to softer, grippier tyres – but the engine remained stubbornly unmoved.

■ LEFT *Once sorted, the Sportster Sport represented a quantum leap in Harley-Davidson engine power, handling and stopping prowess.*

■ BELOW LEFT *The Sportster Sport was extremely popular, and the 1998 model pictured was long-awaited by its devotees.*

SPECIFICATIONS

Engine	ohv V-twin
Capacity	1,203cc
Transmission	5-speed
Power	75bhp
Weight	518lbs (235kg)
Wheelbase	60.2in (1,530mm)
Top speed	110mph (177kph)

Sportster fans had to wait another two years before the model truly reached its peak, but the 1998 Sportster Sport was surely worth the delay. In broad terms, the engine was little changed from previous Sportsters, with its hydraulic tappets, dry sump and triple-row primary chain driving a wet multi-plate clutch and toothed-belt final drive. Naturally, the 1200S carries higher overall gearing: 2.103:1 compared to 2.259:1 on the 883.

However, a comprehensive engine revamp had raised torque figures by an average of 15 per cent throughout the twin's 2,000–5,500rpm operating range. The model now had both the chassis and the engine to justify its "Sport" aspirations at last.

Essential to these improvements was an all-new ignition pack igniting not one, but two spark plugs in each cylinder, promoting quicker, more efficient burning of the incoming fuel/air charge. Although a conventional carburettor was retained – a 1½in (40mm) constant velocity Keihin instrument equipped with an "accelerator" pump – combustion control was further improved by an

■ RIGHT *Clean lines are common, but note improved calipers between this early example and the 2000 Sportster that is pictured below.*

electronic management system even more sophisticated than the V Fire III set-up fitted to its sister models. The system, incidentally, also affords high-tech electronic diagnostic capabilities. These measures allowed Harley-Davidson's engineers to bump up compression from 9:1 to 10:1, offering a substantial increase in mid-range power.

As well as lumpier pistons, the revised powerplant benefited from a larger, less restrictive exhaust system and new camshaft design. The camshafts offer both higher lift and longer duration, again with the emphasis on enhancing mid-range torque. Harley can claim a peak torque figure of 78lb/ft (106Nm) at 4,000rpm, over 50 per cent higher than the 883. With not only much improved power characteristics but better throttle response as well, the Sport feels even stronger than the figures might show. The 1200S looks every inch as mean and muscular as a Sportster should, with its clean lines and understated black engine highlights. Nor is this a deception, for the twin-plug Sport package delivers genuine punch. Better still, it stops and handles in a most un-Milwaukee-like manner – a mantle several more recent models have since adopted, to welcome effect.

In short, this not only proved to be the best XL for years, but perhaps was also the model with which Harley rediscovered the Sportster's roots, and made a great addition to the range.

■ ABOVE LEFT *One of the first examples of the 1200S. Later versions were better.*

■ ABOVE RIGHT *The Sportster is really a joy to ride.*

■ LEFT *Getting back to its roots: the XL1200S.*

Softails

It is a typical Harley irony that the Evolution V2 engine, unveiled in 1984, brought about a revolution in the company's fortunes, whereas the Twin Cam engine launched in 1998 was truly revolutionary in engineering terms. Then came the Twin Cam 88 and its balance-shafted brother, the 88B – so revolutionary that it might aptly be dubbed the Revo V2. It took four years and 2.5 million test miles (4 million km) to bring the project to fruition, resulting in an engine with 18 of 450 components in common with the 80-inch Evo motor. The result has as many benefits over its predecessor as the Evo had over the Shovel. If it does half as well Harley-Davidson can look forward with confidence.

If the Evolution V2 engine was a success, then so was the model in which it first appeared. Softails are the glittering style kings of the Harley range, and the first of these was the seminal FXST Softail of 1984. "Retro-Tech" is something modern in concept but executed and styled in a recognisably "classic" way. To achieve the hardtail illusion, Harley-Davidson engineers designed a massive triangulated rear swinging fork, with twin shock absorbers hidden from normal view beneath the engine. The clean overall lines of the machine emphasized the elegant sweep from head stock to rear wheel spindle, heightening the hardtail effect. Visually, however, the origins were the 1949 HydraGlide, the first Harley model with telescopic front forks. If any modern motorcycle belonged outside a 1950s American diner, the Softail was surely it, until the even more eye-grabbing 1988 Springer Softail brought the same throwback concept to the front end as well. Retro-Tech has since established itself as the fourth major theme in the Milwaukee menagerie, alongside the Sportsters, Dynas and Glides. Indeed, of all Harley models, Softails are invariably in the shortest supply.

FXST Softail, 1984

Certain motorcycles have stood out as memorably special over the years, mobbed for days on end at motorcycle shows. Honda's original CB750F was one, as was Ducati's sensuous 916. In recent years, the Milwaukee equivalent has surely been the first Softail, from 1984. True, all Harley-Davidsons are someone's idea of beauty but the FXST had a quality all its own.

Based on the existing FXWG Wide-Glide – somewhat loosely, to judge by appearances – the Softail had bikers not knowing quite where to look. Did they focus on the all-new Evolution V2 engine or eyeball that strangely elegant rear end? Most probably they did both and Softails are still being eyed covetously to this day.

The Softail's rear suspension was a clever piece of lateral thinking based on an old theme, created for Harley by consulting engineer Bill Davis. The inspiration almost certainly came from custom craftsmen such as Arlen Ness – and even carries a distant echo of the Goudier-Genoud endurance racing Kawasakis. Essentially, it's an inverted cantilever rear end (as per Vincent and Yamaha) in which a triangulated assembly pivots at the top, near the seat, rather than at the usual place. Paired, gas-charged Showa shock absorbers lie unobtrusively under the engine. The layout has little to do with function but a lot to do with style, something it

SPECIFICATIONS

Engine	air-cooled ohv V-twin
Capacity	81.6cu in (1,338cc)
Transmission	4- (later 5-) speed
Power	69bhp
Weight	604lbs (274kg)
Wheelbase	66.3in (1,685mm)
Top speed	106mph (170kph)

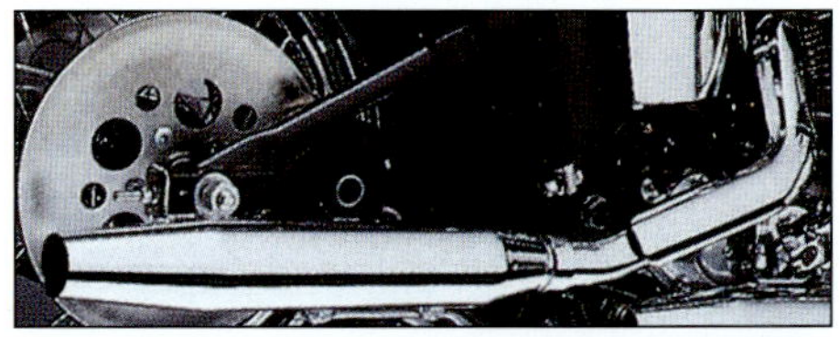

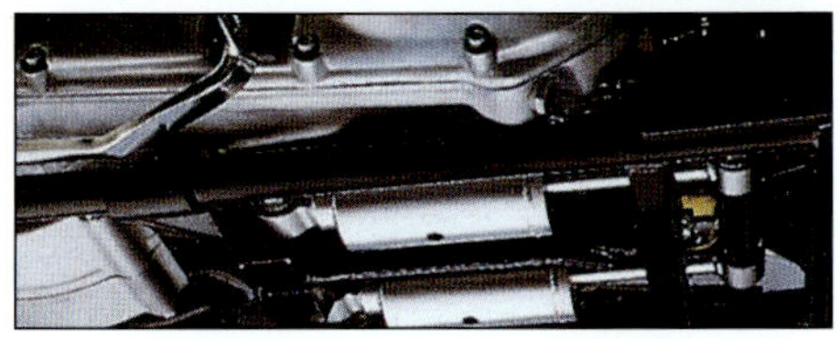

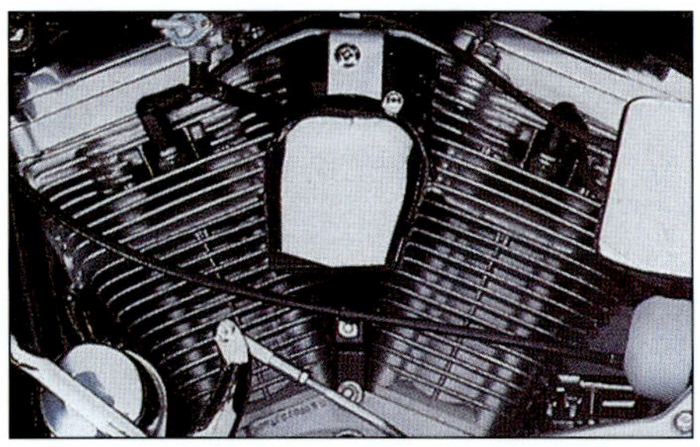

■ TOP RIGHT, CENTRE RIGHT, RIGHT AND ABOVE ***The earliest versions of the Softail featured Evo engines with four-speed transmissions, although contemporary FLs enjoyed five speeds. Even a kick start was originally retained.***

■ LEFT ***With its fake hardtail rear end, the 1984 FXST was the first true "Retro-Tech" model. The series has since become the most stylish and desirable in the range.***

■ BELOW *Based on the existing Wide-Glide model, the Softail was as visually startling as any Japanese "crotch rocket".*

demonstrated superbly. Despite the space constraints inherent in the twin-damper system, Softails in fact boasted more rear suspension travel – 4in (103mm) – than any other models in the Harley range.

Maybe the Softail look wasn't keenly anticipated, since most people didn't know it was coming, but the engine certainly was. Although a few very early 1984 Softails may have been built with Shovelhead engines, every one since has had belt-driven Evo power. With its all-new light alloy top end, the new big twin produced around 70bhp at 5,000rpm and a withering 84lb/ft (114Nm) of torque at just 3,600rpm. Indeed, the spread of power was so immense that almost no-one complained that 1984 examples had to make do with four-speed gearboxes. A five-speed cluster was installed for 1985, by which time a lighter diaphragm spring clutch had also appeared.

The chassis is characterized by an immense 66.3in (1,685mm) wheelbase and a seat height of 1in (25mm) lower than even a Low Rider's seat. Fuel is carried in the familiar, bulbous, two-piece Fat Bob tank, split across the mid-line, with a speedometer set in the centre. Wheels are wire-spoked, 21in (533mm) front and 16in (406mm) rear, carrying a single hydraulic disc apiece. Unlike contemporary Glides, the 80-inch engine is solidly mounted, although rubber-insulated handlebars and footrests compensate to some extent. Softails may be stylish, but smooth they are not.

The low saddle and forward-mounted "highway" pegs impose an appropriately laid-back riding position. As for handling: well, the Softail doesn't – it just sort of rumbles from A to B and all the better if that doesn't include too many fast corners. The suspension at both ends is woefully under-damped, the front forks are characteristically soft and woolly, and the rear is, frankly, harsh. Nonetheless, the expansive wheelbase and conservative steering geometry keep things more or less in line. Besides, this is a bike for cruising.

It's a measure of the overall rightness of the concept that, superficially at least, Softails appear little changed to this day. This disguises the vast improvements Harley-Davidson has made in build quality and detailing since the time of the FXST's launch.

Above all, there's the inescapable fact that this inspired piece of post-modern design was a huge and instant success.

Although not the most practical model that Harley-Davidson has ever built, it certainly can be said that Softails are the most eye-catching and, above all, the most prized.

■ LEFT *The Softail Custom introduced in 1987 was the first of many models inspired by the original FXST.*

FXSTS Springer Softail, 1988-present

■ BELOW *Any Springer simply refuses to be ignored, especially one dripping with tassels and chrome plate as much as with this example.*

In late 1987, the motorcycle world took one look and pinched itself – twice. The Springer Softail unveiled for the 1988 model year looked like no new motorcycle of the previous 40 years. Gone were the telescopic front forks to which we had become accustomed. In their place was a trellis-work of bright-chromed steel members, linkages and springs. It was called "Springer", and was as audacious as it was surreal.

As Harley said at the time, the new front-end wasn't just reborn, it was re-invented. The Springer front end was styled along the lines of the girder forks seen on almost every make of motorcycle from before the 1920s until the late 1940s, but the technology and the detail were all-new. Using computer-aided design (CAD) and the latest materials, Milwaukee had created a system which not only afforded an acceptable level of wheel travel (around 4in/100mm) and suspension control, but which freed its designers to make the styling statement of the year.

We now had Retro-Tech at both ends: Springer at the front to accompany Softail lines at the rear. The engine, naturally, was the doughty 80-inch Evo, styled for its new role and fitted with staggered shorty dual exhausts.

Like all "conventional" Softail models, the new Springer offered defiantly lazy steering geometry. In this case, a shallow 32-degree steering head gave a generous 5¼in (133mm) of trail. The wheelbase was a lanky 64.6in (1,640mm). Unlike standard Softails, Springers roll on slow-steering 21in (533mm) front wheels, with a 16in (406mm) hoop at the rear. Inevitably, the result isn't quite at the cutting edge of modern suspension performance. Any Softail rear end can be harsh, especially

■ ABOVE *A modern damper unit (with Harley sticker) controls the movement of the Springer forks.*

■ LEFT *No-one pretends Springers give state-of-the-art handling, but who needs it on a cruise in the sun?*

SPECIFICATIONS

Engine	air-cooled ohv V-twin
Capacity	81.6cu in (1,340cc)
Transmission	5-speed
Power	69bhp
Weight	625lbs (284kg)
Wheelbase	64.6in (1,640mm)
Top speed	100mph (161kph)

■ RIGHT *The Springer has always been exclusive. Around 1,350 were produced in its first year, compared to more than 14,000 other Softail models.*

■ BELOW RIGHT *Optional screen, trim and running lights give the owner of this Springer even more to polish.*

■ BOTTOM *Aftermarket fishtail silencers and two-tone paint contrive to make this Springer look for all the world like a 1946 FL.*

over freeway seams, and the latter-day girders lack the control of even Fat Boy's massive telescopic forks. Such judgements miss the point, however. Of all the Milwaukee models, Springers are unashamedly machines for stately cruising – and are as far removed from a Japanese "crotch rocket" as a 1959 Cadillac.

If 1987 marked the Springer's debut, then 1997 marked what many regard as its finest hour. As well as offering practical accessories such as leather saddlebags as standard, the 1997 FLSTS Heritage Springer Softail went further down the classic road, combining even more vintage styling with today's retro-technology. "Loaded with chrome and leather," publicity material hailed at the time, "the Heritage Springer Softail screams nostalgia." And so it did, from its bright-chromed fishtail mufflers to its deeply-valanced mudguards and whitewall tyres. Even at first glance, the result is sublime, the level of detail extraordinary. Note the nostalgic front fender-tip light and the "retro-1940s tombstone tail-light once commonplace on Harley-Davidsons decades ago." Admire a seat with a leather fringed valance "embossed with a basket-weave pattern and accented with conchos".

The ultimate factory custom had come a long way from the original SuperGlide. As the man said: "Is it a motorcycle or is it art?"

FLSTN Heritage Softail Nostalgia, 1993

Dubbed the "CowGlide" on its release for the 1993 model year, the limited-edition Heritage Nostalgia was the fanciest incarnation of Milwaukee's fanciest line. The nickname came from its hairy, black-and-white natural cowhide seat and saddlebag inserts, but there were plenty more cosmetic tricks where they came from. Little wonder its creators described it as: "Without doubt, the most distinctive-looking motorcycle in Harley's 1993 line ... nostalgic-looking ... but thoroughly modern." It had already proved a winning formula.

Modern, of course, means something else in Harley-Davidson's wondrous time-warp world – like whitewall tyres and forks straight out of the 1940s. Ever since beginning life in 1986, the Heritage Softail package attempted to re-enact the look of the 1949 HydraGlide, with its "hardtail" rear and gleaming metal fork shrouds.

Fine detail isn't something you'd normally expect from a device scaling almost one third of a ton, but this is a Harley, so the tank badge is a specially fired enamel named "jewelled cloisonné." Yet at heart, it's essentially an even more customized variant on the Heritage Softail Classic, available only in Birch White and Black two-tone, with black and chrome engine trim. Power comes from an identical 80-inch Evo engine booming out the same 69bhp at a mere 5,000rpm and a mammoth 70-or-so pound-feet (95Nm) of torque at an even lowlier 3,500rpm. Like the rest of the 1993 range, the Nostalgia benefited from a taller final drive (61-tooth rear pulley) for lower revs at cruising speeds. Improved brake and clutch levers, master cylinder sight glasses and a new, neater engine-breather system also arrived for the same model year.

■ ABOVE *The engine was an 80-inch Evo like any other, but the Nostalgia package set it apart.*

■ BELOW *The "CowGlide" was derived from the stock Heritage Softail, here seen cruising in company with a LowRider.*

SPECIFICATIONS	
Engine	air-cooled ohv V-twin
Capacity	81.6cu in (1,340cc)
Transmission	5-speed
Power	69bhp
Weight	710lbs (322kg)
Wheelbase	64.2in (1,630mm)
Top speed	100mph (161kph)

To ride, it's inevitably much like any other Softail, particularly the Classic or Fat Boy (with which it shares wheel sizes), steering geometry (32-degrees rake, 5.8in/147mm trail), forks, footboards, handlebars and almost every other relevant dimension. The only significant differences are a fuel tank almost ¼ gallon (1 litre) larger and the addition of a hefty 93lbs (42kg) of mass compared to the basic Softail model.

With suspension springing as soft as the CowGlide's considerable weight will allow, handling falls somewhere between sedate and ponderous. Over bumps, the steering is vague and

■ LEFT *No jewelled cloisonné, but plenty of leather and studs: a standard Heritage Softail.*

■ BELOW LEFT *"CowGlide" nickname comes from the Nostalgia's black and white hide details.*

accompanied by a slow weave whenever the road turns lumpy. As with the brakes, it's adequate if it is ridden with prudence.

Since Softail engines are not rubber-mounted, the vibrations intrude towards the top of the rev range even with its higher overall gearing – or as its makers prefer, the bike "rumbles with the echoes of Harleys past."

At a first glance, most onlookers took the Nostalgia – which was fresh from the factory floor – to be either the real 1949 McCoy or a bespoke special that had been put together at huge expense by one of Hollywood's celebrity custom farms. Harley-Davidson's retro illusion was that good, yet only 2,700 examples of the limited-edition Nostalgia were ever built.

Even at $13,000 – just $3,100 less than the most lavish Glide – demand for these highly-desirable models far exceeded supply.

Second-hand "CowGlide" Nostalgias were soon changing hands at far more than list price. Mark up another masterpiece for Willie G. Davidson and his men.

■ BELOW *They say that nostalgia isn't what it used to be. No, in this case it's much better.*

FLSTF Fat Boy, 2000

■ LEFT *Solid disc 16in wheels have distinguished the Fat Boy since its launch for 1990.*

■ BELOW LEFT *Only Harley could get away with such a derogatory title – and make it sell.*

The irreverently-named Fat Boy has held pride of place in Milwaukee's custom line-up since its debut in 1990. The FLSTF could claim to be the coolest of all the Retro-Techs, with its 16in (406mm) solid-disc wheels, elegant lines and bold but understated paint. For the year 2000, Fatso and its fellow Softails got the biggest shake-up since the line began back in 1984, with only a handful of parts retained from the old model. The new millennium marks the end of the noble 80-inch Evo engine and the adoption of the Twin Cam 88 across the entire heavyweight range.

This is no ordinary Twin Cam, though. Designated the 88B, the engine was developed in parallel with the "stock" 88 and uses essentially the same top ends, including the same 88.42cu in (1,449cc) displacement from identical bore and stroke dimensions. The bottom-end, however, features hardware never seen on any previous Harley: twin counter-rotating balance shafts. The eccentrically weighted shafts, tightly-packed inside the crankcases, rotate in the opposite direction to the crankshaft to eliminate primary engine vibration.

This is necessary because the Softail rear suspension pretty much demands that the engine be mounted rigidly in the frame. As a consequence, the rubber mounting used to such good effect on other heavyweight models is not a practical option.

Since their inception, Softails have been marred by punishing vibration, especially at high revs, reducing their long-haul capability. Rideability has been dramatically improved with the 88B, offering true long-distance comfort. In keeping with this, fuel capacity was increased to 5 gallons (19 litres) and the tank is now one-piece, obviating the irritation of earlier twin fillers.

Although somewhat less powerful than Twin Cam Dynas and Glides, the 88B also offers more power and torque

SPECIFICATIONS

Engine	air-cooled ohv V-twin
Capacity	88.42cu in (1,449cc)
Transmission	5-speed
Power	63bhp
Weight	666lbs (302kg)
Wheelbase	64.5in (1,637mm)
Top speed	106mph (170kph)

■ LEFT *The first of the breed. Fender trim, backrest and saddlebags are non-standard.*

■ RIGHT *The Fat Boy is actually no more of a fatso than other Softails, and its lines are cleaner, as these late-Evo versions clearly show.*

with substantially improved tractability. Maximum power is some 63bhp at 5,300rpm, with torque peaking at 78lb/ft (106Nm) at 3,500rpm. Uprated gearbox internals offer slicker, lighter gearshifts, easier neutral-finding and less transmission noise.

At the rear, a new drive belt is stronger and longer-lasting than before yet, at 1⅛in (28mm), almost ¼in (6mm) narrower in section. This permits a wider rear tyre, although – with less than 30 degrees of lean angle on offer – this is scarcely likely to promote scratching.

In addition, year 2000 Softails ride on an all-new frame, stiffer than before but fabricated from half as many parts – just 17 – as previous models. This is complemented by a redesigned swing arm which also contributes to a more stable ride. When it comes to hauling this 666lb (300kg) brute down from speed, even the brakes – long a Milwaukee blind-spot – have been substantially improved. Four piston callipers now grace both ends of the Fat Boy, and the disc rotors are more resistant to heat distortion. The effect is improving braking power and a 20 per cent reduction in brake-lever effort.

This is a considerable catalogue of real improvements on any model, let alone one cherished more for its looks and style than its functional elan. The 2000 Fat Boy has received a few cosmetic touches – notably, restyled exhausts and rear mudguard – without losing any of its essential character, but Milwaukee has surely got it right by making it work far better, too.

■ LEFT *The very first FLSTF in metallic grey was widely considered the most handsome.*

■ BELOW *For year 2000 the Fat Boy benefited from the new 88B balance-shafted Twin Cam engine.*

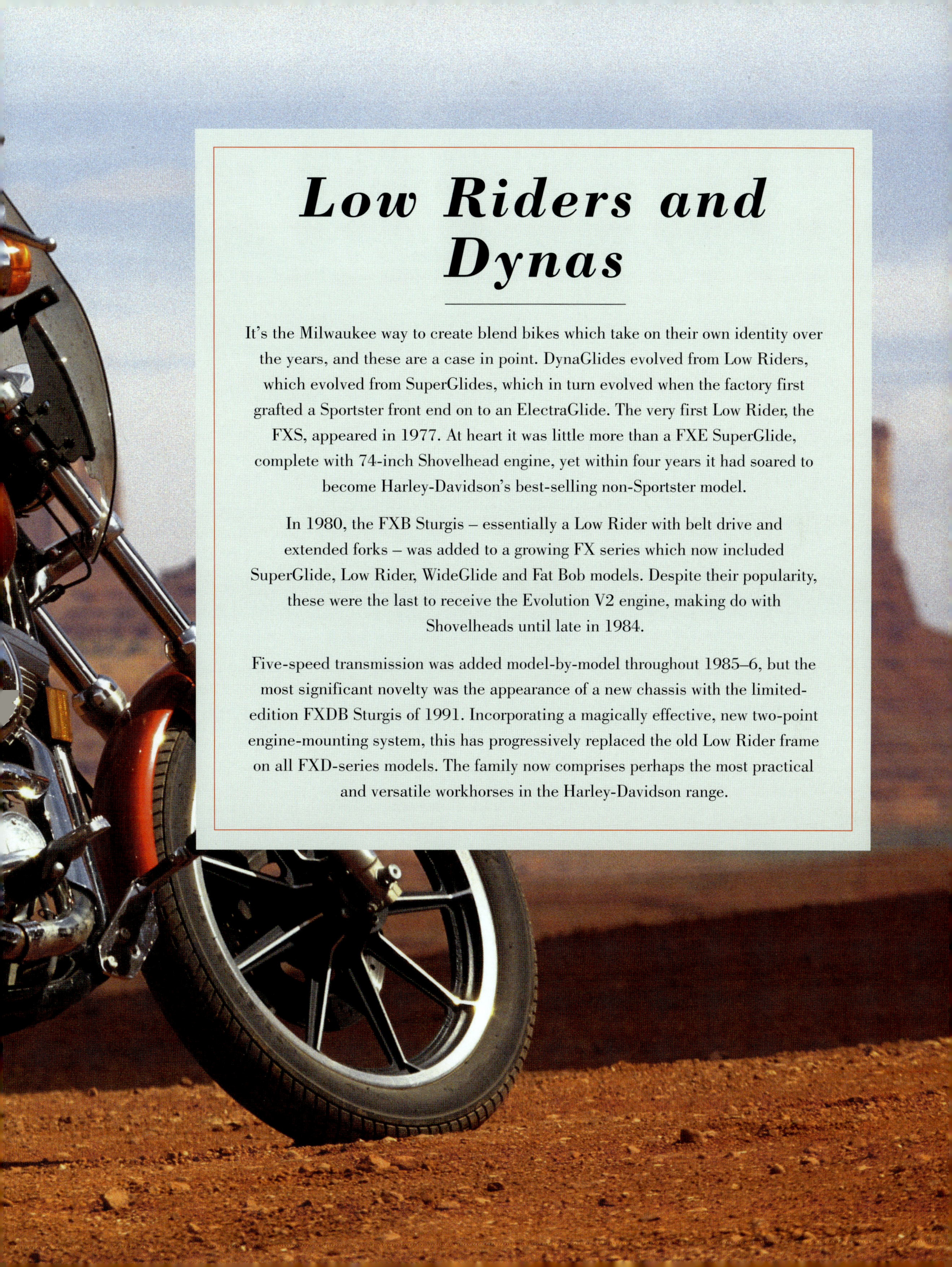

Low Riders and Dynas

It's the Milwaukee way to create blend bikes which take on their own identity over the years, and these are a case in point. DynaGlides evolved from Low Riders, which evolved from SuperGlides, which in turn evolved when the factory first grafted a Sportster front end on to an ElectraGlide. The very first Low Rider, the FXS, appeared in 1977. At heart it was little more than a FXE SuperGlide, complete with 74-inch Shovelhead engine, yet within four years it had soared to become Harley-Davidson's best-selling non-Sportster model.

In 1980, the FXB Sturgis – essentially a Low Rider with belt drive and extended forks – was added to a growing FX series which now included SuperGlide, Low Rider, WideGlide and Fat Bob models. Despite their popularity, these were the last to receive the Evolution V2 engine, making do with Shovelheads until late in 1984.

Five-speed transmission was added model-by-model throughout 1985–6, but the most significant novelty was the appearance of a new chassis with the limited-edition FXDB Sturgis of 1991. Incorporating a magically effective, new two-point engine-mounting system, this has progressively replaced the old Low Rider frame on all FXD-series models. The family now comprises perhaps the most practical and versatile workhorses in the Harley-Davidson range.

FXRS-CONV LOW RIDER CONVERTIBLE, 1989–93

■ BELOW *The Convertible became the ultimate Harley all-rounder upon its launch for 1989.*

Characterized by their brutal, low lines, fat rear wheels and skinny front ends, Low Riders represented one of the core "families" of Milwaukee models from 1977 until the mid-1990s. Beginning with the 74-inch Shovelhead FXS in 1977, the range grew to include seminal spin-offs such as the FXEF Fat Bob and FXB Sturgis. Along the way, Low Rider capacity grew to 80cu in (1,338cc) for 1980 and adopted toothed-belt final drive for the FXSB of 1983. The first Evolution-engine Low Rider, the FXRS Custom Sport, appeared for the 1985 model year, gaining five-speed transmission one year later. By 1987, Harley's "broadest and most versatile range" included Standard, Custom and Sport Edition models, as well as sister models such as the quintessential Super-Glide and SportGlide.

Harley-Davidson literature was always keen to stress Low Riders' unrivalled "combination of style and comfort", and it was certainly true that the range always veered towards the practical end of the style scale: cruisers that are as adept on the open road as on the city streets.

"They're in their element anywhere there's pavement" was how the brochures put it. It was no idle boast.

This was never more apparent than with the Low Rider Convertible released for the 1989 season.

Although not exactly a convertible in the Cadillac sense, this model was as close as any two-wheeler needed to be. No longer did owners need to lash luggage wherever they could – this Convertible came complete with leather saddlebags. There was a large, wind-cheating Lexan screen, too. The real beauty of both was that they were detachable, and quickly. Riders setting out for the long haul could leave them on – or, in just a few moments, whip them off for a cruise downtown.

■ LEFT AND ABOVE LEFT *Easily detached screen and saddlebags made the FXRS equally at home in the western deserts as cruising city streets. The 1991 model (above) is en route from the Harley factory at York, Pennsylvania to San Francisco.*

SPECIFICATIONS

Engine	air-cooled ohv V-twin
Capacity	81.6cu in (1,340cc)
Transmission	5-speed
Power	69bhp
Weight	585lbs (265kg)
Wheelbase	64.7in (1,643mm)
Top speed	106mph (170kph)

■ BELOW *Successor to the FXRS-Conv is the DynaGlide Convertible, now with 88 Twin Cam power.*

As a touring alternative to Electra-Glide overkill, the Convertible was supreme. Its plush seat, standard sissy bar and highway pegs offered reasonable comfort (although the pillion pad was always something of a style-dictated joke), while the screen kept off the worst of road grime and weather. It handled tolerably well, too. The 1½in (39mm) front forks featured air-adjustment and anti-dive. For a heavyweight Harley, ground clearance was also good. Stopping was better than the Milwaukee norm – courtesy of twin hydraulic discs at the front and one at the rear.

■ LEFT *Hot dry air and stinging dust make the screen essential in desert conditions.*

■ BELOW *Possibly not the most handsome chunk of Milwaukee iron, but very definitely one of the most practical. This is a 1992 example.*

The Low Rider look came largely from the choice of wheels: a 19in (483mm) front rim with a 100/90 tyre, compared to a 16in (406mm) rear hoop with a fat, 5⅛in- (130mm-) wide tread. Power came from the Evo 81.6cu in (1,340cc) mill. Although the rubber-mounting wasn't quite in the same league as modern Dyna models, it was pretty good. For five years until it gave way to the Dyna series at the end of 1993, the Low Rider Convertible was perhaps the most practical Harley-Davidson model. It was a neat adaptation of a well-sorted design, so there were few improvements during the time. A 1⅗in (40mm) Keihin carb and improved clutch were introduced in 1990, and other minor details, but essentially the first one was as good as the last. In 1994, the FXRS gave way to another Convertible, the Dyna-series FXDS.

FXDB Sturgis, 1991

On the face of it, the "Mark II" Sturgis added little to the Low Rider family from which it sprang. Named after the annual North Dakota bike rally, the FXDB looked like little more than a midnight-black FXRS with modest changes to its rear shocks and oil tank. Indeed, the two models shared the same front end. The major attributes of the FXDB Sturgis were simplicity itself – just two hard-to-spot pieces of rubber – and with them, a motorcycle was transformed. The Sturgis was a limited-edition model – just over 1,500 were produced – but its impact lives on in every DynaGlide built since. The frame itself, an all-steel structure developed by advanced computer-aided design, is fabricated from a mixture of tubular and forged components with a large-diameter box-section backbone.

The engine isolation system differed from the existing Glide series and Low Rider mounts. These had used three location points with rubber-bonded

bolts, rather than the two more sophisticated composite blocks of the Sturgis. The result was startling. The big twin's effective rev range had been limited by low-speed shudders at the

SPECIFICATIONS	
Engine	air-cooled ohv V-twin
Capacity	81.6cu in (1,340cc)
Power	69bhp
Transmission	5-speed
Wheelbase	65.5in (1,665mm)
Weight	597lbs (271kg)
Top speed	106mph (170kph)

bottom end and intrusive vibes at the top. With the Sturgis, that all changed. One could now happily ride at engine speeds where other Hogs would rattle. Softails have the highest overall gearing of any model to reduce revs to comfortable vibration levels at cruising speeds. Fittingly, another Sturgis, the FXB, had been associated with two other momentous bits of rubber a decade earlier – the toothed rubber belts of its revolutionary primary and final drive.

■ ABOVE TOP AND CENTRE ***Named after a major motorcycle rally, the Sturgis was a major leap forward in Harley affairs. It was to give rise to the stunningly successful Dyna-Glide series.***

■ LEFT ***Stars and stripes had less to do with the Sturgis legacy than did two deceptively simple rubberized blocks.***

FXDWG DYNA WIDEGLIDE, 1993–PRESENT

By 1992, the Sturgis no longer existed, but it had spawned a growing DynaGlide family – first the Dyna Daytona, then the SuperGlide Dyna Custom. By 1993, the Dyna Low Rider was closer to the original but the WideGlide harked back to its namesake of the 1980s. Both, however, went one stage further than the Sturgis in the anti-vibration stakes, with revised "directionally-controlled" mounting blocks.

Harley's idea was "to combine the look of Low Riders of the late 1970s, with the handling and rubber-mounted ride of today", and it worked startlingly well. The 1993 DynaGlides were the smoothest Hogs yet, by a margin. Milwaukee's engineers had made a good bike better, even more than they had with the Sturgis. Without so much as laying a hand on the engine, the company had broadened the big V's effective powerband by a quantum amount – a bigger bonus than adding another ten horsepower.

Much of the rest, as is Harley's way, was in the hands of the blend-men and cosmetic engineers. There are "factory ape-hangers", a "tucked-in tail light", "air-foil directionals" and a wide front fork (hence the "WideGlide") with a 21in (533mm), wire-spoked front wheel, as well as a new, one-piece Fat Bob tank, which removed the need of having to fill up two separate fuel tanks each time you ran short on petrol (gas).

■ RIGHT *An original 1993 WideGlide, so named because of the obvious width between the fork legs.*

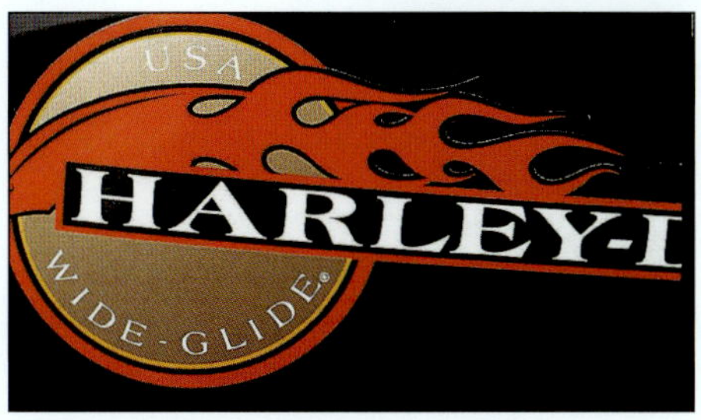

■ BELOW *The badge might be fiery, but the vibrations were not, thanks to a revolutionary system of engine mounting.*

To ride the WideGlide is to marvel at the unprecedented smoothness of the experience – especially after you've grown accustomed to having only forward-mounted footpegs and controls. The ape-hanger handlebars tower somewhere above you, but after a couple of miles it all feels fairly natural and comfortable.

In that uncanny Harley-Davidson way, the steering is light with excellent low-speed balance.

Turns, however, reveal a lot about the WideGlide. Even by Harley-Davidson standards, ground clearance is poor. The stand scrapes on the left, the muffler on the right, both with sufficient force to pitch you off line.

But on the straight, wide highway, it's great to ride.

■ BELOW *For 1999 the new Twin Cam 88 engine was bestowed upon the redoubtable WideGlide.*

SPECIFICATIONS

Engine	air-cooled ohv V-twin
Capacity	81.6cu in (1,340cc)
Transmission	5-speed
Power	69bhp
Weight	598lbs (271kg)
Wheelbase	66.1in (1,680mm)
Top speed	106mph (170kph)

FXDX Dyna SuperGlide Sport, 1999–present

■ BELOW *With its understated lines, the FXDX is as stylish as previous Dynas.*

The FXDX Dyna SuperGlide Sport is much more than just the first model to be fitted with the new Twin Cam powerplant. True, the 88.42cu in (1,449cc) engine will attract the most fuss and gives the latest Dyna more get-up-and-go than any previous Milwaukee model, but the rest of the bike offers even more surprises – this is a Harley that stops and handles. For once, the "Sport" in the title means what it says.

Compared to the 80-inch Evo, the Dyna's blacked-out Twin Cam 88 engine runs a bigger 3¾in (95.25mm) bore with a shortened 4in (101.6mm) stroke. Despite a ten per cent increase in capacity, the result is a powerplant that spins up faster yet with less vibration and a higher rev ceiling of 5,500rpm. The high-pressure, die-cast aluminium crankcases possess a strengthened vertical rear face across which four high-tensile bolts connect the engine to the five-speed transmission. The resulting structure is more rigid than before, reducing stress on the inner primary drive and reducing overall vibration levels. The crankcases themselves are lighter and stronger due to design changes in high-stress areas, redesigned tappet guides and the relocation of the oil pump. Chain cam drive, in place of the previous straight-cut gears, is not only cheaper to produce but also one of several measures aimed at reducing mechanical noise in the face of increasing environmental concerns. Great effort has also been put into improving even the Evo's record of durability, with the all-new pressed-up

■ ABOVE *The FXDX was the first Harley to be fitted with the Twin Cam powerplant, the chain drive to which can be seen here.*

■ LEFT *The Dyna can be adjusted to suit any riding style.*

■ RIGHT *Gliding along on the open road.*

crankshaft featuring new forged flywheels, beefier connecting rods and an uprated crank pin – all of which should easily withstand the Twin Cam's prodigious torque – over 78lb/ft (106Nm) at a mere 2,900rpm. O-rings replace the Evo's cylinder base gaskets, allowing a sturdier and more oil-tight joint between the crankcase and cylinders, as well as enhancing temperature tolerance and reducing bore distortion. Of course, Harley's trademark air-cooling is retained, but a 50 per cent increase in fin area on the cylinders and cylinder heads improves its effect.

If the 88's eager power makes it a real joy to ride, the chassis is at least as rewarding. The frame is substantially similar to previous Evo-engined Dynas, with the same highly effective rubber mounting system insulating rider and passenger from vibration. By the standards of many Harley-Davidson heavyweights, the Dyna runs relatively little trail at just over 4in (104mm) and thus turns more eagerly, but it's the suspension that makes the difference – as big a departure as was the DuoGlide's more than four decades earlier. Both the forks and the Japanese Showa rear shock absorbers now feature full adjustment of preload, rebound and compression damping. Whatever type of riding you have in mind, the Dyna can be adjusted to suit.

Winding up the damping at both ends won't turn the 614lb (279kg) FXDX into a sports bike, but it certainly allows it to corner like no previous big Hog. It still wallows to a degree through fast, bumpy turns, but handles with reassuring precision even at three-figure speeds. Ground clearance is also better. When the time comes to slow down, the latest Dyna is up to the challenge, thanks to a trio of four-piston Hayes calipers biting hard on 11½in (292mm) discs.

Cosmetically, the newcomer sports the same understated lines as previous Dynas, with flat, dirt track style handlebars, a low-line saddle, acres of moody black and a relatively restrained sprinkling of chrome.

Maybe that's just how it should be, for perhaps more than any other Milwaukee musclebike, this is the one that least needs to shout about its virtues.

SPECIFICATIONS

Engine	air-cooled ohv V-twin
Capacity	88.42cu in (1,449cc)
Transmission	5-speed
Power	86bhp
Weight	614lbs (279kg)
Wheelbase	64in (1,623mm)
Top speed	115mph (185kph)

■ LEFT *The Twin Cam FXDX – a thoroughly modern Harley.*

Glides

For more than half a century, the Glide series has stood at the pinnacle of the Harley-Davidson hierarchy – the plushest, best equipped and most expensive models. The line began with the 1949 HydraGlide, a long, low cruiser of which the current Heritage Softail is more than faintly reminiscent.

With their big, slow-tempo engines and long, slow-steering chassis, Glides have always been the long-haul kings of America. In the old days, though, the rider needed to be at least as tough as the Hog, for the bikes had few concessions to comfort. The 80-inch Shovelhead on the FLH-80 was introduced in 1978. Twelve months later, essentially the same machine metamorphosed into the ultimate grand tourer as the FLHC. As well as a luxurious frame-mounted saddle, standard equipment included a fairing and windshield, saddle bags, crash bars, luggage rack and running boards – previously available only as "Tour Pak" optional extras.

At the time, no other motorcycle in the world was so comprehensively equipped, but the Glide story hasn't stopped there. Subsequent models have added a bewildering array of touring extras to top-of-the-range touring models. At the same time, other models have moved nearer to the family's roots with leaner, stripped-down variants, such as the Road King.

FLTCU TourGlide Ultra, 1989–96

After the ElectraGlide, Sportster and SuperGlide, the TourGlide was one of the most enduring packages in the entire Milwaukee line up. The concept – the most "loaded" machine Harley-Davidson engineers could imagine – began with the basic FLT TourGlide of 1980. At the time, the TourGlide offered the nearest thing you could buy to a two-wheeled limousine. Small refinements to the already profoundly refined machine followed year-on-year, not to mention the adoption of belt final drive and Evo V2 power in 1984. The basic concept was still fine, but as the decade was drawing to a close, an even more luxurious carriage was needed. It arrived in 1989 with the awesome TourGlide Ultra Classic, 81.6cu in (1,340cc) of imposing, luxurious brawn. As well as obvious features, such as new fairing "lowers" to protect the rider, a welter of electronics graced the big Glide. From the saddle, the rider now had control of a mouth-watering array of on-board refinement. At the rider's fingertips, there was now electronic cruise control, CB radio and a sophisticated stereo hi-fi system. Even the pillion was provided with separate speakers and a built-in intercom allowed rider and passenger to chew the fat. A cigarette lighter was

■ ABOVE *A 1991 TourGlide in its element, easing across the high desert plateau of Utah, in the south-western United States.*

■ LEFT *The last of a majestic line, a fuel-injected FLTCUI Ultra Classic TourGlide from the 1996 model year.*

■ LEFT *Copious luggage capacity and excellent rider protection are clear from this image of a TourGlide crossing Nevada's wide-open spaces.*

In 1990, I rode a TourGlide from the Harley-Davidson factory in York, Pennsylvania, to San Francisco, California, on America's west coast. Along the way, the big Glide had thumped up endless gradients to more than 11,000ft (3,300m), rumbled across baking deserts for hour after hour, splashed through thunderstorms and scarcely missed a beat. It carried me and everything I needed for 4,000 miles (6,500km), and everyone I met smiled in appreciation. For this sort of experience – traversing the vast emptiness of the United States – no other motorcycle comes anywhere close to it. It was almost as though the TourGlide evolved there – which, come to think of it, it did.

The TourGlide story has ended – for the time being, at least. After 16 years as the long-haul king of America's open roads, the name was dropped from the Harley line-up after the fuel-injected FLTCUI model of 1996. However, its spirit still lives on in the extravagantly equipped Ultra Classic ElectraGlides.

SPECIFICATIONS

Engine	air-cooled ohv V-twin
Capacity	81.6cu in (1,340cc)
Transmission	5-speed
Power	69bhp
Weight	765lbs (347kg)
Wheelbase	63in (1,600mm)
Top speed	105mph (169kph)

■ ABOVE *The rider's cockpit perspective of the Ultra Classic TourGlide.*

■ BELOW *The majestic spirit of the Glides lives on in this 1992 TourGlide.*

standard and even the self-cancelling indicators were microprocessor-controlled. To cope with this plethora of added electrical demands, a new high-output 32-amp alternator was also fitted.

Overkill? Perhaps, but profoundly practical too. The panniers and capacious "Tour-Pak" top-box easily swallowed two weeks' luggage. The plush, upholstered saddle was good for long, long days on the road, while the screen kept dust and dry desert winds at bay. True, a sound system as good as the one at home isn't strictly necessary on a motorcycle, but who can resist cruising enchanted landscapes to a favourite blues tune, all to a backbeat of a thundering Milwaukee twin?

FLHR ElectraGlide Road King, 1994–present

As standard equipment became even more comprehensive at the top of the ElectraGlide range, there came a demand for a model more like the stripped-down FLs of the 1960s. Harley-Davidson's response was the FLHS Sport of 1987 – a real lightweight at "only" 690lbs (313kg). Today's handsome FLHR Road King is in much the same mould.

Launched for the 1994 season, the Road King was an attempt to bridge the gap between Milwaukee's custom and touring models. Although in essence a full-on ElectraGlide minus the fairing, with a "retro" chromed headlight and tank-mounted speedometer, its long, low silhouette belied its super-heavyweight roots. Here was a machine that could hit the highway with the same authority as any other Glide – once the detachable windscreen was installed. As well as the QD windshield (an idea borrowed from the Low Rider Convertible), the panniers and pillion perch were also easily removed, changing the machine's profile and character in the wink of an eye. Thus stripped, the King had all the languid grace of a custom cruiser.

■ ABOVE *Cleaner, lower lines distinguish this king of the road from other heavyweight FLs.*

■ BELOW *Adding a few of Milwaukee's many accessories can undermine the effect.*

To most eyes this is the best looking of all the Glides, the normally ponderous lines replaced by a machine which, if not exactly svelte, has a certain grace. Where fully-loaded FLs tend to obesity, the Road King has style. It's a Harley-Davidson for those who want their heavyweight cake in custom clothes.

Equally, its touring roots make the King an eminently practical custom bike. Six hours in the saddle is hard work on any Softail but a Glide can comfortably knock that off – and more.

SPECIFICATIONS

Engine	air-cooled ohv V-twin
Capacity	81.6cu in (1,340cc)
Transmission	5-speed
Power	69bhp
Weight	692lbs (314kg)
Wheelbase	62.7in (1,590mm)
Top speed	100mph (161kph)

■ LEFT AND BELOW *The "Road King" badge and overall detailing is pure 1960s, although the other chromework (below) is aftermarket kit.*

The rubber-mounted Evo engine keeps vibration at bay but lets that evocative rumble pour through. Parked anywhere it looks good; on the open road, it works.

The first fuel-injected Road King, the FLHRI came in 1996, although carburetted versions continued to be produced in parallel. The ESPFI (Electronic Sequential Port Fuel Injection) system is based on a similar Italian Magneti Marelli design to that of Ducati V-twins, although in this case the emphasis is on user-friendliness rather than sheer power. Though some owners may prefer the reassuring simplicity of a stock single carb poking out of the right-hand side, the new fuel-injection system is a major bonus. As well as improving emissions, it offers slightly higher torque (83lb/ft rather than 79lb0/ft) and much better driveability, particularly at high altitude. The fuel system was improved across the Injection range for 1997.

High-tech is largely absent elsewhere, except of course for Harley-Davidson's trademark belt final drive. Suspension is adjustable only for air pressure in the twin rear shock absorbers. Both wheels are cast light alloy, 16in (406mm) in diameter, wearing characteristically fat Glide rubber.

Twin hydraulic disc brakes grace the front, with a single disc at the rear. All three of these brakes have a lot of work to do on a machine that scales 692lbs (314kg), but these days, Harley-Davidson stoppers work fairly well. Like most of the Glide family, the Road King's top speed is maybe a shade over 100mph (161kph), although screaming the big twin that hard is a futile pursuit.

The Road King is happiest when it is ambling along at a disdainful 75mph (120kph); if you travel at much above 85mph (140kph), a disconcerting weave has sometimes been known to intrude.

To be king of the road the Milwaukee way, you don't need to be the fastest – just the coolest.

■ LEFT *A 1996 Road King – or should that be FLHR-Convertible? Both the windshield and pillion seat are quickly detachable.*

FLHTCU-I Ultra Classic ElectraGlide, 1997–present

For a supposedly conservative model from a fairly cautious company, the top ElectraGlide has undergone a relentless battery of changes during the past few years. Fuel injection (ESPFI) first hit the family on the FLHTC Thirtieth Anniversary in 1995, before becoming standard on Road King and top-of-the-range ElectraGlides for the following model year. Then, scarcely had 1997 brought a new frame with lower saddle height (27in/685mm) and many other detail changes, than Harley-Davidson's first new engine for 15 years graced the good old ElectraGlide.

The Twin Cam 88 is not only "glittering with chrome" but gives the massive ElectraGlide a welcome boost to more than 80bhp, with a prodigious peak torque of 86lb/ft (117Nm). With a wider spread of torque and the driveability that only fuel injection brings, the big Glide's legendary ability to gobble up countless miles is improved. Now it shrugs off gradients and altitude with even greater ease than before. Everything about the big Glide, from its fat tyres and sofa-like saddle to lazy, laid-back steering geometry, marks it out as the grandest of open-road tourers.

Scaling a thundering 776lbs (352kg) without so much as a drop of fuel in the tank, this is the heaviest Hog of them all. Most of that weight is good, solid Milwaukee metal, but much of the rest aims to pamper the rider like no other bike known to humanity. The amply

■ ABOVE *With its luxuriously cushioned seat, riding the Ultra Classic is a dream.*

■ BELOW *An Evo-engined predecessor to the full-on Ultra Classic 88. But who'd want his electricity bill?*

SPECIFICATIONS	
Engine	air-cooled ohv V-twin
Capacity	88.42cu in (1,449cc)
Transmission	5-speed
Power	80bhp
Weight	776lbs (352kg)
Wheelbase	63in (1,600mm)
Top speed	105mph (169kph)

■ RIGHT *With plenty of room to store luggage, this is the ultimate long-haul Hog.*

padded seat is huge and welcoming, while the adjustable footboards give room to move and relax. Harley's neat method of rubber mounting the engine in the steel square-backbone frame ensures that engine vibration is enough to say "Harley" but not so that it will intrude. Meanwhile the panniers, fairing pockets and copious, carpet-lined "King Tour-Pak" top box simply swallow up luggage.

Harley-Davidson describes its top model as "fully loaded" and you'd better believe it. Depending on the market, it comes with passing and running lamps, more instruments than a Boeing and even a cigarette lighter. There's a voice-activated intercom, CB radio and electronic cruise control complete with "Resume" and "Accelerate" modes. The 40-watts-per-channel AM/FM cassette radio contains weatherband, four speakers, separate passenger controls and dual antenna, all controlled from a myriad of switches on the left handlebar and able to respond automatically to ambient noise levels.

If any Harley-Davidson is as much fantasy as motorcycle, this top ElectraGlide takes the dream to the next level. Imagine cruising over Arizona's high plateaux, the warm desert wind tugging at your sleeves and caressing your designer sunglasses. Slip in your favourite blues cassette or tune in to a passing country music station, and the Glide will transport you to Hog heaven. Come service time, it can even talk to Harley-Davidson mechanics as well, since the engine management system contains full diagnostic capability – and that's only part of the story.

Some bikers mock the ElectraGlide as a two-wheeled Cadillac de Ville. Certainly, it's as far from a sports bike as it is possible for a motorcycle to get.

Absurd, to some.

Over-the-top, probably.

But glorious – definitely yes.

■ LEFT ***The biggest, most expensive and most magnificent model in the Harley-Davidson range, the mighty fuel-injected ElectraGlide Ultra Classic.***

FLHRCI Road King Classic, 2000

■ BELOW *The aristocratic Road King Classic, a new breed of style machine.*

The Classic version of the Road King takes up where the standard model left off. In terms of straight specification, there is little to set the two models apart. Yet the Classic, as the name suggests, is a different sort of hybrid: a full-on tourer which is also a custom machine.

With laced (spoked) wheels and fat whitewall tyres, chrome-fringed saddlebags and swept-back lines, the King Classic is almost as svelte as the ElectraGlide is gross – or, as Harley puts it, "has enough traditional styling to drop jaws throughout the continent". Indeed, throughout any continent.

So, for a tourer, the Classic screams "style". As well as those wheels and tyres, it's in the custom metal emblems on the tank, fender tips and seat. It's in that bold trademark , chromed headlamp and twin 35-watt passing lights. It's in the chrome dual mufflers and stainless-steel "Buffalo" handlebars and – new for 2000 – in classic two-tone paint.

As with all year 2000 big-twin models, power comes from the Twin Cam 88 engine first unveiled the previous year. The 88.42cu in (1,449cc) ohv V-twin features electronic fuel injection via 1½in (38mm) inlet stacks – and, not least, an attention-grabbing chrome-and-black engine finish. Other than its long-legged lump, the King's touring credentials lie with its leather saddlebags (with rigid inserts to prevent their going out of shape), well-upholstered seat, Lexan windshield (quickly detachable for town riding) and 5-gallon (19-litre) fuel tank. In addition, both rider and pillion foot-boards can be adjusted to the right height.

SPECIFICATIONS

Engine	air-cooled ohv V-twin
Capacity	88.42cu in (1,449cc)
Transmission	5-speed
Power	80bhp
Weight	710lb (322kg)
Wheelbase	63½in (1,612mm)
Top speed	110mph (177kph)

Once upon a time, Milwaukee might have been content with leaving it at that, but not any more. In recent times, it has actively sought greater user-friendliness and better performance on all fronts. So, in common with its fellow heavyweights (except the Springer Softail), the feeble old brakes give way to four-pot calipers (heavy-weights have two at the front), squeezing uprated friction pads on to much-improved 11½in (292mm) rotors. Both braking power and feel are improved as a result, while lever effort is reduced substantially.

There are new wheel bearings, maintenance-free for 100,000 miles (160,000km). The same goes for the new sealed, long-life, 28Ah battery.

The King Classic is built as vast as only Harley-Davidson knows how, scaling over 700lbs (320kg) without so much as a drop of fuel in its Fat Bob tank. Tying the plot together is a massive mild-steel frame with heavyweight box-section spine and twin tubular cradles.

Suspension at both ends is air-adjustable, although wheel travel is less than generous.

The HydraGlide-style forks offer 4.6in (117mm) of movement while the twin rear shock absorbers afford (3in) 76mm. The King Classic will change direction in its own good time, and has 6.1in (155mm) of trail and a gargantuan wheelbase of 63½in (1,612mm). Which is precisely the point: where's the dignity in rushing?

■ ABOVE *An Evo-engined 1997 Heritage Springer Softail. The latest version benefits enormously from the smoothness of the Twin Cam 88B powerplant.*

Buell

Buell

The name might be unfamiliar and Buell may not have the length of pedigree of the Harley-Davidson company, but they do have deep and fertile roots. The breed arose from the efforts of former racer Erik Buell, who began creating his idiosyncratic line of racing specials in 1983. The first of these, the RW750, had a four-cylinder 750cc two-stroke engine and was capable of around 180mph (290kph) – very un-Harley fare. When this was outlawed by a change in racing regulations, Buell began his first Harley-engined project, the RR1000.

A total of 50 of these XR1000-engined machines were produced during 1987–8, before the focus switched to the new 1,200cc Evolution powerplant and the RR1200 model. Tuned versions of the same 1200 Sportster engine have powered all Buell models since. All bore tribute to Buell's innovative approach to design, particularly with respect to their lightweight monoshock chassis with advanced suspension and braking components.

It is precisely these attributes that now differentiate Buell Harleys from the more traditional Harley-Davidson models. Buell does not build cruisers or customs – or tourers in the heavyweight Milwaukee sense. Buells are sports bikes, sports tourers or "in your face" streetfighter machines. They still have Harley-Davidson soul and presence, but they have added muscle and attitude, too.

M2 Cyclone & S3 Thunderbolt

■ RIGHT *The Cyclone has style, speed and attitude. What more could you want?*

■ BELOW *Sleek yet brutal – the Buell Thunderbolt.*

■ M2 CYCLONE

"It came from a motorcyclist's soul, not from a product planning committee," is the Buell promotional slogan, and it fits the streetfighting Cyclone to a "T". The base model of the East Troy range when launched in late 1996, the Cyclone is propelled by a tuned 1,200cc Sportster mill. Claimed peak power is a shuddering 86bhp – more than even the new Twin Cam 88. A wickedly broad torque band peaks at 79lb/ft (107Nm) at 5,400rpm.

The Cyclone runs on slightly less exotic chassis components than its siblings, notably conventional Showa teles rather than upside-down forks. All Buell models employ a single White Power rear unit located under the engine. Bodywork is kept to a minimum, showing the chrome-molybdenum steel perimeter frame off to maximum effect. The big twin engine is located using Buell's patented "Uniplanar" mountings, with tie-rods to reduce the effects of vibration. Final drive is via a reinforced toothed-belt similar to the mainstream Harley range. Although bestowed with only a single front disc, this offers an enormous friction area swept by a huge six-piston caliper. Both wheels are cast aluminium and of lightweight, three-spoke design. With a frame weighing a mere 26lbs (12kg), the Cyclone is fully 77lbs (35kg) lighter and more than 10bhp stronger than a 1200S Sportster. With these impressive numbers and this quality of chassis kit, the Cyclone and its kin handle and stop like no conventional Harley. Soul and speed are not mutually exclusive.

■ S3 THUNDERBOLT

The Thunderbolt, launched for 1997, was based around a chassis assembly similar to the then top-of-the-range S1 Lightning, mated to the Cyclone's 86bhp carburetted big twin engine. The race-bred chassis features fully-adjustable inverted White Power forks and under-slung rear suspension unit, with similar wheels and brakes to the Cyclone's. The Sportster-derived engine produces a claimed 86bhp at a giddy 6,000rpm and 79lb/ft (107Nm) of torque. The motor enjoys the same Uniplanar anti-vibration mountings as other Buell models, allowing plenty of gutsy rumble to reach the rider but damping out more destructive vibes. Visually, the T-bolt is distinguished by its swooping rear bodywork and aerodynamic fairing. Buell produces a sports-touring version, the S3T, with legshields and panniers.

SPECIFICATIONS: CYCLONE (THUNDERBOLT)

Engine	ohv 45 degree V-twin
Capacity	1,203cc
Transmission	5-speed, toothed-belt final drive
Power	86bhp
Weight	434lbs/197kg (450lbs/204kg)
Wheelbase	55½in/1,410mm
Top speed	126mph/203kph (133mph/214kph)

BUELL HISTORY

Following the modest success of the Sportster-powered RR1200 (of which 65 were built), 1989 marked the debut of the first two-seater Buell, the RS1200 from which the single-seat RSS1200 evolved two years later. By this time, inverted telescopic forks and six-piston disc-brake calipers had become the norm for a marque which was rapidly grabbing the attention of the motorcycle community. By the end of 1992, the company had built a total of 442 machines and brought its founder a solid reputation for engineering and design.

In February 1993, Buell became part of the Harley-Davidson empire when Milwaukee bought a 49 per cent stake in the company. The merger gave Buell access to development funds and Harley-Davidson expertise while offering Harley a direct avenue into Buell's creative engineering. Buell was in fact collaborating with Harley on design as early as the late 1970s when he contributed to the original belt-drive Sturgis project.

■ LEFT ***A rare Buell RS1200 from around 1989. Its heritage is evident.***

■ BELOW LEFT ***The Buell assembly line in East Troy, an hour from Milwaukee, shown before Harley bought in.***

■ BELOW ***The Buell's raw lines and radical engineering are abundantly clear with body-work removed.***

Buells are now built at East Troy, Wisconsin, using engines made at the "small powertrains" plant on Milwaukee's Capitol Drive. Now marketed in parallel with mainstream Harley-Davidson machines, the current generation of Cyclone, Thunderbolt and Lightning Buell models was first launched in the United States in 1994.

Buell X1 Lightning, 1999

Sharing a name with a 3,000mph (5000kph) jet plane, the X1 Lightning replaced the S-series Lightning when launched for 1999. This is a mean and purposeful "Streetfighter" from the makers of "Harleys with attitude".

The X1 is a truly credible sports machine. It bristles with character, and its power and handling are vastly improved compared to more traditional Milwaukee fare. At the X1's heart is a reworked "Thunderstorm" version of the familiar 1,203cc Sportster engine with higher compression pistons, larger valves and ports re-profiled for improved gas flow. Lighter flywheels improve engine response and at the same time quicken the Sportster's normally leisurely gearchange.

Best of all is the X1's new and ultra-sophisticated Dynamic Digital fuel injection. The system uses state-of-the-art computer control to ensure that the big V-twin delivers its best under all conditions, virtually eliminating flat-spots, improving fuel economy and cleaning up exhaust emissions. The result is one of the sharpest Harley-Davidson's ever built – and perhaps the most powerful.

According to independent dyno tests, peak power is 85bhp at 5,300rpm – more than any other stock Harley; the X1's torque is even more impressive:

SPECIFICATIONS

Engine	ohv 45 degree V-twin with EFI
Capacity	1,203cc
Transmission	5-speed, toothed-belt final drive
Power	95bhp (see main text)
Weight	439lbs (199kg)
Wheelbase	55½in (1,410mm)
Top speed	135mph (217kph)

■ ABOVE ***The X1 Lightning: a real mean street-fighting machine.***

■ LEFT ***With its minimalist seat design, this is a far cry from the ElectraGlide.***

■ LEFT *Understated, fast and stylish, the Lightning lives up to its name.*

92lb/ft (125Nm) at just 3,300rpm, guaranteeing a broad range of solid, usable power (Buell actually claims 95bhp and 85lb/ft (115Nm).

With this engine there is almost no such thing as being in the wrong gear: simply wind open the throttle and the big twin will deliver the goods at almost any rpm. Top speed is around 136mph (220kph), although this can vary as some markets receive models with raised gearing to help meet local noise limits.

Pinning all of this to the road is a rugged tubular steel trellis chassis, with new Japanese Showa suspension components at both ends. At the front are sturdy inverted forks which are adjustable for pre-load, compression and rebound damping.

The monoshock rear end offers built-in rising rate, plus pre-load and two-way damping tuning. The stainless-steel exhaust is tucked tight in, providing maximum room and comfort for one- or two-up riding and giving the best cornering ground clearance of any Milwaukee roadster, allowing the X1 to exploit to the full its Dunlop rubber. Although the Lightning boasts only a single front disc, braking is excellent as well, with a brawny 13.4in (340mm) rotor grabbed by a huge, six-piston "Performance Machine" caliper. A simple single-piston caliper and 9in (230mm) disc adorn the rear.

Handling, too, is top notch. With its short, nimble wheelbase and only 3½in (89mm) of trail, the X1 turns quickly by Harley standards, inviting riders to dive hard into turns. Stability, too, is surprisingly good, allowing the machine to be ridden with confidence under almost any circumstances. Its minimalist seat and overall ergonomics may fall a long way short of ElectraGlide territory, but the sort of owners the X1 is aimed at will not mind that.

This impressive package is cloaked in the sort of eye-catching yet understated muscular styling for which the East Troy streetfighting machines have become renowned.

With a Buell, what you see is what you get – and you get the best Buell yet with the X1 Lightning.

■ LEFT *Burnouts are easy thanks to tuned 1,200cc Sportster power.*

■ BELOW *Truly awesome: the Buell X1 Lightning.*

HARLEY-DAVIDSON
SPECTRO
EBC

Racers

The first Harley-Davidson "racers" were nothing more than standard production machines in the hands of some adventurous private individuals.

These days, although competition is a long way from Harley-Davidson's corporate image, it's still very much part of the company soul. The American motorcycle racing scene was effectively founded by the Indian and Curtiss companies, but Harley soon picked up the gauntlet and eventually became the dominant force. Even some of the founders were keen competitors – Walter Davidson himself recorded the first "factory" win in an endurance trial in 1908. By the First World War, daredevil riders were hurtling along on Harley twins at three-figure speeds – with no brakes and almost no suspension.

Since the innocent enthusiasm of the pioneer years, a wealth of Harley-Davidson racing machines have become legendary, from the first eight-valvers to the booming XR750 which still runs rampant on America's dirt tracks. For Harley-Davidson, as for almost everyone else, racing has improved the breed.

EARLY RACERS

■ **EIGHT-VALVE, TWO-CAM**
Although a special "7-E" competition version of Harley-Davidson's first V-twin was built for selected customers as early as 1910, the first model created specifically for racing was the eight-valve twin which appeared in 1916. The multi-valve layout had already been amply proven by the exploits of Indian's similar engine, already the winner of the Isle of Man TT.

Displacing 61cu in (999cc), the Harley-Davidson eight-valve was the device on which the Harley Wrecking Crew began their domination of the American racing scene.

Private individuals were less fortunate, since the machine's price – $1,500 – was deliberately inflated to ensure that it could only fall into serious hands.

A 65cu in (1,065cc) twin-cam racer followed. Like the eight-valve model, the Two-Cam had inlet-over-exhaust valve layout, no brakes and direct drive by chain to the rear wheel (although some examples may have used three-speed transmissions). Once started – no easy task due to the use of very high compression ratios – these monsters were capable of well over 100mph (160kph). To promote its wares overseas, Harley-Davidson freighted its top racing machines all over the world. In Britain, both Freddie Dixon and D.H. Davidson took the Two-Cam to numerous records at the famed banked Brooklands circuit in Surrey. In September 1923, at Arpajon in France, Dixon took the same machine to a world-record speed of 106.5mph (171.4kph).

■ LEFT *A handsome 74-inch J-series racer dating from 1924. Note the total lack of any sort of brakes.*

■ LEFT *A 1924 74-inch F-head racer. Exhaust silencing was not a prime concern.*

■ BELOW *Another F-head, a 1920 board racer ridden by Dewey Sims. The plunger on the left side of the tank feeds engine oil.*

■ **OHV TWINS**
During the mid-1920s, the F-head Two-Cam was the mainstay of Harley-Davidson's factory twin-cylinder racing efforts, but they were seriously hampered when the AMA introduced the new "Class C" racing formula. This was

■ LEFT *The legendary eight-valve racer, one of the most potent motorcycles in the world in its day.*

for production-based 45cu in (750cc) machines, of which at least 25 had to be built. Overnight, the old Class A and Class B factory specials were relegated to the sidelines in much of American racing – especially in the buoyant "slant-shooting" (hill-climbing) scene.

At the time, Milwaukee produced no eligible machine, but by 1926 it did have the remarkably fast 21-inch ohv Peashooter single, and any darn fool could see that two times 21 wasn't far from 45. It wasn't long before someone investigated the possibility of grafting Peashooter heads on to existing V-twin bottom ends.

The first such ohv Harley-Davidson twin was probably a machine dubbed "Home Brew", ridden with some success by Oscar Lenz in 1927. A similar device, also based on a 61-inch bottom end, was built by Ralph Moore of Indianapolis.

By 1928, Harley-Davidson had given in to popular demand and released "roadster" versions of its Two-Cam racing twins, the 61-inch JH and 74-inch JDH and it wasn't long before Juneau Avenue followed the example of creative privateers with a number of factory specials featuring ohv Peashooter top ends grafted on to JD Two-Cam crankcases.

These first hit the tracks in 1928 at Fond du Lac, just a few miles north of Milwaukee. However, there is some dispute as to whether they were actually created in Harley's competition shop or by a local dealer, Bill Knuth, with the factory's knowledge and support.

In either case, this was an interim measure, because twelve months later a 45-inch factory racer, the DAH, first appeared.

Unlike the Two-Cam-based machines, the DAH was substantially a new engine from the ground up, although it still depended on cylinder heads derived from the Peashooter's.

Displacing 45.44cu in (744cc), the DAH retained the 88.9mm stroke of the JD, but with a bore reduced to 70.6mm.

The DAH was dominant for a while, but Knuth came back with a four-cam hybrid reputed to produce fully 45 horsepower, which continued to give the official factory machines a run for their money. There are even records of a 61-inch ohv racing twin, designated FAR, being built for export.

It is highly likely that, in some measure or other, these exotic racing models were to inspire the later Knucklehead ohv twin. What is for certain is the profound influence that they had on the racing world at large.

■ ABOVE *Four overhead valves per cylinder can clearly be seen in this view of the same 1923 eight-valver. Note the single carburettor between the cylinders.*

■ BELOW *Compared to the exotic factory eight-valvers, F-head board racers such as this were relatively low-tech, but still capable of frightening speeds.*

PEASHOOTER, 1929

As legendary in its way as was the exotic Two-Cam, the Peashooter began life as a standard roadster model. The Peashooter was based on the overhead-valve Model AA magneto version of the 21.1cu in (346cc) single produced from 1926 to 1935, which proved itself more than amenable to race tuning. Perhaps this was not altogether surprising, as the cylinder head – the most crucial performance element in any four-stroke engine – was designed by the great Harry Ricardo, the British engineering genius. Only a few years earlier, Ricardo had created Triumph's first four-valve motor, the Model R. Sir Harry, as he was later to become, practically invented the art of petrol- (gas-) flowing and, during

■ LEFT *The cylinder head of the Peashooter was designed by Harry Ricardo, a British engineer.*

■ BELOW *This single became a legend on the race tracks of the United States.*

■ BELOW *Chains were commonly fitted for extra grip on hill climbs.*

SPECIFICATIONS

Engine	ohv single
Capacity	21.1cu in (346cc)
Transmission	1- or 3-speed
Weight	290lbs (132kg)
Wheelbase	55in (1,400mm)
Top Speed	over 80mph (128kph)

the course of developing the concept of octane ratings for fuel, gained an unparalleled understanding of the combustion process.

Central to the Peashooter's success were two things. One was the engine's hemispherical "squish" heads, in which the outer portion of the piston crown almost touches the cylinder head as it rises up the bore. This in turn creates a fierce turbulence, promoting fuel/air mixing and combustion. This made the 'Shooter's combustion more efficient than its rivals over a broader range of revs, also permitting the safe use of higher compression ratios. Even in roadster form, the "21" generated only 20 per cent less power than an F-head twin with almost three times the displacement.

The Peashooter's other "ace" was Joe Petrali who (along with Scott Parker) is surely the most successful racer ever to grace the race tracks of America. In 1935, towards the end of the model's racing career, he won every one of the 13 dirt track races in the national series. The diminutive Californian was equally adept whether board racing or tackling towering hill-climbs, proving virtually unbeatable until his retirement in 1938.

Petrali and the single first hit the headlines when the AMA adopted a new 21-inch racing class in 1925. In the first race under the new formula, fittingly held in Milwaukee before a crowd of over 20,000, Petrali, Jim Davis and Eddie Brock simply blasted the opposition into the Wisconsin weeds. Board-racing versions of the ohv roadster were stripped to the bare essentials, with tiny seats, "Speedster" drop handlebars and neither brakes nor mudguards. Such abbreviated devices were easily capable of speeds in excess of 80mph (128kph). Depending on the type of competition, they were built with single-speed (Model SM) or three-speed (SA) transmission.

Despite the ohv single's instant track success, Juneau Avenue was oddly disposed towards its side-valve sidekick since the flathead roadster was seen as the likeliest seller. However, others quickly saw the potential of high-revving overhead-valve engines, and the Peashooter became the single of choice on the American racing scene (although a speedway version, inspired by the all-conquering British JAP, was far less successful).

The final, flattering piece in the Peashooter jigsaw came with the introduction of the ohv Knucklehead in 1936.

Although the factory was developing overhead-valve DAH competition twins during the late 1920s, the Knuckle bears many detail similarities with the Peashooter top end.

Whether this was by design or accident, no-one can now tell.

■ LEFT *"Speedster" drop handlebars were a feature of the Peashooter.*

WR/WRTT, 1940–51

■ ABOVE *This "45" wears telescopic forks manufactured long after the side-valve racer was history.*

Harley-Davidson's racing mainstay of the 1940s, the side-valve WR, had the humblest of beginnings, evolving by degrees from the unpretentious Model D of 1929. Essentially, this was powered by little more than a pair of Ricardo heads grafted from the 21.1cu in (346cc) single (which had almost the same bore diameter) onto a common crankcase. The machine developed rapidly year-on-year, becoming the Model R in 1932, at which time its hottest roadster derivative was the RLD Special Sport Solo.

Racing efforts at the time, both official and private, were concentrated on overhead valve engines, both singles and 45-inch twins. However, by 1933 the RLDE twin with magnesium alloy pistons was available from the factory by special order.

Two years later still, the Series R range included five models based on the familiar flathead "45", crowned by the lean and purposeful RLDR Competition Special – a snip at $322. For 1937, a Knucklehead-inspired restyle and a welter of engine improvements metamorphosed the R into the enduring Model W. Other than the change of prefix letter, the 45-inch range continued as before, now with the WLDR Competition Special at its head – a WR in all but name. Harley-Davidson put this right in 1941: the WLDR still existed, but now as a mere Special Sport Solo roadster.

Taking its place as the hottest 45 was the plain WR, a race machine available only to special order. Initially, availability was poor – just 36 WRs were produced in 1941 – but both

SPECIFICATIONS

Engine	side valve 4-stroke V-twin
Capacity	45.3cu in (742cc)
Transmission	3- or 4-speed
Power	40bhp
Wheelbase	60in (1,525mm)
Top speed	around 105mph (169kph)

■ ABOVE AND LEFT *Although substantially similar engines propelled American postmen, the WR carried Harley's racing banner for a decade in both factory and private teams.*

■ RIGHT *The main advantage of the side-valve twin wasn't its potency, but its capacity, which kept it competitive in American racing.*

■ LEFT *A competitor fettles his "45" during a modern classic race meeting.*

■ BELOW *The "pillion" pad helped the rider stretch out to cheat the wind.*

demand and supply picked up dramatically in the aftermath of war. A total of 292 were produced in 1948, 121 in 1949 and 23 in the last year of production.

These purpose-built racing machines were, of course, very much stripped down compared to their roadster cousins (the WR had not so much as a front mudguard, and later examples also benefited from a lightweight chrome-molybdenum steel chassis). The WRTT, produced as a specific model only late in the WR's career, retained the heavier roadster frame. Being a flat-track machine, the WR also had no brakes, while the road-racing TT machine was equipped with standard WL wheels and brakes – scarcely state-of-the-art stopping power. The WR's suspension was no more impressive, with old-fashioned girder front forks and a rigid rear end. For good measure, the gearbox, although available with close-ratio racing cogs, was hand-change. It may have been crude, and 40bhp from 45 inches was unimpressive. Yet this, and sheer weight of numbers, was enough to rival the much more sophisticated but sorely handicapped overhead-valve twins and overhead-camshaft singles from Europe. The brute toughness of the WRTT, in particular, made it a surprisingly capable "Class C" racer. This formula had first been introduced for roadster-based machines in the 1920s to reduce the spiralling cost of Class A and B factory specials.

For more than a decade, these outwardly primitive machines gave a good account of themselves on the race tracks of America – taking 19 out of 23 championship victories in 1948 alone.

This was partly because they were rugged and dependable, and partly because the AMA was as eager then as it has been since to adjust the rules in favour of domestic hardware.

In this case the AMA, which is the governing body of American motorcycle sport, greeted the arrival of fast European overhead-valve machines with a decree that said they would be limited to 500cc, while side-valves of 750cc were permitted. And guess who made the only flathead racers in the frame?

KR/KRTT 1952–69

■ LEFT *Few racers have remained competitive for as long as the KR, although it needed help from the rules to survive.*

■ BELOW LEFT *The 45-inch (750cc) engine in close-up. The push-rod tubes to the side valves are clearly seen.*

What Harley-Davidson needed to replace the elderly WR was a machine reflecting the technology of its era. In the KR, the company most certainly didn't get it. What it got instead was yet another long-stroke flathead racer derived from a road bike, in this case the 45.3cu in (742cc) Model K which was about to be so comprehensively licked by British machines on America's streets. In racing, the KR had an edge: the AMA's 500cc limit on overhead-valve engines still applied.

As with the WR a decade earlier, production began slowly, with just 17 KRs built in the first year. Yet by 1955, the special equipment range encompassed no less than five specific models: the KHK Super Sport Solo, KHRM off-roader, KR dirt track racer, and KRTT and KHRTT "Tourist Trophy" machines.

All three KH models boasted the new 55cu in (883cc) long-stroke K-Series engine and were essentially "race replicas" intended as much for the private enthusiast as the racer. Serious racers remained limited to what the regulations allowed: 750cc.

In 1955, the factory built 90 45-inch competition models, declining to 33 by the decade's end. Unlike the WR/WRTT, all variants now enjoyed a lightweight racing frame, although only the road-racing TT model received the new swinging-arm rear end.

The flat-track KR had a smaller tank, fatter wheels and tyres and no need of brakes. Bore and stroke were identical to the WR's at 70 x 97mm (the slow-revving 55's stroke was even longer at 116mm).

However, the cylinders were commonly re-bored after bedding-in. By using the maximum permitted piston oversize – more than 0.04in (1.1mm) mechanics could raise the displacement legally to 46.8cu in (767cc).

At 9:1, the compression ratio was high by side-valve standards and a single 33mm Linkert carburettor was

SPECIFICATIONS	
Engine	side-valve 4-stroke V-twin
Capacity	45.3 cu in (742cc)
Transmission	4-speed
Power	48bhp
Weight	377–385lbs (171–175g)
Wheelbase	56in (1,420mm)
Top speed	150mph (240kph) (with road-race streamlining)

■ LEFT *A very original example of a 1962 KR dirt-tracker. Note the lack of rear suspension or brakes.*

■ RIGHT *Rear springing identifies this KR as the TT version.*

standard. Power was around 48bhp at 7,000rpm, with 50lb/ft (68Nm) of torque at 5,000rpm. British Norton, Matchless and Triumph machines, as well as putting out far more specific power than the KR, handled and stopped far better. Yet the old KRs just kept rolling on.

While they were heavy (around 380lbs/172kg) and ill-suited to any circuit with proper corners, they remained surprisingly competitive elsewhere – not least because every race grid in America seemed to be packed with them.

Since a dirt-track KR actually cost $95 less than a stock road-going Sportster during the mid-1960s, perhaps this wasn't too surprising.

The road racers, too, were capable of surprising feats. At the super-fast Daytona Speedway, streamlined KRs have been recorded in excess of 150mph (240kph), an astonishing achievement for a side-valve machine.

For all their shortcomings, in the hands of racing aces such as Markel and Resweber, they managed to win a round dozen American national titles during their 18 years on the grid.

The KR's astonishing span came to an end in 1969 when the AMA ended discriminatory limitations on overseas machines.

Faced with a level playing field, there was no way that the redoubtable old flathead "45" could compete with the machines that were coming in from abroad.

■ ABOVE RIGHT *A KRTT in Harley's famous orange and black factory racing colours.*

■ RIGHT *This dirt tracker wears TT-type rear suspension and brakes, although both the shock absorbers and front forks are non-period items.*

XR750 Flat-Tracker, 1970–present

To many people's eyes – and ears – the XR750 dirt-track machine is the most handsome, the raunchiest and the most purposeful piece of kit ever to rumble out of Milwaukee. Certainly no other Harley-Davidson has enjoyed so much competition success over so many years as the seminal XR. After almost two decades plugging along on the side-valve KR twin, the arrival of an overhead-valve replacement in 1970 must have been keenly anticipated. Yet its debut year was to prove a deep disappointment when Mert Lawwill and Mark Brelsford could manage only a disappointing sixth and seventh in the AMA championship. Just 12 months earlier, Lawwill had won the title on a side-valve KR.

The problem was the new engine's iron cylinders. They were heavy and conducted heat much less efficiently than aluminium components. This in turn meant that the motor's compression ratio had to be drastically reduced – to around 8:1 – if fatal breakdowns were to be avoided. With lumpier pistons, the iron XR had proven fast – but it just couldn't last the distance. In 1970, race boss Dick O'Brien admitted to a lowly 62bhp at 6,200rpm. In June 1971, light alloy replaced iron, and the XR750 hasn't looked back.

SPECIFICATIONS	
Engine	ohv V-twin
Capacity	45.8cu in (750cc)
Transmission	4-speed
Power	around 95 bhp
Weight	290lbs (132kg)
Top speed	130mph (210kph)

■ ABOVE LEFT ***Despite troubled beginnings, the XR went on to sweep away all before it in American dirt-track racing – with only occasional help from the rules when Honda's RS750 got too close.***

■ LEFT ***Only that ugly California-mandated silencer mars the XR750's brutal yet beautiful lines.***

■ LEFT *The XR was also briefly successful in road racing, notably with Cal Rayborn in control. This is the iron-head machine on which he won the 1972 Transatlantic Series.*

On dirt, Mark Brelsford took the XR to the 1972 American Number One plate in its maiden season. At Easter the same year, the great Cal Rayborn whipped all comers in the annual USA v Great Britain road-race series.

At the heart of the XR is that rarest of beasts, a short-stroke Harley-Davidson. "Iron-head" XRs used what were essentially de-stroked 883cc Sportster engines, retaining the road machine's 72mm bore but with a shorter 82mm stroke. The 1972 engine's cylinders measured 79.4 x 75.8mm – by comparison, the side-valve KR measured an ultra-long-stroke 70 x 97mm. This, allied to a much stronger crankshaft, permitted more revs as well as a substantially higher 10.5:1 compression ratio made possible by the use of light alloy. The result was a dramatic rise in power and reliability. Shortly after Rayborn's Transatlantic road-race triumph (which was, ironically, on an iron-head engine), peak power was reputed to be around 80bhp at 8,000rpm. Even so, for many years even the light alloy XR ran dangerously hot – road-racers employed two oil coolers yet were worn out after only 200 miles (320km) – until the internal oil circulation was improved.

At the outset, carburation was by twin 1½in (36mm) Japanese Mikuni instruments (often larger on the road racers). Sparks were provided by a Fairbanks-Morse magneto, an unreliable system sometimes dubbed "Can't Get Worse" by unhappy riders. The lightweight, high-grade steel frame used Ceriani forks and paired Girling rear shock absorbers. Dry weight was a feather-light 291lb (132kg), although the road racers, with a fairing and brakes, were somewhat heavier.

■ ABOVE *They still fight for it: the coveted AMA Number One plate.*

■ BELOW *Nine times AMA Number One Scott Parker, here in action at Sacramento. All his titles have been XR-powered.*

Almost 30 years of detailed development have left the XR engine little changed visually, but without equal for the demands of dirt-track competition.

These days, power is around 95bhp at 7,800rpm, with a strong spread from 4,500 to more than 8,000rpm. On one mile (1.61km) ovals, this is good for a top speed of around 130mph (210kph), although it's the way that the big twin finds grip that really sets it apart from the others on the field.

True, the XR soon became obsolete as a road racer, but has gone from strength to strength on the dirt tracks of the United States.

In the hands of men like Brelsford, Gary Scott, Jay Springsteen and Scott Parker, the XR has simply swept away all before it, taking three-quarters of all the subsequent AMA championships.

RR250, RR350 1971–6

The twin cylinder, two-stroke racers built at Varese during the 1970s brought Harley-Davidson its sole successes in post-war grand prix road racing. These were state-of-the-art machines, broadly similar to the stroker twins produced by Yamaha and Kawasaki, with fierce powerbands, strident exhaust notes and performance belying their relatively small engine displacement. To cope with the narrow band of usable revs, the gearbox held six speeds – and might well have held more if this were not prohibited by FIM regulations.

The 250's 56.2 x 50mm cylinders were fed via rotary disc valves by twin 34mm Mikuni carburettors. The earliest examples were air-cooled but the factory soon switched to liquid-cooling, bringing far greater temperature stability and reliability during long grand prix races. Primary drive was by gear, to a multi-plate dry clutch and thence to the six-speed "box". Power output was prodigious (particularly by Milwaukee's four-stroke standards), with the 250 producing 58bhp at 12,000rpm and the 350 a dozen horsepower more at 11,400rpm. The 250's figure equates to over 232bhp per litre, compared to a mere 65 for the KR750 which had been Harley-Davidson's racing mainstay at the time RR250 development began.

■ LEFT *The great Walter Villa at speed on the RR250 at the notorious Nurburgring circuit in 1978. He failed to finish. Note that the machine still relies on a drum front brake.*

SPECIFICATIONS: RR250

Engine	liquid-cooled twin cylinder 2-stroke
Capacity	15.1cu in (248cc)
Transmission	6-speed
Peak power	58bhp @12,000rpm
Weight	230lbs (104kg)
Top speed	140mph (225kph)

■ BELOW LEFT *A disc-braked factory two-stroke twin shares pride of place with a classic four-stroke single.*

■ BELOW RIGHT *Villa on the RR350 at Hockenheim in 1977, carrying the world champion's Number One. He finished third in the 250cc world championship that year, but the 350 proved less competitive.*

The chassis featured a conventional twin cradle of high-grade tubular steel. Italian Ceriani suspension graced the front end with a pair of English Girling shock absorbers at the rear. The whole package weighed just 230lbs (104kg). If the machine had a shortcoming, it was the use of drum brakes (albeit a double-sided twin-leading shoe affair at the front) when hydraulic discs were already in widespread use and far superior. Discs finally arrived in 1976, by which time the great Walter Villa had already taken two 250cc world titles.

With better brakes, he repeated the feat in 1976, adding the 350cc title for good measure. RRs also campaigned successfully in American road races, ridden by Gary Scott, Jay Springsteen, Cal Rayborn and others.

MX250 1977–8

■ ABOVE AND LEFT *Harley's Italian-designed and built MX250 motocrosser benefited from lessons learned in grand prix road racing and might have gone on to great things had Varese not been sold.*

Harley-Davidson's only venture into mainstream motocross produced a highly competitive machine which could have become better still had Milwaukee not severed its Italian links after just two years of MX production. By the time the MX250 came on stream in 1977, Varese had developed a formidable pool of two-stroke know-how, not least from its successful grand prix road-racing experience.

Four years after its official demise, the great Jay Springsteen mischievously used an MX-based machine to win the first AMA event of the 1982 season in Houston. We can only speculate about where this potential might have led.

The single-cylinder stroker used a short-stroke (72 x 59.6mm) engine which drove an integral five-speed transmission via gear primary drive and wet multi-plate clutch – such as you might find on any dirt-bike today.

Initial examples were air-cooled, but a liquid-cooled version came later. A 38mm Italian dell'Orto carburettor provided the fuel (mixed 20:1 with oil for lubrication), while sparks came from a CDI generator on the left end of the crankshaft. During development, peak power rose to a ferocious 58bhp at a giddy 12,000rpm. Telescopic forks provided a generous 9in (228mm) of travel with a similar degree of movement that came from the twin rear shock absorbers.

Light alloy Akront rims were laced to simple 5½in (140mm) drum brakes (as discs were not yet used on dirt-bikes).

SPECIFICATIONS	
Engine	single-cylinder 2-stroke
Capacity	14.8cu in (242cc)
Transmission	5-speed
Peak power	58bhp @12,000rpm
Weight	233lbs (106kg)
Wheelbase	57.3in (1,455mm)
Top speed	n/a

■ RIGHT *Harley's only current single is this Rotax-engined device.*

Aermacchi OHV Racers 1961–78

Originally an aircraft factory – hence the name – Aermacchi diversified into motorcycle production in 1948, in Varese, Italy. Its first models were 123cc (7.5cu in) singles – two-strokes but already possessing the horizontal cylinder which was to become so typical of the marque. Overhead valve four-stroke singles followed, both road bikes and the potent Ala D'Oro (Golden Wing) production racer. A generation of elegant racing models were developed from the late 1950s onwards, based on this Alfredo Bianchi-designed machine.

Although the racers were built in both 250cc (15cu in) and 350cc (21cu in) versions, it was the latter which achieved the greater success. Even during the 1960s, a single-cylinder push-rod machine was an anachronism among the exotica then crowding the grands prix grids, yet the "Macchi" exploited its fine handling, light weight and slim aerodynamic profile to the fullest. Its best world-championship performance came in 1966 when the late Renzo Pasolini – the "Paso" in the Ducati model of the same name – took third place in the 350cc grand prix championship.

■ LEFT *An Aermacchi 250 at speed. Light weight and a slim profile made them astonishingly fast.*

■ BELOW LEFT *A CRTT 250 in factory racing livery.*

SPECIFICATIONS: 350	
Engine	ohv horizontal single
Capacity	344cc (21cu in)
Transmission	5-speed
Power	38bhp
Weight	245lbs (111kg)
Wheelbase	not known
Top Speed	130mph (210kph)

It was as a privateer mount that the little "Macchi" achieved its greatest popularity and success however, although it also had a reputation for being temperamental unless expertly set up. Perhaps its most remarkable performance came in the 1970 Isle of Man TT races when Alan Barnett lapped the daunting Mountain Course at a stunning 99.32mph (159.84kph) on a Syd Lawton 350, recording well over 40mpg (15km/litre) in the process.

Nor were the ohv single's exploits confined to the track. On 21 October 1965, a 250cc Aermacchi established a world mile record of 176.817mph (284.55kph) and kilometre record of 285.21kph (177.225mph) at Utah's Bonneville salt flats. Although nominally a Sprint roadster, the machine in question used a 1966-specification CR racing engine on standard pump fuel. Officially, Milwaukee dubbed its Italian singles CR, CRS and CRTT, although in Europe these designations were largely ignored.

The single was produced with many variations over the years, but the 350's

■ BELOW *A brace of ex-factory racers. Note the racing dry clutch.*

■ BELOW *A 350 'Macchi contesting the 1984 Historic Isle of Man TT. Ironically this was the only TT ever won by an American – on a British Matchless machine.*

typical power output was around 38bhp at 8,400rpm. Bore and stroke were under-square at 74 x 80mm, although this incurred a dangerously high piston speed (almost 4,400ft/1,340m) at maximum revs. As a result, other configurations were also built, including short stroke and ultra-short stroke examples. Compression was high – around 11.4:1 – and the engine breathed through a 35mm dell'Orto carburettor tipped almost vertically to feed fuel into the horizontal cylinder. A short megaphone exhaust swept down the right side of the machine.

The racer was available with a choice of "A" or "B" gear clusters, the latter offering the closer ratios, although the engine delivered a reasonable spread of power considering its high state of tune.

The chassis was simple in the extreme, using a large-diameter tubular steel spine, which was reputed to flex but in a controlled, user-friendly way which gave the rider ample feedback.

A variety of suspension and brake components were employed, invariably with telescopic forks (usually Ceriani), twin rear shock absorbers and drum brakes. On later versions, the front drum was often twin-sided.

A measure of the machine's excellence is the sheer joy – and speed – with which many contest classic races today.

■ LEFT *Pictured here, the engine of a 1969 350 Aermacchi.*

■ BELOW *In the USA, Aermacchis derived from the Sport roadster were also popular for dirt-track racing.*

LUCIFER'S HAMMER, 1983

■ BELOW *Lucifer's Hammer's engine was based on that of an XR750 competition model.*

In the spring of 1983, Lucifer's Hammer was the first big twin for a decade to carry Harley-Davidson's famous black and orange racing livery on to the Daytona speed bowl. It certainly did so with distinction, taking the great Jay Springsteen – better known as a dirt-track rider but certainly no slouch on tarmac – to victory in the Battle of the Twins event. In October of the same year, Gene Church began a love affair with the same machine when he rode it triumphantly in the BoT finals, also held at Daytona.

The Hammer represented one of those bouts of enthusiasm and expertise with the big twin that were often typical of Harley-Davidson. The germ of the project began when Dave McClure rode a prototype XR1000 street bike at Daytona the previous autumn, which suggested that a full-on racer project might succeed. Once race-boss Dick O'Brien got the go-ahead to build what would become the Springsteen machine, he set his hand-picked team into action. Engine work was put in the hands of Don Habermehl, while racing legend Carroll Resweber (four times AMA champion for Harley, 1958 to 1961) put his considerable talents into the chassis, and Peter Zylstra oversaw the design. To some extent, the machine was also a test-bed and publicity statement for the XR1000 roadster unveiled at the same Daytona meeting, another project which very much carried the O'Brien imprint.

SPECIFICATIONS	
Engine	ohv V-twin
Capacity	60.9cu in (998cc)
Transmission	4-speed
Power	104bhp
Weight	286lbs (130kg)
Wheelbase	56in (1,420mm)
Top speed	158mph (254kph)

The engine consisted of a modified competition XR750 bottom end and light alloy heads mated to iron Sportster barrels. Twin 42mm smoothbore Mikuni carburettors took care of induction, feeding exotic 110 octane aviation fuel – for nothing less would handle the engine's giddy 10.5:1 compression ratio. To improve combustion, each cylinder boasted twin spark plugs, fired by a total-loss racing ignition system.

In dyno tests, this device had put out a brutal 106bhp at 7,500rpm, but fears

■ BELOW *The Hammer with fairing removed, at Daytona in 1983.*

about reliability caused Habermehl to impose a rev ceiling of 7,000rpm, at which point the big twin was pumping out 104bhp. Since even this equated to a dizzying mean piston speed of 4,430 ft/min (1,350m/min), the precaution must have been wise. Not only was power prodigious but the spread was enormous, too, coming in strongly by 4,000rpm. A four-speed gearbox was more than adequate. Resweber's chassis employed the very XR750 frame comprehensively crashed by then-AMA champion Mark Brelsford at Daytona fully ten years before the Hammer's 1983 win. The basic single spine and twin tube cradle was heavily reworked with extra gussets and bracing, mated to an all-new box-section swing-arm.

The rest was essentially an Italian affair: front suspension was in the hands of a pair of 1.57in (40mm) Forcelli Italia forks, with twin Fox gas shock absorbers at the rear. Brembo supplied the brakes: twin 11.8in (300mm) floating-front disc brakes, with a 9.8in (250mm) disc at the rear. These ran on Campagnolo magnesium wheels, 16in (406mm) front wheel, 18in (457mm) rear, both shod with Goodyear racing slick tyres. Dry weight was a remarkably lean 285lbs (130kg) and top speed an even more impressive 158mph (254kph).

After its winning Daytona debut, Gene Church went on to take the HOG-sponsored Hammer to three AMA Battle of the Twins titles.

All of this success was not really too bad for a bike that began its life as a ten-year-old scrap!

■ ABOVE *The Hammer owed many of its engine parts to the XR750 flat-tracker.*

■ RIGHT *The road-going XR1000 (shown here) is blood brother to the awesome Lucifer's Hammer.*

VR1000, 1994–PRESENT

■ ABOVE *Chris Carr in action on the VR1000 at Daytona Raceway. In 1999, Carr returned to dirt track and claimed the AMA title.*

The VR1000, which has been flying Milwaukee's road-racing flag through the latter half of the 1990s is a Harley even the faithful scarcely believe. It's a V-twin, true, but with twin overhead camshafts, and its cylinders are liquid-cooled and splayed at a sacrilegious 60 degrees. True, its four valves per cylinder have been done by Milwaukee before – but not for 70-odd years.

Clearly the VR is not your typical Hog. It's built in the United States, says "Harley-Davidson" on the side, and is decked out in classic black and orange racing livery. But it probably doesn't share a single part with any other Milwaukee model.

The machine uses Harley's own purpose-built powerplant, which looks for all the world like one quarter of a V8 car engine in its design and construction. Almost everything else is bought-in from quality suppliers, such as Swedish Ohlins suspension and Italian Marchesini magnesium-alloy cast wheels. The whole is tied together, not by American steel, but by a massively stiff twin-beam aluminium chassis. Erik Buell was one of the original development engineers on the project, while the race team is run by Steve Shybee.

In its early years, ridden by the mercurial Miguel du Hamel, the VR proved surprisingly potent, pumping out more than 120bhp at 10,800rpm. Yet it did not make the progress for which Harley fans might have hoped. This was not for the want of talented riders. Among others, the twin has been ridden

SPECIFICATIONS

Engine	dohc V-twin
Capacity	60.8cu in (996cc)
Transmission	6-speed
Power	171bhp
Weight	373lbs (169kg)
Wheelbase	55.1in (1,400mm)
Top speed	179mph (288kph)

■ ABOVE *As brutally black as the old XLCR, the factory racer has failed to live up to expectations on the track.*

■ RIGHT *A private racing VR with special lightweight frame. The 60-degree engine layout is apparent with bodywork removed.*

by AMA Number 1 Chris Carr, Thomas Wilson, Doug Chandler and former World Superbike champion Scott Russell. The bike continued to improve, but not quickly enough. Observers were often surprised at the lack of all-out effort the factory appeared to put into the project. As a racer, it had one fatal and embarrassing flaw: it didn't win. No wonder onlookers – Harley devotees and not – struggled to comprehend quite what the VR1000 was for.

Even the VR's noted tractability could not overcome this sort of deficit. Although it could be competitive in wet conditions, it lacked at least 30bhp compared to similar Ducati twins. During 1998–9, however, an intensive programme of development work began to show startling results. Peak power soared to more than 170bhp, giving a measured top speed of 179mph (288kph) around the Daytona banking. Rider Pascal Picotte, in particular, posted some impressive results during 1999, although he could manage no better than twelfth place in the American MBNA Superbike championship. Team mate Scott Russell placed twentieth.

Some VRs have been sold to private teams, with an odd route to racing legality. To qualify for competition, these must be street-legal – not necessarily in the USA, but somewhere. The United States is a very expensive place to make any motorcycle legal, so a limited-edition run of 50 "roadster" VRs flew a flag of convenience. No, not Liberia, but the truth is almost as absurd. The VR1000 met the relevant standards for road-going motorcycles – in Poland.

Nonetheless, this high-tech device – the only racer in the world, for instance, to run a carbon multi-plate clutch – remains a puzzle. What is the purpose of the VR1000? Is it a rolling test-bed for hardware that might appear on future roadsters? Or is it the basis for a future roadster model? Racing people close to the factory team have suggested that a road-going liquid-cooled sports bike may be a genuine possibility. Some even believe that such a device could blow away even a Ducati V-twin; traditional Harley die-hards must throw up their hands in horror at the very thought. Wherever you stand, like the rest of us, you'll just have to wait and see.

■ FAR LEFT *Note the slim lines of the Superbike VR. The ventilated dry clutch would later be replaced by an exotic multi-plate carbon assembly.*

■ LEFT *What the future might hold: a sneak shot of a prototype roadster VR1000.*

GLOSSARY

Air cleaner: A filter for removing dust from the air entering the engine.
Air-cooled: An engine which is cooled directly by the air flowing over it, rather than via a liquid-filled radiator.
Alternator: An electrical generator producing alternating current which must then be converted to direct current by a rectifier.
AMA: American Motorcycle Association (governing body of American bike racing).
Bearing: Placed between two rubbing or turning components to reduce friction. Can be "plain" or with moving balls or rollers.
bhp (brake horsepower): Engine power as measured on a dynamometer, on which the engine is run against a resistance or "brake". Horsepower is essentially torque times revs.
Big end: The connection between con-rod and crankshaft.
Bore: Diameter of the cylinder in which the piston travels.
Bottom end: The engine below the cylinder, containing crankshaft, bearings, oil pump, etc.
CAD: Computer-aided design.
Camshaft: A lobed shaft turning at half engine speed which operates the valves.
Carburettor: Instrument that mixes fuel and air for combustion.
Choke: A device that enriches the fuel and air mixture to facilitate cold starts; also the carburettor venturi.
Clutch: A device which allows the rear wheel to be isolated from the turning of the engine.
Coil: An electrical device which turns low-voltage current into high-voltage for the spark plug.
Compression: The extent to which the piston "squeezes" the fuel and air mixture, expressed as a ratio of maximum to minimum volume.
Con-rod (connecting rod): A (usually steel) member connecting the crankshaft to the piston.
Crankcases: The (usually aluminium) housing containing bottom end components. These are commonly split into pairs.
Crankshaft: An eccentric (cranked) shaft on which the con-rods run, held in the crankcases by the main bearings; it turns the piston's reciprocating action into rotary motion.
Cylinder: A cylindrical "barrel" in which the piston moves up and down.
Disc: A type of brake in which "pads" of friction material are squeezed against rotating disc(s) attached to the wheel.
Displacement: An engine's capacity, i.e. total volume displaced by an engine's pistons.
Drum: A type of brake in which a mechanism forces "shoes" against the inside of a drum in the wheel hub.
Dry-sump: An engine in which lubricating oil is located in a separate tank rather than the sump.
Evo: The 1,340cc V2 Evolution engine produced from 1984.
F-head: An ioe cylinder head.
Flathead: Any side-valve engine.
Flywheel: A heavy disc spinning with the crankshaft which stores engine inertia and "smooths out" power pulses.
Gearbox: A housing in which lie the shafts on which the transmission gears run.
Gudgeon pin (wrist pin in the USA): A steel tube connecting the piston to the small end.
Hardtail: A rigid, i.e. unsprung, motorcycle rear end.
Hog: Nickname given to any Harley-Davidson model.
HOG: Harley Owners' Group.
Horsepower: Torque times revs, the actual power output of an engine. However, in the early years, an engine's rated horsepower was simply a function of engine displacement.
Hydraulic: Operated by pressure in a fluid, as with disc brakes or hydraulic "lifters".
ioe (inlet-over-exhaust): The earliest type of valve arrangement, with a side exhaust valve facing an overhead inlet valve. The latter could be "automatic" or mechanically operated.
Knucklehead: Harley's first ohv engine, 1936–47.
Lifter (USA): A push-rod. Also hydraulic lifters.
Magneto: An early, free-standing device which generates (and times) the ignition spark.
Mudguard: fender (USA).
ohv (overhead valve): Both valves contained in the cylinder head and actuated by rockers.
Panhead: An ohv Harley engine produced 1948–65.
Piston: An inverted cylindrical "tub" in the cylinder which transmits combustion forces to the crankshaft via the con-rod.
Piston ring: A flexible iron or steel ring located in a groove near the top of the piston which seals against the leakage of combustion gases or oil.
Power: See bhp.
Push-rod (also, solid lifter in the USA): A metal rod which transmits camshaft motion to the valve via the rocker.
Rake: The effective angle of the front forks, expressed in degrees from vertical.
Revs (rpm): Engine revolutions per minute.
Retro-Tech: Modern technology that mimicks old, such as Springer forks.
Rocker: A rocking arm which transmits motion from lifter to the valve.
Shovelhead: An ohv Harley engine produced 1966–84.
Side-valve: "Flathead" engines with both valves below the level of the cylinder head.
Small end (little end): The connection between the piston's gudgeon pin and the con-rod.
Softail: Rear suspension with swing arm and underslung shock absorbers, that is designed to look like a hardtail.
Springer: A modern "Retro-Tech" version of the sprung fork; any Harley-Davidson so fitted.
Sprung fork: Pre-1948 front suspension with solid legs, and (usually) coil spring(s) at the top.
Stroke: The distance travelled by a piston between its top-most and bottom-most points.
Swing-arm: Also known as swinging fork, a pivoting suspension member allowing the rear wheel to move up and down.
Sump: An extension at the bottom of the crankcase containing oil. "Dry sump" engines hold their oil in a separate tank.
Tachometer (rev-counter): An instrument that measures engine revs.
Telescopic fork: Front suspension in which one tube (containing a spring) slides within another, damped by oil.
Timing: Arranging that the spark is delivered (or the valves open and close) at the correct time.
Top end: The engine "above" the base of the cylinder, including the cylinder head.
Trail (castor): The extent to which the front tyre's contact patch trails the point at which the steering angle intersects the ground. Harley-Davidson favours high trail figures which tend to give slower steering and greater stability.
Torque: The turning force applied to the crankshaft (and ultimately the rear wheel) by the force of combustion on the piston.
Venturi: The part of the carburettor through which incoming air passes; also its diameter.
Wheelbase: Distance between the front and rear wheel centres.
Wrist Pin: see gudgeon pin.

HARLEY-DAVIDSON MODEL CODES

The Harley-Davidson company has always favoured a particularly cryptic method of model designation, although the system is in most cases quite simple once the "code" is understood. The first model made in any numbers was the 1908 Model 4 – indicating the fourth year of production. A suffix letter identified the precise model type, such as "A" for magneto ignition, with the most basic model simply known by its model year number. The first "suffix" was actually a prefix: in 1912, "X" before the model year indicated a rear wheel clutch.

Thus, the Model 5 followed in 1909, the Model 6 in 1910 and so on, until all models adopted the last two digits of their year of manufacture from 1916 (Models 16). Thus, Model 16B was a base-model 1916 single, a 16E was the most basic twin and a 16J was a three-speed twin with full electrical system. Unfortunately, Harley's long-standing habit of having lead times – by which you could buy most "year 2000" models in late 1999, for instance, often creates additional ambiguity.

Later, as the range became entirely composed of V-twins, the suffix letters became more elaborate and numerous but the basic year-prefix system continued publicly until 1969 (and technically still does). Initially, there was little attempt to marry a suffix letter logically with what it represented, although in recent times the connection has – usually – been more clear.

Not quite every letter of the alphabet has been used ("Y" is the exception) which would be daunting enough, but several have enjoyed different meanings at different times. Equally, the same "feature" has also commanded different code letters. Thus, electric start has been indicated variously by "B" and "E", while the latter has also represented the 61-inch Knucklehead and Panhead engines (as opposed to "F" for the 74-inch models) and even police spec. In recent times, "B" has variously represented Belt drive, Daytona and Bad Boy, to name but three.

All current Harley-Davidsons start with a pair of letters, denoting certain engine and chassis combinations. Therefore, XL is the Sportster range, with solidly-mounted 883cc or 1,200cc engines. The suffix dates back to the original 55-inch XL Sportster of 1957.

"FX" first appeared for the 1971 SuperGlide when the "X" indicated that the model had borrowed the lighter Sportster front end. The FX suffix now refers to a welter of models with Twin Cam or 81.6cu in (1,340cc) Evo engines. FXD now represents the Dyna series with two-point rubber-mounted engines dating from the FXDB Sturgis frame of 1991. FXST denotes Softails, with engines rigidly mounted in a chassis based on the previous FX range.

"Heavyweight" models (not that most others are light) have enjoyed the FL suffix since 1941, when "F" indicated the new 74-inch Knucklehead engine, of which the Special Sport version was designated "L". These days, it refers to rubber-mounted big twin engines: Electra and TourGlides. Exceptions to this are rigidly-mounted FLST Softail models, such as the Fat Boy and Heritage Softail.

The table on the right outlines a selection of the suffix letters that have been employed.

Suffix	Modern meaning	Historical meaning
A	–	Army (military spec)/without tow bar (on Servi-Car)
B	Bad, as in Bad Boy, Belt Drive and Daytona	Electric start/previously aluminium piston(s)
C	Custom, Classic, Café (as in Café Racer)	"Competition"/Commercial /Canadian spec
CH	–	"Competition Hot": super sports with magneto
D	Dyna, Daytona	At least four other uses
DG	Disc Glide	–
E	(Formerly) electric start. Previously 61-inch ohv engine and some police models	–
F	Fat Boy	As a prefix, 74-inch ohv engine; as suffix, foot change
H	Notionally extra power but largely redundant	Extra power/high compression/larger engine
I	Fuel injection	–
J	–	Battery electrical system (as opposed to magneto)
L	–	Sports specification; "LD" signified Special Sports models
LR	Low Rider	–
N	Nostalgia	Iron piston
P	–	Police model/sprung fork on 1949 ohv models
Q	–	Two passenger sidecar
R	Road King	Racing/pseudo racing (XR1000)
S	Springer, as in the last letter of FXSTS (Springer Softail) or Sport, as in FLHS (ElectraGlide Sport)	Sidecar specifications/ sometimes Sport
SP	Sport Edition, as in FXRS-SP Low Rider Sport Edition	–
ST	Softail	–
T	Touring, with frame-mounting fairing	Reverse gear/Twin
U	Ultra	"Restricted" engines
WG	WideGlide	–
X	Some Sports models	Rear wheel clutch

INDEX